MW01094782

Databricks Certified Data Engineer Associate Study Guide
In-Depth Guidance and Practice

Derar Alhussein

Databricks Certified Data Engineer Associate Study Guide

by Derar Alhussein

Copyright © 2025 Derar Alhussein. All rights reserved.

Published by O'Reilly Media, Inc., 1005 Gravenstein Highway North, Sebastopol, CA 95472.

O'Reilly books may be purchased for educational, business, or sales promotional use. Online editions are also available for most titles (*http://oreilly.com*). For more information, contact our corporate/institutional sales department: 800-998-9938 or *corporate@oreilly.com*.

Acquisitions Editor: Aaron Black	**Indexer:** Ellen Troutman-Zaig
Development Editor: Shira Evans	**Interior Designer:** David Futato
Production Editor: Aleeya Rahman	**Cover Designer:** Karen Montgomery
Copyeditor: Liz Wheeler	**Illustrator:** Kate Dullea
Proofreader: Kim Wimpsett	

February 2025:   First Edition

Revision History for the First Edition
2025-02-14:   First Release

See *http://oreilly.com/catalog/errata.csp?isbn=9781098166830* for release details.

The O'Reilly logo is a registered trademark of O'Reilly Media, Inc. Databricks Certified Data Engineer Associate Study Guide, the cover image, and related trade dress are trademarks of O'Reilly Media, Inc.

The views expressed in this work are those of the author and do not represent the publisher's views. While the publisher and the author have used good faith efforts to ensure that the information and instructions contained in this work are accurate, the publisher and the author disclaim all responsibility for errors or omissions, including without limitation responsibility for damages resulting from the use of or reliance on this work. Use of the information and instructions contained in this work is at your own risk. If any code samples or other technology this work contains or describes is subject to open source licenses or the intellectual property rights of others, it is your responsibility to ensure that your use thereof complies with such licenses and/or rights.

978-1-098-16683-0

[LSI]

Table of Contents

Preface

Innovative technologies in data engineering empower companies to leverage their growing data effectively, leading to improved business outcomes. In this context, platforms like Databricks have emerged as essential tools for managing, processing, and analyzing vast amounts of data. However, this evolution also brings the need for skilled professionals who can navigate the Databricks platform efficiently and implement robust data solutions that meet business needs.

Why I Wrote This Book

With over ten years of experience in the data sector, I've seen firsthand how Databricks unlocks the power of big data to drive business growth across various industries. Throughout my journey, I have also witnessed how certification programs like the Databricks Data Engineer Associate can serve as a meaningful benchmark, validating the skills needed to succeed in the real world of data engineering.

This book is the result of my passion for teaching and my deep belief in the importance of hands-on learning. The goal is simple: to guide you through the concepts, tools, and techniques that you will need to not only pass the certification exam but also excel as a data engineer in practical scenarios. By combining fundamental knowledge with practical exercises, I hope to provide you with a study guide that is as useful for building your day-to-day data engineering skills as it is for earning your certification.

Who This Book Is For

This book is designed for anyone seeking to advance their data engineering skills, whether you're just beginning your journey or already have some experience in the field. It's tailored specifically for those preparing for the Databricks Data Engineer Associate certification, but it also serves as a practical guide for anyone who wants to gain a deeper understanding of the Databricks platform and its many capabilities.

The book is ideal for individuals who already have a strong foundation in SQL and a basic understanding of Python. If you are familiar with manipulating data using SQL and are looking to apply those skills within the Databricks platform, this guide will help you bridge that gap. The choice to focus primarily on SQL in this book reflects the structure of the certification exam, where most code-based questions are demonstrated using SQL. However, for more complex operations where SQL alone is insufficient, Python is introduced to complement your learning.

What You Will Learn

This book is designed to provide a comprehensive, hands-on learning experience, covering every topic you'll encounter on the Databricks Certified Data Engineer Associate exam. The curriculum aligns with the latest version of the certification (V3), ensuring that you are well-prepared for the current exam requirements.

Throughout the book, you'll gain a deep understanding of essential topics, categorized into five broad areas related to the exam topics:

Databricks Lakehouse Platform
: Explore the foundational aspects of the lakehouse architecture, which brings together the benefits of data lakes and data warehouses, enabling you to manage data efficiently.

ELT with Spark SQL and Python
: Learn how to extract, transform, and load data using Spark SQL and Python, focusing on practical techniques that will enhance your data processing skills.

Incremental data processing
: Understand the methodologies for processing data incrementally, allowing for real-time data updates.

Production pipelines
: Discover best practices for building robust production pipelines using Delta Live Tables and Databricks Jobs, ensuring your workflows are reliable and scalable.

Data governance
: Familiarize yourself with the governance aspects of data management, including the introduction of Unity Catalog and its integration with the Hive metastore.

A main emphasis in this book is on the Hive metastore, which remains an essential part of the current exam version. Although Databricks has introduced a new governance model, Unity Catalog, the Hive metastore continues to be a valuable learning resource, particularly for those starting out in data engineering. The book leverages the simplicity and accessibility of the Hive metastore to explain fundamental concepts, such as managing Delta Lake, which are integral to mastering Databricks.

As Databricks evolves, so do its tools, and Unity Catalog is one of the newest additions to its data governance model. Although the Hive metastore remains essential for certification purposes, this book also introduces Unity Catalog and explains how it extends beyond the existing metastore, ensuring you are up to speed with the latest features. By the time you reach Chapter 8, you'll understand how both systems work together and be ready to handle the new governance features.

To help solidify your learning, each chapter ends with a "Sample Exam Questions" section. These questions mirror the complexity of the actual certification exam, giving you a clear sense of what to expect. This practical approach ensures that, by the end of the book, you'll have not only covered the necessary technical content but also developed the exam techniques and confidence to tackle the real test. Solutions to these questions are included in Appendix C for your reference.

What Not to Expect

While this book is comprehensive in preparing you for the Databricks Certified Data Engineer Associate exam, certain advanced topics and cloud-specific details fall beyond its scope. Given that Databricks operates as a multi-cloud platform, you may work on Microsoft Azure, AWS, or Google Cloud. However, the exam content is cloud-agnostic, focusing solely on Databricks fundamentals rather than cloud-specific configurations or integrations.

For beginners setting up a Databricks workspace, Appendix A provides guidance on creating workspaces across different cloud providers. However, the core chapters focus strictly on Databricks itself, omitting platform-specific instructions such as configuring access to cloud-specific storage systems (e.g., AWS S3 or Azure Blob Storage). For these specialized cloud configurations, please consult Databricks documentation pertinent to your provider.

This book focuses on preparing you for the Associate-level certification, concentrating on foundational skills and concepts. For those looking to delve into more advanced aspects of Databricks or data engineering beyond the certification exam, consider exploring further resources, documentation, or advanced-level training. This way, you'll be equipped with the foundational knowledge needed to progress smoothly into more complex areas.

GitHub Repository and Community

To complement your learning experience, this book includes hands-on examples and exercises designed to reinforce the concepts presented in each chapter. The source code for all these examples is hosted on GitHub (*https://github.com/derar-alhussein/oreilly-databricks-dea*). This allows you to experiment with the material as you progress and see the concepts in action.

For the best experience with these code examples, I recommend using Databricks Runtime 13.3 LTS. This specific runtime version ensures compatibility with the certification exam content and minimizes the risk of encountering discrepancies from newer, untested features. By following along with this runtime, you'll maintain alignment with the exam requirements and be better equipped to handle exam-related tasks without unexpected behavior.

The exercises in this book are designed to run on classical compute resources within Databricks. Serverless clusters are intentionally avoided, as they do not permit runtime version selection and might default to newer versions outside the scope of the certification exam. With classical clusters, you'll have more control over your learning environment, ensuring each example runs consistently and matches the exam experience.

As you progress through the exercises and explore the Databricks platform, you may encounter questions or technical challenges that require assistance. For these situations, the Databricks Community Forum is an excellent support resource. The forum, accessible at *https://community.databricks.com*, allows you to search for previously answered questions or post your own if you can't find the information you're seeking. The community is active, and responses are often quick and insightful, coming from both experts and peers within the field.

Conventions Used in This Book

The following typographical conventions are used in this book:

Italic
: Indicates new terms, URLs, email addresses, filenames, and file extensions.

`Constant width`
: Used for program listings, as well as within paragraphs to refer to program elements such as variable or function names, databases, data types, environment variables, statements, and keywords.

`Constant width bold`
: Shows commands or other text that should be typed literally by the user.

`Constant width italic`
: Shows text that should be replaced with user-supplied values or by values determined by context.

 This element signifies a tip or suggestion.

This element signifies a general note.

 This element indicates a warning or caution.

Using Code Examples

If you have a technical question or a problem using the code examples, please send email to *support@oreilly.com*.

This book is here to help you get your job done. In general, if example code is offered with this book, you may use it in your programs and documentation. You do not need to contact us for permission unless you're reproducing a significant portion of the code. For example, writing a program that uses several chunks of code from this book does not require permission. Selling or distributing examples from O'Reilly books does require permission. Answering a question by citing this book and quoting example code does not require permission. Incorporating a significant amount of example code from this book into your product's documentation does require permission.

We appreciate, but generally do not require, attribution. An attribution usually includes the title, author, publisher, and ISBN. For example: "*Databricks Certified Data Engineer Associate Study Guide* by Derar Alhussein (O'Reilly). Copyright 2025 Derar Alhussein, 978-1-098-16683-0."

If you feel your use of code examples falls outside fair use or the permission given above, feel free to contact us at *permissions@oreilly.com*.

O'Reilly Online Learning

 For more than 40 years, *O'Reilly Media* has provided technology and business training, knowledge, and insight to help companies succeed.

Our unique network of experts and innovators share their knowledge and expertise through books, articles, and our online learning platform. O'Reilly's online learning platform gives you on-demand access to live training courses, in-depth learning paths, interactive coding environments, and a vast collection of text and video from O'Reilly and 200+ other publishers. For more information, visit *https://oreilly.com*.

How to Contact Us

Please address comments and questions concerning this book to the publisher:

> O'Reilly Media, Inc.
> 1005 Gravenstein Highway North
> Sebastopol, CA 95472
> 800-889-8969 (in the United States or Canada)
> 707-827-7019 (international or local)
> 707-829-0104 (fax)
> *support@oreilly.com*
> *https://oreilly.com/about/contact.html*

We have a web page for this book, where we list errata, examples, and any additional information. You can access this page at *https://oreil.ly/databricks-associate-study-guide*.

For news and information about our books and courses, visit *https://oreilly.com*.

Find us on LinkedIn: *https://linkedin.com/company/oreilly-media*

Watch us on YouTube: *https://youtube.com/oreillymedia*

How to Contact the Author

Follow the author on LinkedIn: *https://www.linkedin.com/in/deraralhussein*

Follow the author on Facebook: *https://www.facebook.com/DerarAlhussein*

Follow the author on GitHub: *https://github.com/derar-alhussein*

Visit the author's website: *https://derar.cloud*

Acknowledgments

I would like to express my deep gratitude to Lamia Jaafar, my former manager, who opened the door to my first role as a data engineer. Her trust and guidance laid the foundation for my journey in this field. A special thanks to Thomas Lamy, the lead data architect on my team, for his continued support and encouragement throughout this journey. His expertise and leadership have been invaluable, motivating me to elevate my work to new heights.

I would also like to extend my appreciation to the technical reviewers, Tristen Wentling, a lead solutions architect at Databricks and co-author of the O'Reilly book *Delta Lake: The Definitive Guide*; Holly Smith, a staff developer advocate at Databricks; and Yasir Khan, a Databricks instructor at O'Reilly Media, for their valuable feedback that helped enhance the quality of this work.

Additionally, it has been a true pleasure to work with the O'Reilly team! I would like to especially acknowledge Aaron Black for his early confidence in the project, and my development editor, Shira Evans, for her excellent organization and assistance.

CHAPTER 1

Getting Started with Databricks

Databricks is transforming the way data and artificial intelligence (AI) are managed with its innovative Data Intelligence Platform. This platform offers a unified solution that addresses the limitations of traditional data systems, providing a more comprehensive approach to work with data. In this chapter, we will explore the Databricks Data Intelligence Platform and its capabilities. We will begin with an overview of the platform's architecture and then delve into its key features, including compute resource creation, notebook execution, and Git integration.

Introducing the Databricks Platform

Traditional data management has long relied on two primary paradigms: data lakes and data warehouses. Each approach comes with its own strengths and limitations, particularly in the context of big data processing. Data lakes, while flexible, often struggle with data quality and governance due to their unstructured nature. Data warehouses, though structured, can be rigid and costly, limiting their adaptability to the evolving demands of diverse, high-volume, and high-velocity data. To overcome these challenges, enterprises often deploy multiple systems—data lakes for storing raw data for AI applications, and data warehouses for business intelligence (BI) purposes. However, this strategy leads to increased complexity, requires frequent data transfers, and complicates data governance. Databricks addresses these issues by offering a unified platform that supports both data lake and data warehouse functionalities in a single environment, known as the *data lakehouse*.

Understanding the Databricks Platform

The Databricks Data Intelligence Platform is an AI-powered data lakehouse platform built on Apache Spark. A data lakehouse represents a hybrid solution that combines the best aspects of data lakes and data warehouses. Specifically, it integrates the openness, scalability, and cost efficiency of data lakes with the reliability, strong governance, and performance features of data warehouses.

To illustrate the concept of a data lakehouse, imagine you have a vast collection of books (data) that contains various genres, formats, and authors. Traditionally, two separate systems would be employed to manage these books:

Data warehouse

An organized library where books (data) are carefully curated, processed, and stored in a specific format, facilitating efficient analysis and querying. However, maintaining this system is costly, and its rigid structure makes it challenging to accommodate new or unconventional book formats.

Data lake

A vast, inexpensive, and unstructured repository where all the books are stored without extensive organization or processing. It resembles an endless, disordered storage shelf where various items can be easily stored; however, locating a specific item can be problematic.

A lakehouse represents a smart, adaptable library that combines the best of both worlds: the vast, flexible, and economic storage of a data lake with the structured, organized, and analyzable system of a data warehouse.

In the real world, such integration ensures that enterprises can store vast amounts of diverse data in low-cost cloud storage while maintaining the ability to analyze it efficiently and securely. This facilitates performing a wide variety of tasks in one place, including data engineering, machine learning, and analytics. Thus, the data lakehouse serves as a unified platform where data engineers, data scientists, and analysts can all work together. Figure 1-1 illustrates this convergence of capabilities into a single, comprehensive platform.

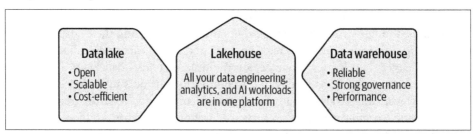

Figure 1-1. Convergence of data lakes and data warehouses into a unified data lakehouse platform

To understand how Databricks achieves this, let's examine the underlying architecture of its data lakehouse.

High-Level Architecture of the Databricks Lakehouse

The Databricks lakehouse is designed with a layered architecture that consists of four fundamental layers: the cloud infrastructure, Databricks Runtime, data governance, and the workspace. Figure 1-2 illustrates the high-level architecture of the Databricks lakehouse, showcasing the relationships among these layers.

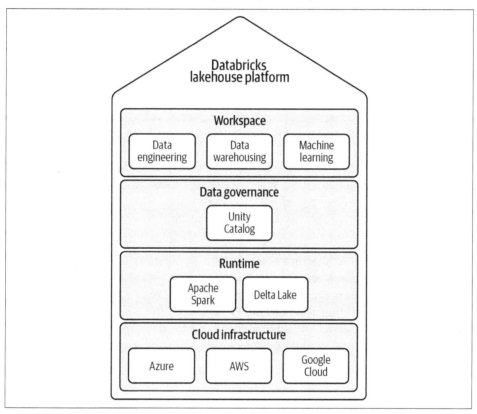

Figure 1-2. High-level architecture of the Databricks lakehouse

Each of these layers plays a vital role in ensuring the platform's scalability, reliability, and security. To gain a deeper understanding of their individual contributions, let's examine each layer in detail, starting from the bottom:

Cloud infrastructure

At the foundation of the Databricks lakehouse architecture lies the cloud infrastructure layer. Databricks is a multi-cloud platform, meaning it is available on major cloud service providers, including Microsoft Azure, Amazon Web Services (AWS), and Google Cloud Platform (GCP). This layer is responsible for providing the underlying hardware resources that Databricks accesses on behalf of users. It enables the provisioning of essential components, such as storage, networking, and the virtual machines (VMs) or nodes that form the backbone of a computing cluster running Databricks Runtime.

Databricks Runtime
Databricks Runtime is a pre-configured virtual machine image optimized for use within Databricks clusters. It includes a set of core components, such as Apache Spark, Delta Lake, and other essential system libraries. Delta Lake enhances traditional data lakes by providing transactional guarantees similar to those found in operational databases, thereby ensuring improved data reliability and consistency. In Chapter 2, we explore Delta Lake in detail to understand its transformative impact on data lake reliability.

Data governance with Unity Catalog
At the core of the Databricks lakehouse architecture is Unity Catalog, which provides a centralized data governance solution across all data and AI assets. Unity Catalog is designed to secure and manage data access across the Databricks environment, ensuring that sensitive information is accessible only to authorized users. This layer is crucial for maintaining data security, integrity, and compliance across the lakehouse platform. Chapter 8 provides an in-depth look at Unity Catalog and its comprehensive features and capabilities.

Databricks workspace
At the top of the architecture is the Databricks workspace, which serves as the user interface for interacting with the platform. It provides an interactive environment where users can perform data engineering, analytics, and AI workloads using a variety of languages, such as Python, SQL, R, and Scala. The workspace offers a range of services, including notebooks for development, dashboards for visualizing data, and workflow management tools for orchestrating data pipelines.

Deployment of Databricks Resources

When deploying Databricks resources within your cloud provider's environment, the architecture is divided into two high-level components: the control plane and the data plane. Figure 1-3 illustrates these two components and the interaction between them.

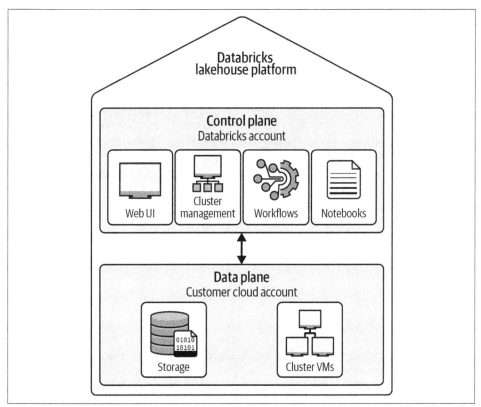

Figure 1-3. Databricks resource deployment architecture

Understanding the distinction between these components is essential for effectively managing and securing your Databricks environment. Let's take a closer look at each component to ensure a clear understanding of their individual roles:

Control plane

The control plane is managed by Databricks and hosts various platform services within the Databricks account. When you create a Databricks workspace, it is deployed within the control plane, along with essential services such as the Databricks user interface (UI), cluster manager, workflow service, and notebooks. Thus, the control plane handles tasks such as workspace management, cluster provisioning, and job scheduling. It also provides the interface through which users interact with the platform, including the web-based notebooks, the Databricks REST API, and the command-line interface (CLI).

Data plane

The data plane, on the other hand, resides within the user's own cloud subscription. This is where actual storage and classic compute resources (non-serverless) are provisioned and managed. When a user sets up a Spark cluster, the virtual machines that comprise the cluster are deployed in the data plane, within the user's cloud account. Similarly, storage resources, such as those used by the Databricks File System (DBFS) or Unity Catalog, are also deployed in the data plane.

This separation of control and data planes offers several advantages. First, it ensures that the compute and storage resources remain within the user's cloud environment, providing greater control over data security and compliance. Second, it allows Databricks to manage the operational aspects of the platform, such as updates and maintenance, without impacting the user's data or compute resources.

Apache Spark™ on Databricks

Apache Spark, an open source data processing engine, is a cornerstone of the Databricks platform, enabling fast and scalable analytics. Databricks, founded by the original creators of Apache Spark, has deeply integrated Spark into its platform, making it one of the most optimized environments for running Spark applications.

The key features of Apache Spark on Databricks include the following:

Distributed data processing
Spark's architecture is designed to process data in parallel across multiple nodes in a cluster. On Databricks, this capability is enhanced by the seamless integration with cloud-based clusters, which can be scaled up or down depending on the workload.

In-memory processing
One of Spark's most significant advantages is its in-memory processing capability. By keeping data in memory across the cluster, Spark significantly reduces the time required for iterative algorithms and complex computations.

Multi-language support
Databricks supports all the programming languages that Spark does, including Scala, Python, SQL, R, and Java.

Batch and stream processing
Apache Spark on Databricks supports both batch and stream processing, making it suitable for a variety of use cases. Batch processing is ideal for historical data analysis and data transformations, while stream processing enables real-time analytics and processing of continuous data streams.

Flexible data handling
Databricks, powered by Spark, can handle structured, semi-structured, and unstructured data. This flexibility is crucial in modern data ecosystems where data comes in various forms, such as CSV files, JSON objects, images, videos, and even complex nested data structures.

Databricks File System (DBFS)

A key feature that enhances Spark's distributed processing capabilities on Databricks is the Databricks File System (DBFS). The DBFS acts as an abstraction layer that simplifies file management across the distributed environment. It allows users to interact with cloud files as if they were stored on a local file system.

When a file is created in a Databricks cluster and stored in the DBFS, it is actually persisted in the underlying cloud storage associated with your cloud provider. This is illustrated in Figure 1-4.

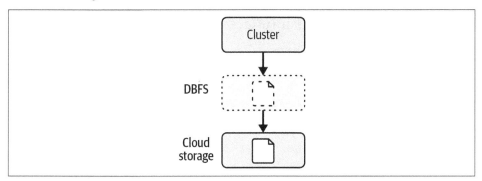

Figure 1-4. Data persistence in the DBFS and the underlying cloud storage

For instance, a file stored in the DBFS on Azure Databricks would really be stored in Azure Data Lake Storage (ADLS). This design ensures that data remains durable and accessible, even after the Spark cluster is terminated.

Setting Up a Databricks Workspace

Creating a Databricks workspace is the first step toward leveraging the platform's capabilities for data engineering, analytics, and machine learning. To set up a workspace, an active Databricks account is required. Databricks offers a 14-day free trial, allowing you to explore its features using your cloud account on Azure, AWS, or Google Cloud. The setup instructions vary slightly depending on the cloud provider you choose; however, it's important to note that the certification exam does not include cloud-specific questions. This means that you won't be tested on the details of creating a workspace on a specific cloud platform.

For detailed instructions on setting up a Databricks workspace on each of these cloud platforms, refer to Appendix A. This section provides step-by-step guidance on how to sign up for a free trial with Databricks and create your first workspace. If you do not have a cloud account or prefer a simpler environment for personal use or training, Databricks also offers the Community Edition. This is a lightweight version of

Databricks, which provides access to the key platform's features at no cost. To learn how to sign up for Databricks Community Edition, refer to Appendix B.

Exploring the Databricks Workspace

The Databricks workspace provides an easy-to-use and intuitive interface, enabling users to interact with their data objects and perform a wide variety of essential tasks. This represents a unified working environment for data engineers, data analysts, and machine learning engineers.

Overview of the Workspace Interface

Figure 1-5 illustrates the home page of the workspace interface, highlighting several key platform navigation areas.

> The Databricks platform is frequently updated with enhancements and new features. As a result, the workspace interface in newer versions may differ from the examples provided here. While the core functionality remains the same, the appearance and specific layout elements might vary.

Figure 1-5. The home page of Databricks workspace

The interface displays a dynamic landing screen that shows recently accessed items and suggested content, providing a personalized experience. The layout is intuitively organized into two primary sections: the sidebar and the top bar. To break it down further, let's explore the key components of each section.

Sidebar

The sidebar, located on the left side of the interface, offers quick access to the platform's key services. It is organized into several categories, each serving a specific function:

Common categories

Workspace
This is an integrated browser where you can organize and manage all your resources, such as folders, notebooks, and other files.

Catalog
This tab allows you to manage your data and AI assets, such as databases, tables, and machine learning models.

Workflows
Here, you can deploy and orchestrate jobs, allowing for automated processing and execution of your data tasks.

Compute
This tab is where you create and manage your compute resources, such as classic clusters and pools. We'll cover cluster management in detail in the following section.

SQL
The SQL section provides access to Databricks SQL, a service designed for running SQL workloads on your data. It is particularly useful for analytics and reporting tasks. Chapter 7 provides an in-depth look at Databricks SQL and its capabilities. However, it's important to note that Databricks SQL is not available in the Community Edition. This is one of the reasons why it is recommended to use the full trial in your cloud environment instead of the Community Edition.

Data Engineering
This section focuses on collaboration among data engineers for performing advanced data engineering tasks. It includes tools and features that are essential for ingesting data and creating data pipelines and jobs. In Chapter 6, we delve into these topics to learn how to build production-grade pipelines and orchestrate jobs effectively.

Machine Learning
 This section offers a range of options tailored for machine learning (ML) engineers. It includes features such as ML experiments, feature stores, and capabilities
 for registering and serving ML models. It's worth noting that these topics are not
 included in the Data Engineer Associate certification exam.

Top bar

The top bar spans across the top of the workspace interface and provides several
important functions:

Search bar
 This AI-powered search tool allows you to efficiently search for various items
 within your workspace, including tables, notebooks, dashboards, and more. It is
 an essential feature for quickly locating resources in your workspace using natu-
 ral language.

Switch Workspaces
 If you manage multiple workspaces or need to navigate between different
 projects, the Switch Workspaces option allows you to easily toggle between them.

Databricks Assistant
 This is an AI-based workspace assistant designed to enhance your experience
 with developing notebooks, queries, and dashboards. It provides a conversational
 interface that facilitates code generation, explanation, and troubleshooting,
 thereby boosting your productivity inside the platform. It also integrates with
 Unity Catalog to offer features such as table searching with context awareness.

Profile settings
 The profile settings give you access to user-related options, such as managing
 your preferences, linking external services, and setting up notifications. They also
 provide access to admin-specific settings that help configure your workspace
 environment.

Navigating the Workspace Browser

The workspace browser is a central feature of the Databricks platform, providing an
organized and structured environment where you can manage all your project items,
such as folders, notebooks, scripts, or other files.

When you navigate to the Workspace tab from the left sidebar, you enter your Home
directory, where all your resources are stored, as illustrated in Figure 1-6.

Figure 1-6. The workspace browser in the Databricks platform

The workspace is structured hierarchically, making it easy to organize your work. The left-hand menu includes several key directories to help you manage your workspace effectively, such as the following:

Home directory

The Home directory is your default location within the workspace. It is personalized to each user's personal directory, providing a semi-private space where you can store your files and folders.

Workspace directory

This is the root folder that contains all users' personal directories. From here, you can also access your Home directory by going to *Users > yourname@example.com*.

Repos

This is the legacy service used for integrating your workspace with Git repositories. It has now been replaced by Git folders, which we cover in detail at the end of this chapter in "Creating Git Folders" on page 42.

Trash

This folder contains deleted items, which are retained for 30 days before being permanently removed.

To add a new item in your Home directory, click the Create button on the right side of the workspace browser. This allows you to create various types of resources like folders and notebooks, as shown in Figure 1-7.

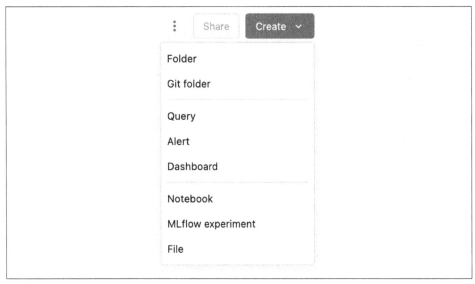

Figure 1-7. Create button in the workspace browser

As an example, use the Create button to add a new folder named *Demo*; then open the folder to begin organizing your files. Within any folder, you can further organize your resources by creating subfolders, which helps to keep your workspace clean and well-organized.

Next to the Create button, you will notice a menu icon represented by three vertical dots, as displayed in Figure 1-8.

Figure 1-8. Menu icon in the workspace browser

This menu provides additional options for managing your resources, such as importing code files from your local system into your Databricks workspace and exporting the contents of the current folder as an archived file.

Importing Book Materials

The exercises and examples provided in this book are hosted on a GitHub repository (*https://github.com/derar-alhussein/oreilly-databricks-dea*). Importing these materials into your Databricks workspace is an essential step to being able to follow along with the content of the book. This section will guide you through the process of importing these resources using two primary methods: Git folders and DBC (Databricks Cloud) files.

Option 1: Git folders

For those using the full version of Databricks on a cloud platform, such as AWS, Azure, or Google Cloud, the Git folders feature offers a seamless integration with Git providers. This allows you to clone remote repositories directly into your Databricks workspace. To clone our book repository from GitHub, follow these steps:

1. Navigate to your workspace browser: In your Databricks workspace, navigate to the Workspace tab to access your Home directory.

2. Create a Git folder: At the top of your directory, click the Create button and select "Git folder" from the drop-down menu, as illustrated in Figure 1-9.

Figure 1-9. Adding a Git folder using the Create button in the workspace browser

This action will open a dialog box where you can specify the GitHub repository you want to clone, as shown in Figure 1-10.

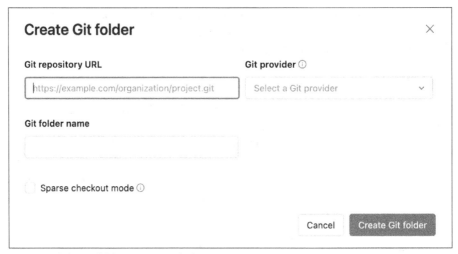

Figure 1-10. Git folder creation dialog

3. Paste the GitHub repository URL: In the Git folder creation dialog, paste the URL of the book's GitHub repository (*https://github.com/derar-alhussein/oreilly-databricks-dea*). The interface will automatically detect the Git provider (e.g., GitHub) and fill in the repository name based on the URL provided.

4. Create the Git folder: After confirming the details, click the Create Git folder button to clone the repository. The cloned repository will then appear as a folder in your workspace, and you can navigate through its contents just as you would with any other directory.

It's important to note that this feature is available only in the full version of Databricks. Users of the Databricks Community Edition should refer to the alternative method outlined next.

Option 2: DBC files

On the Databricks Community Edition, Git integration through Git folders is not supported. However, you can still import the book's materials by utilizing DBC files, which are archive files designed for directly importing source code into Databricks workspaces. To import the DBC file of our book's resources, follow these steps:

1. Download the DBC file from GitHub: Navigate to the book's GitHub repository (*https://github.com/derar-alhussein/oreilly-databricks-dea*) and locate the *Exports* folder. From this folder, download the file named *book_materials.dbc* to your local machine.

2. Navigate to your workspace browser: In your Community Edition workspace, navigate to the Workspace tab to access your Home directory.

3. Use the Import option: At the top of your directory, click the menu icon (represented by three vertical dots) and select the Import option, as illustrated in Figure 1-11.

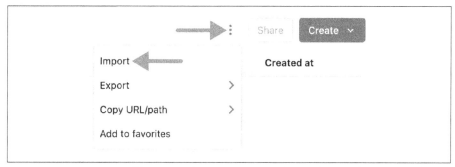

Figure 1-11. Importing files using the menu icon in the workspace browser

This action will open a dialog box where you can specify the file you want to import, as shown in Figure 1-12.

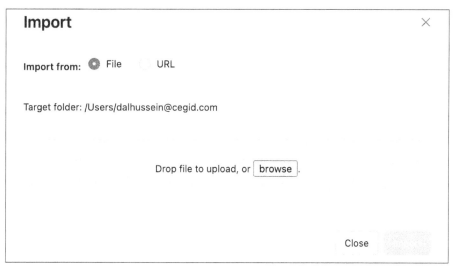

Figure 1-12. File import dialog

4. Upload the DBC file: In the Import dialog, browse to select the DBC file you downloaded earlier and import it into your workspace.

By following these steps, you will have all the book's resources in your workspace, allowing you to replicate the solutions within your own environment.

Creating Clusters

Clusters in Databricks form the backbone of data processing and analytics on the platform. A cluster is essentially a collection of computers, often referred to as *nodes*, instances, or virtual machines, working together as a single entity. In the context of Apache Spark, which powers Databricks, a cluster comprises a master node known as the *driver* and several worker nodes, as illustrated in Figure 1-13. The driver node is primarily responsible for orchestrating the activities of the worker nodes, which execute tasks in parallel, thereby enabling efficient processing of large-scale data.

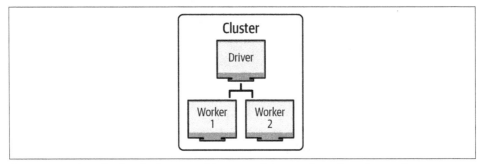

Figure 1-13. Apache Spark cluster architecture: driver node and worker nodes

Databricks offers two primary types of clusters: all-purpose clusters and job clusters. Each serves distinct purposes and use cases, tailored to different stages of the data engineering and analytics lifecycle. Table 1-1 summarizes the differences between these two types of clusters.

Table 1-1. Comparison of all-purpose clusters and job clusters

	All-purpose cluster	Job cluster
Usage	Interactive development and data analysis	Automated job execution
Management	Manually created and managed by the user	Automatically created by the job scheduler
Termination	Manual or auto-termination after inactivity	Automatic termination upon task completion
Cost efficiency	Comes at a higher expense	Less expensive

Let's dive deeper to gain a comprehensive understanding of these two types of clusters.

All-Purpose Clusters

All-purpose clusters are designed for interactive, exploratory tasks, making them ideal for development, and ad hoc analysis. They offer flexibility and control to users who need a dynamic environment to work with their data:

Usage

All-purpose clusters are mainly used for interactive tasks where a user is actively involved. This includes writing and testing code in notebooks and performing exploratory data analysis (EDA). The interactive nature of these clusters makes them essential for development and testing environments.

Management

Users can manually create and manage their all-purpose clusters depending on their needs. This can be achieved using the Databricks workspace interface, command-line interface, or REST API.

Termination

All-purpose clusters can be terminated manually by the user when they are no longer needed. Additionally, Databricks provides an auto-termination feature, where you can specify a period of inactivity after which the cluster will automatically shut down. This feature is particularly useful in reducing costs, as it prevents unnecessary resource consumption when the cluster is idle.

Cost efficiency

All-purpose clusters cost more to run when compared to other types of clusters. Additionally, they can become even more expensive due to the need for manual control and termination. Although auto-termination helps with cost savings, it still enforces a minimum runtime of 10 minutes, which can add to the overall expense.

In the next section, we will learn how to create and manage all-purpose clusters within the Databricks workspace. These clusters will be our primary tool for executing hands-on exercises throughout this book.

Job Clusters

Job clusters, on the other hand, are optimized for automated workloads. These clusters are designed to be ephemeral, spinning up only when a job is triggered and terminating immediately after the job is completed:

Usage

Job clusters are used primarily for running automated tasks, such as scheduled jobs and data pipelines. They are particularly useful in production environments where tasks need to be executed without manual intervention. Examples include extract, transform, and load (ETL) jobs, database maintenance, and training machine learning models on a scheduled basis.

Management
> Unlike all-purpose clusters, job clusters are not created manually by the user. Instead, they are automatically provisioned by the Databricks job scheduler when a job is triggered. This automation simplifies cluster management in production, as there is no need for manual intervention to start or stop clusters.

Termination
> Job clusters are designed to be used for a single purpose and terminate automatically once the assigned task is completed. This ephemeral nature ensures that resources are utilized only when necessary, which helps in optimizing costs and enhancing the efficiency of resource allocation.

Cost efficiency
> From a cost-efficiency standpoint, job clusters are generally more economical than all-purpose clusters. Therefore, it is recommended to use job clusters for production environments to optimize costs.

In Chapter 6, we explore job clusters in the context of Databricks Jobs and Delta Live Tables (DLT) pipelines.

Databricks Pools

In addition to offering various types of clusters, Databricks provides cluster pools to further optimize resource usage and reduce operational latency. Cluster pools are a powerful tool for users who need to minimize the time it takes to spin up clusters, especially in environments where job execution speed is critical.

Understanding cluster pools

A cluster pool in Databricks is essentially a group of pre-configured, idle virtual machines that are ready to be assigned to clusters as needed. The primary advantage of using a cluster pool is the reduction in both cluster start time and autoscaling time whenever there are available nodes in the pool. This can be particularly beneficial in scenarios where time is a critical factor, such as in automated report generation and real-time data processing tasks.

Cost considerations

While cluster pools offer significant operational benefits, they come with important cost considerations. It's essential to understand that even though Databricks itself does not charge for the idle instances in a pool, your cloud provider does. This is because these instances, although idle, are actively running on your cloud infrastructure, and as such, they incur standard compute costs. Therefore, when using cluster pools, it is important to balance the need for rapid cluster availability with the associated cloud costs.

Creating All-Purpose Clusters

This guide walks you through the process of creating an all-purpose cluster, from initial navigation to final configuration.

1. Navigating to the Compute tab

To begin, access the Compute tab from the left sidebar in your Databricks workspace. This page is the central hub for managing all your Databricks clusters, as illustrated in Figure 1-14.

Figure 1-14. Compute page in the Databricks workspace

This page presents various tabs at the top, including "All-purpose compute," "Job compute," and Pools, each corresponding to the different types of compute resources discussed earlier. Additionally, there's a tab for SQL warehouses, which are dedicated compute resources for executing SQL workloads within Databricks SQL. In Chapter 7, we delve deeply into Databricks SQL and explore the nuances of SQL warehouses. For the moment, let's focus on setting up an all-purpose cluster to get started with running interactive workloads.

2. Initiating the cluster creation

Under the "All-purpose compute tab," click the blue "Create compute" button. This action opens the configuration page for your new cluster, as illustrated in Figure 1-15.

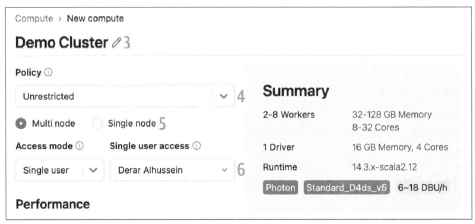

Figure 1-15. Compute cluster configuration page

3. Naming your cluster

The first step in the configuration process is naming your cluster. The system provides a default name, but you can change it by clicking the name field at the top. For example, you might name your cluster "Demo Cluster" to reflect its purpose.

4. Setting the cluster policy

Next, you'll encounter the Policy setting. By default, this is set to Unrestricted, allowing you full control over the cluster's configuration. In environments with stricter governance or where specific configurations are mandated, other policies may be in place to limit certain settings.

5. Configuring the cluster: Single-node versus multi-node

Databricks allows you to choose between creating a single-node cluster or a multi-node cluster:

Single-node cluster
    This cluster operates with just a driver node, eliminating the need for additional worker nodes. In this configuration, the driver handles both driver and worker responsibilities, executing all Spark jobs on a single machine. This setup is more cost effective as it consumes fewer resources.

Multi-node cluster
    If you need to handle larger datasets or more complex processing tasks, you can opt for a multi-node cluster, which includes one driver node and multiple worker nodes. This setup allows parallel processing, making it suitable for heavier workloads.

For demonstration, this guide will focus on configuring a multi-node cluster to show-case the advanced configuration options available.

6. Configuring the access mode

Databricks clusters offer different access modes depending on how the cluster is intended to be used:

Shared access mode
    This allows multiple users to share the cluster simultaneously but restricts work-loads to SQL and Python only. Shared clusters are useful in collaborative envi-ronments where several users need to access the same cluster.

Single user mode
    This mode is appropriate if you are the only one using the cluster. It ensures that the cluster resources are dedicated solely to your tasks, potentially improving performance and efficiency.

For this demonstration, select "Single user" mode as you are the only user of this cluster.

7. Performance: Selecting the Databricks Runtime version

The Databricks Runtime version is a critical choice, as it determines the software environment in which your clusters will operate. Databricks Runtime is a pre-configured virtual machine image that includes specific versions of Apache Spark, Scala, and various other libraries essential for data processing.

For this guide, choose Databricks Runtime 13.3 LTS (long-term support), as illustra-ted in Figure 1-16. This runtime version aligns with the version covered in the latest certification exam. Newer versions might offer additional features and optimizations that are not yet included in the exam. Sticking to the recommended version ensures you're studying the relevant content for the test.

Figure 1-16. Compute cluster configuration page (continued)

8. Enabling Photon

Photon is an optional feature you can enable to further enhance your cluster's performance. Photon is a high-speed query engine developed in C++, designed to accelerate the execution of SQL queries in Spark. Enabling Photon is particularly beneficial for workloads that involve heavy SQL processing or operations with many files, as it can significantly reduce query execution times and enhance overall performance. However, it's essential to consider the additional costs associated with this feature.

9. Configuring worker nodes

Worker nodes are the backbone of a multi-node cluster, responsible for processing the distributed tasks assigned by the driver node. Here, you'll configure the type and number of worker nodes, as illustrated in Figure 1-17.

Figure 1-17. Compute cluster configuration page (continued)

VM size selection
> Databricks allows you to choose from various virtual machine types and sizes provided by your cloud provider (e.g., Azure). These differ in terms of CPU cores, memory, and storage options, which should be selected based on the specific demands of your workloads. For simplicity, you may choose to keep the default VM size.

Number of workers
> Databricks offers an autoscaling feature, which dynamically adjusts the number of workers based on the cluster's workload. Enabled by default, the "Enable autoscaling" option allows you to specify a minimum and maximum range for the number of workers. Databricks will automatically increase or decrease the number of worker nodes within this range based on demand. Alternatively, you can disable autoscaling and set a fixed number of workers, such as 3, ensuring

that the cluster always operates with the specified resources regardless of changes in workload.

10. Configuring the driver node

After configuring the worker nodes, you can set the configuration for the driver node, which coordinates all tasks across the cluster. You can either choose a different configuration for the driver or simply match it with the worker nodes, depending on your workload requirements.

11. Enabling auto-termination

To manage costs and optimize resource usage, Databricks provides an auto-termination feature, which is also enabled by default. By setting a specific duration of inactivity (e.g., 30 minutes), you can ensure that the cluster automatically shuts down if it remains idle for that period. This feature is particularly useful in preventing unnecessary charges for clusters that are no longer in use.

12. Reviewing the cluster configuration

As you configure the cluster, Databricks provides a summary on the right side of the screen, giving you a clear overview of your selections, as shown in Figure 1-18.

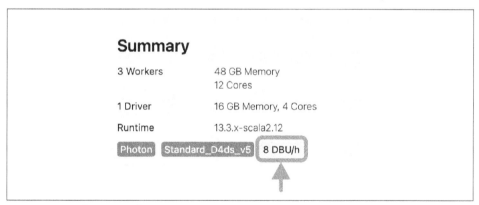

Figure 1-18. Cluster configuration summary

This summary includes important details such as the total number of worker cores and RAM, the runtime version, and the number of Databricks units (DBUs) the cluster will consume. A DBU is a measure of processing capacity per hour, which helps estimate the costs associated with running the cluster. For example, a single-node cluster will generally consume fewer DBUs compared to a multi-node cluster, making it a more cost-effective choice for less demanding workloads. For precise DBU pricing specific to your cloud and region, consult the Databricks pricing page (*https://oreil.ly/kCCy_*).

13. Creating the cluster

Once you have reviewed the configuration and ensured that it meets your needs, click the Create button. Databricks will then proceed to provision the required virtual machines, apply the configurations, and install Databricks Runtime and any additional specified libraries.

 If you are using the free tier on Microsoft Azure cloud, there is a compute limit of four cores. To avoid a quota exceeded error, ensure that you use a single-node cluster with a maximum of four cores.

Managing Your Cluster

Once your cluster in Databricks is provisioned and running, indicated by a fully green circle next to its name, you have several options for managing and monitoring it.

Controlling your cluster

To access your cluster at any time, simply navigate to the Compute tab in the left sidebar of your Databricks workspace. This page lists all your clusters, displaying their current status, whether running or terminated, as illustrated in Figure 1-19.

Figure 1-19. Compute page in the Databricks workspace

From this page, you can quickly start or terminate your cluster by clicking the play/ stop button located on the right side of each cluster's entry. Next to this button is a menu icon represented by three vertical dots. Clicking this icon opens a drop-down menu with additional management features, including cloning the cluster, editing its permissions, and deleting it.

By clicking the cluster's name, you can access the configuration settings and make adjustments as needed. For example, you might want to change the instance type, adjust the number of workers, or enable additional features like Photon. However, be aware that changing the cluster configuration may require a restart of the cluster, which interrupts any running jobs.

Managing your cluster

Effective cluster management goes beyond just starting and stopping the cluster. Databricks provides tools to monitor the cluster's activity and troubleshoot any issues. These tools are accessible from the cluster configuration page, as illustrated in Figure 1-20.

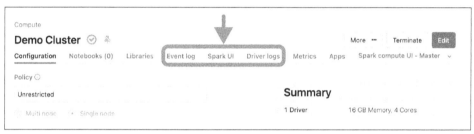

Figure 1-20. Compute cluster configuration page

Event log
> The "Event log" records all significant actions related to the cluster, such as when the cluster was created, terminated, edited, or encountered any errors. This detailed tracking enables effective monitoring and troubleshooting of cluster activities.

Spark UI
> The Spark UI provides a comprehensive interface for monitoring and debugging Apache Spark applications. It provides detailed insights into job execution, stages, and tasks that enable you to easily track performance and identify bottlenecks.

Driver logs
> "Driver logs" contains logs generated by the driver node within the cluster. This log captures output from the notebooks and libraries running on the cluster, making it an essential tool for diagnosing and resolving issues during development.

With our cluster up and running, we're now ready to execute code within Databricks notebooks. This will be the focus of the following section.

Working with Notebooks

Databricks notebooks are interactive development environments that enable you to write, debug, and execute code in a collaborative setting. These notebooks offer advanced capabilities that extend beyond those of traditional environments like Jupyter Notebooks. Databricks notebooks support multiple programming languages, including Python, SQL, Scala, and R. In addition, they integrate seamlessly with Spark clusters, allowing users to leverage distributed computing resources directly from the notebook interface.

Creating a New Notebook

To begin working with notebooks in Databricks, navigate to the Workspace tab in the left sidebar of your Databricks workspace. To create a new notebook, click the blue Create button and choose Notebook from the drop-down menu, as illustrated in Figure 1-21.

Figure 1-21. Adding new notebooks using the Create button in the workspace browser

This action will create and open a new notebook, initially named "Untitled Notebook." The notebook is immediately ready for use, but it's good practice to rename it to something more descriptive. To rename your notebook, simply click the title at the top of the notebook interface and enter a new name, such as **Demo Notebook**.

Setting the Notebook Language

Databricks notebooks default to Python, but they support multiple languages, including SQL, Scala, and R. If you need to work in a language other than Python, you can easily change the notebook's default language. To do this, click the language indicator at the top of the notebook, where it says "Python," and select the desired language from the drop-down menu, as shown in Figure 1-22.

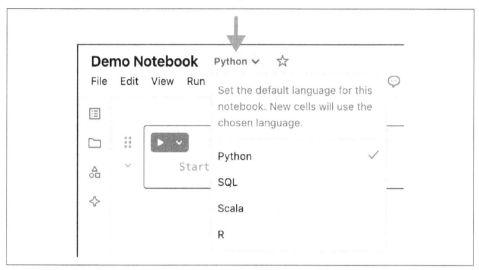

Figure 1-22. Changing the default language in Databricks notebooks

Executing Code

Before executing any code, it's necessary to connect your notebook to an active cluster. Click the Connect button in the top-right corner of the notebook interface, as illustrated in Figure 1-23, and select the desired cluster, such as Demo Cluster created earlier.

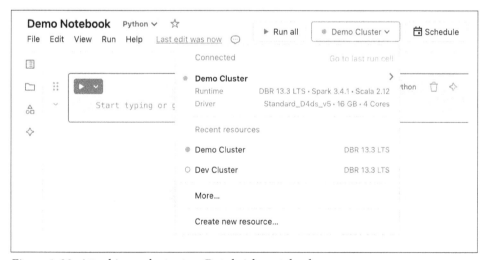

Figure 1-23. Attaching a cluster to a Databricks notebook

If the cluster is currently terminated, selecting it will automatically start it. Starting a terminated cluster can take a few minutes, depending on factors like the cluster's size and configuration.

 Databricks offers serverless compute for notebooks, which allows you to run code without the need to configure and deploy infrastructure. To use this feature, your workspace must be enabled for Unity Catalog, and serverless compute must be activated in your Databricks account (*https://oreil.ly/KNUXM*).

Once the cluster is running, indicated by a fully green circle next to its name, your notebook is ready to execute code.

Running code cells

Databricks notebooks use a cell-based structure, where each cell can contain a block of code. This structure allows for interactive development, where you can run each cell independently, see immediate results, and make adjustments as needed.

Let's start by printing a simple "Hello World" message in our notebook. To do this, enter the following Python command into the first cell:

```
print("Hello World!")
```

To run the cell, click the play button on the left side of the cell, as displayed in Figure 1-24. Alternatively, you can use the Shift+Enter keyboard shortcut to run the current cell and move to the next one. This tends to be more efficient, especially when running lots of cells in succession.

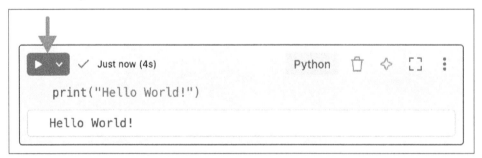

Figure 1-24. Running code cells in Databricks notebooks

The output of the cell—in this case, "Hello World!"—will appear directly below the cell. This immediate feedback is one of the key advantages of working with notebooks, allowing you to experiment and iterate quickly. Other types of outputs can have richer displays, and you'll also see error messages, tool tips, or other warnings here as you work.

Managing cells

Notebooks provide a flexible environment for organizing your code. You can add, move, and remove cells to structure your code logically. To add a new cell, hover your mouse just below an existing cell, and you'll see a + Code button appear, as illustrated in Figure 1-25. Click this button to insert a new cell.

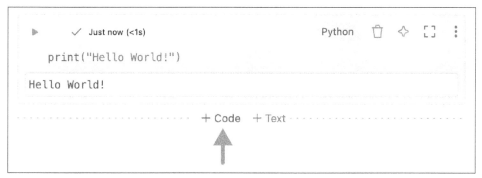

Figure 1-25. Adding a new cell in Databricks notebooks

This approach allows you to break your code into manageable sections, making it easier to develop, debug, and maintain.

Magic Commands

Magic commands in Databricks notebooks are special cell instructions that provide additional functionality in the notebook environment. These commands, which are prefixed with a %, allow you to execute tasks that go beyond standard code execution. Let's explore these commands in detail, highlighting their benefits and how to use them effectively.

Language magic command

By default, a notebook is set to one primary language, but you may often need to use a different language within the same notebook for specific tasks. Language magic commands allow you to execute code cells in a language other than the notebook's default without changing the entire notebook's settings.

To switch the language for a specific cell, you just need to add the language magic command at the beginning of the cell. For example, if your notebook's default language is Python, but you need to run a SQL query, you would use the %sql magic command. This command instructs the notebook to interpret and execute the cell as SQL code:

```
%sql
SELECT "Hello world from SQL!"
```

When you enter a SQL query in a cell, Databricks automatically prepends the %sql magic command if the cell's content is detected as SQL. The cell's language indicator, located on the right side of the cell, will also change to reflect the active language, as shown in Figure 1-26.

Figure 1-26. Language magic command in Databricks notebooks

If you want to manually change the language of a cell or convert it to a text Markdown cell, you can also do so by clicking this language indicator. This action will bring up a drop-down menu that allows you to select the desired option.

Markdown magic command

Beyond code execution, Databricks notebooks support rich-text formatting through the use of Markdown, which is enabled by the %md magic command. Markdown is an annotation language that allows you to format text and insert elements such as images or links directly within the notebook. This feature is particularly useful for documenting your analysis, adding notes, or structuring your notebook into sections.

To add formatted text, simply start a cell with the %md magic command, followed by your Markdown syntax. For instance, to create headers of different levels, you might use the following commands:

```
%md
# Title 1
## Title 2
### Title 3
```

When you press Esc, the text will be rendered as headers with varying levels of emphasis, as illustrated in Figure 1-27.

Figure 1-27. Markdown magic command in Databricks notebooks

Double-clicking a Markdown cell reopens its editor, where you'll find a toolbar with a range of formatting options such as bold, italic, and list creation. It also offers the ability to add images and hyperlinks, which enriches your notes or documentation.

Enhancing notebook navigation with Markdown

One of the significant advantages of using Markdown headers in Databricks notebooks is that they automatically generate entries in the notebook's table of contents. The table of contents is a navigational aid that allows you to quickly jump between sections in your notebook.

To access the table of contents, click its icon in the left-hand panel of the notebook editor, as shown in Figure 1-28.

Figure 1-28. Table of contents in Databricks notebooks

As you add more Markdown headers, these will populate the table of contents, providing an organized overview of your notebook's structure.

Run magic command

The %run magic command in Databricks notebooks is a powerful tool that allows you to execute another notebook within the current notebook. This feature is particularly useful for supporting code modularity and reusability.

The %run command is designed to import and execute all the content of a specified notebook into the current notebook. This means that any variables, functions, or classes defined in the referenced notebook become accessible in the notebook that invoked the %run command. This is highly beneficial for scenarios where you need to share common configurations and functions across multiple notebooks.

To illustrate the use of the %run magic command, let's walk through a practical example where you have two notebooks—our primary notebook named "Demo Notebook" and a secondary notebook named "Setup":

1. Creating the Setup notebook: First, create a new notebook called "Setup" in your Home directory. In this notebook, you define a simple variable, book_publisher, and assign it the value OReilly:

   ```
   book_publisher = "OReilly"
   ```

2. Using the %run command: Now, switch to your demo notebook, where you want to access the variables of the Setup notebook. In a new cell, use the %run magic command followed by the path to the Setup notebook. Since both notebooks are in the same directory, you can use the dot symbol (.) to refer to the current directory, or alternatively, you could use the full workspace path to specify the exact location of the Setup notebook:

   ```
   %run ./Setup
   ```

3. Accessing the imported variable: After running the previous command, the entire contents of the Setup notebook are executed, bringing any defined variables and functions into the scope of the demo notebook. To verify this, you can print the book_publisher variable in a new cell in the demo notebook.

Figure 1-29 displays the output of the print command, confirming that the book_publisher variable was successfully imported from the Setup notebook into our demo notebook.

Figure 1-29. Run magic command in Databricks notebooks

The %run magic command is an essential feature for anyone working with Databricks notebooks, offering a seamless way to create modular, maintainable, and reusable code.

FS magic command

When working within the Databricks environment, managing files and interacting with the file system is a common task. The %fs magic command provides a simple way to execute file system operations directly within your notebook cells. This command allows you to perform various tasks, such as copying, moving, and deleting files and directories within your cloud storage.

One of the most common uses of the %fs magic command is listing the contents of a directory. For instance, if you want to explore the sample datasets directory provided by Databricks, you can use the following command:

```
%fs ls '/databricks-datasets'
```

Running this command will list all files and folders within the */databricks-datasets* directory, displaying 55 items by default, as illustrated in Figure 1-30.

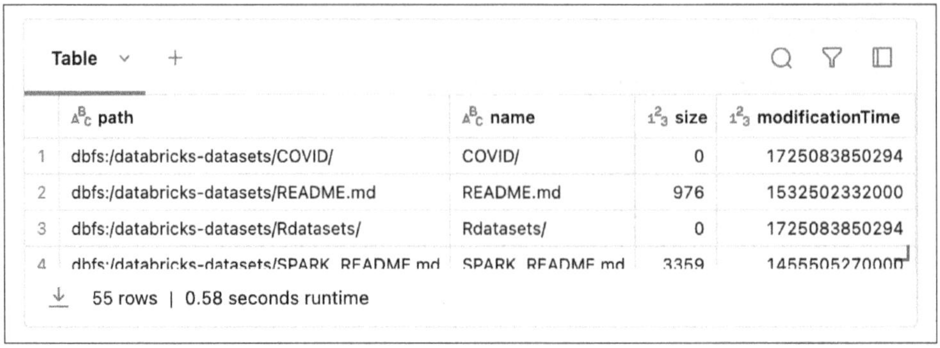

	A^B_C path	A^B_C name	1²₃ size	1²₃ modificationTime
1	dbfs:/databricks-datasets/COVID/	COVID/	0	1725083850294
2	dbfs:/databricks-datasets/README.md	README.md	976	1532502332000
3	dbfs:/databricks-datasets/Rdatasets/	Rdatasets/	0	1725083850294
4	dbfs:/databricks-datasets/SPARK_README.md	SPARK_README.md	3359	1455505270000

⤓ 55 rows | 0.58 seconds runtime

Figure 1-30. Output of the %fs ls magic command on the /databricks-datasets directory

While the `%fs` magic command is convenient, Databricks provides a more flexible and powerful tool called `dbutils`. This tool is particularly useful for integrating file system operations directly into your Python code.

Databricks Utilities

Databricks Utilities (`dbutils`) provides a range of utility commands for interacting with different services and tools within Databricks, including the file system (`dbutils.fs`).

To explore all available commands and their usage within `dbutils`, you can use the help function:

```
dbutils.help()
```

If you're interested in a specific utility within `dbutils`, you can request detailed help for that particular module. For example, if you want to learn more about the file system commands provided by `dbutils.fs`, you can use this:

```
dbutils.fs.help()
```

This command will provide information about the file system operations available, including how to perform common tasks such as listing directories. To achieve similar functionality as the `%fs` command using `dbutils`, you can list the contents of the same directory with the following code:

```
files = dbutils.fs.ls("/databricks-datasets/")
```

This command not only lists the files but also stores the output in a variable (files), which can be further manipulated within your code.

Displaying the output

Directly printing the "files" variable might result in an output that's difficult to read:

```
print(files)
```

To present this information in a more user-friendly way, Databricks provides the display function, which formats the output in a tabular layout:

```
display(files)
```

Using this function, the results are neatly organized into columns, such as filename, size, and type, making it easier to understand and work with the data. Additionally, the display function offers advanced features, like downloading the data as a CSV file or visualizing the results in a graph, as shown in Figure 1-31.

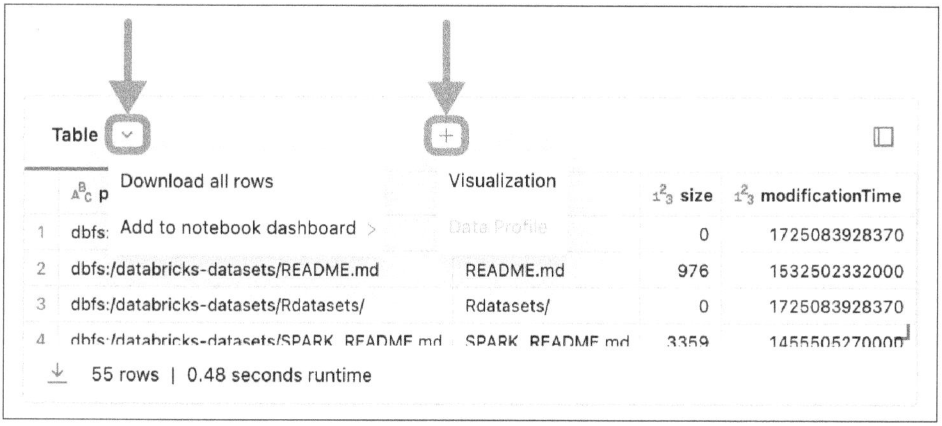

Figure 1-31. Advanced features of the preview display, including data download and visualization options

It's important to be aware that while the display function is useful, it has limitations when previewing large datasets, as it shows only a subset of records.

Comparison: %fs magic command versus dbutils

Choosing between the %fs magic command and dbutils depends on the complexity and requirements of your task. If you need to perform a quick, one-off file system operation, the %fs magic command is straightforward and easy to use. For more complex tasks, especially when you need to manipulate the output programmatically, dbutils is the better choice. It allows you to store the results in variables, apply conditional logic, loop through files, and more—all within your Python code.

Download Notebooks

You may want to download a notebook to your local system for various reasons, such as sharing with others or simply keeping a local copy. Databricks offers a straightforward way to export your notebooks by following these steps:

1. Navigate to the File menu: In the upper menu of your notebook editor, click the File menu, as illustrated in Figure 1-32.

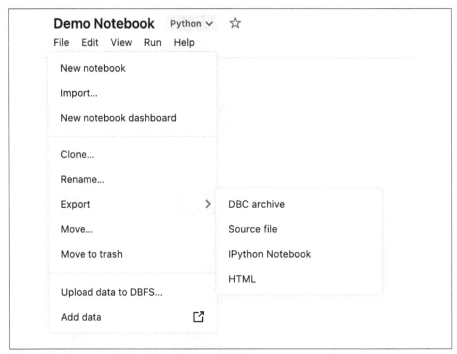

Figure 1-32. File menu in the Databricks notebook editor

2. Select Export: From the drop-down menu, choose the Export option. This will present you with several formats for downloading your notebook.

3. Choose file format: Click "Source file" to download the notebook as a plain Python script (*.py* file). For an HTML output, select IPython Notebook, which is useful for sharing results without needing to render them within a workspace.

The downloaded file can be edited locally or easily imported into a different Databricks workspace for further use. To import a file into a specific folder on Databricks, simply click the menu icon in the target folder and select the Import option, as shown in Figure 1-33.

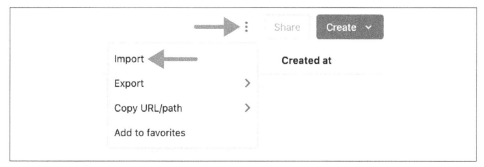

Figure 1-33. Importing files using the menu icon in the workspace browser

By following these steps, you can ensure that you have the flexibility to work with your notebooks across different environments.

Notebook Versioning

As you develop your code in Databricks, you will likely make numerous changes and refinements, which can be challenging to track. To address this issue, Databricks provides a built-in versioning system within its notebooks, allowing you to easily manage and revert to previous versions of your code.

Accessing version history

To access the version history of a notebook, look for the "Version history" icon located in the right sidebar of your notebook editor. Clicking this icon opens a panel displaying the version history, as illustrated in Figure 1-34.

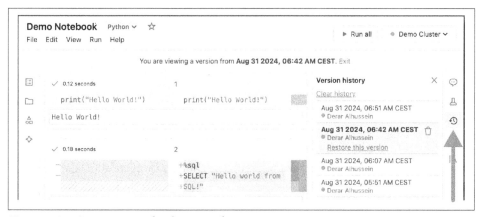

Figure 1-34. Accessing notebook version history

This "Version history" panel shows a chronological list of all changes made to the notebook. Each entry in the list corresponds to an auto-saved version of the notebook, capturing the state of the notebook at that point in time.

Restoring a previous version

If you need to revert to a previous state of the notebook, simply select the desired version from the list and click "Restore this version." This action reverts the current state of the notebook to the selected version, undoing any changes made since that version.

While this versioning feature is helpful for tracking changes, it has limitations, especially in complex or collaborative projects. It lacks advanced capabilities such as merging changes or creating branches. Additionally, users can easily delete this history, which may compromise its reliability. For a more robust solution, Databricks provides integration with Git providers, offering enhanced version control capabilities.

Versioning with Git

Databricks offers Git integration, allowing users to manage their data projects using familiar Git workflows, including branching, merging, committing, and pushing changes to remote repositories. This feature is particularly beneficial for users who need to manage complex projects, collaborate with team members, or maintain a history of changes in a more controlled and secure manner than what the basic notebook versioning can offer.

This seamless integration is facilitated through Git folders, formerly known as Databricks Repos, which enable source control directly into your Databricks workspace. With Git folders, you can synchronize your code with remote Git repositories and perform common Git operations.

Setting Up Git Integration

When importing source code from a public repository like our book's GitHub repo, Git folders work seamlessly without additional setup. However, for private repositories or when performing Git operations like committing and pushing changes, you must link your Databricks workspace with your Git service provider. This setup ensures that you can perform all necessary Git operations from within Databricks.

Prerequisites

Before setting up Git integration, ensure the following:

Access to a full version of Databricks
The Git integration feature is not available in the Databricks Community Edition, so you'll need access to a full version of Databricks on a cloud platform like AWS, Azure, or Google Cloud.

Git service account
You should have an account with a supported Git service provider, such as GitHub or Azure DevOps.

Configuring Git integration

To configure Git integration in your Databricks workspace, follow these steps:

1. Access your profile settings: In the Databricks workspace, click your username profile icon located in the upper-right corner. From the drop-down menu, select Settings.

2. Link your Git provider: In the Settings page, navigate to the "Linked accounts" tab from the left side panel, as displayed in Figure 1-35. Here, you will find options to link your Databricks account with various Git service providers, including GitHub, Azure DevOps, and Bitbucket. Select your desired provider from the drop-down menu.

3. Authenticate your Git provider: If you are linking with GitHub, you can use a more secure method through the Databricks GitHub App, instead of using a personal access token (PAT). Select the "Link Git account" option, and click the Link button to start the process. You will be redirected to GitHub to authorize the Databricks app to access your GitHub account. Follow the on-screen instructions to complete the process.

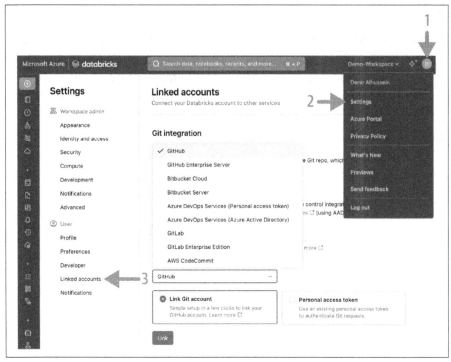

Figure 1-35. Git integration settings in Databricks

4. Install the Databricks app on GitHub: After authorizing the Databricks GitHub App, click Configure in GitHub, as shown in Figure 1-36, to configure the app installation on your GitHub account.

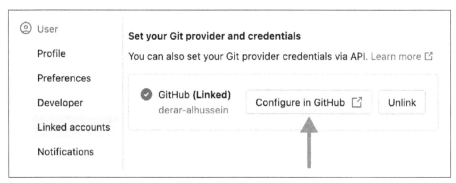

Figure 1-36. Configuring GitHub integration in Databricks

In the configuration page, you can choose to grant access to all your repositories or select specific repositories that Databricks can interact with, as displayed in Figure 1-37.

Once you confirm your selections, click Install to complete the setup. With this, your Databricks workspace is now fully integrated with your chosen Git provider, enabling seamless version control and collaboration.

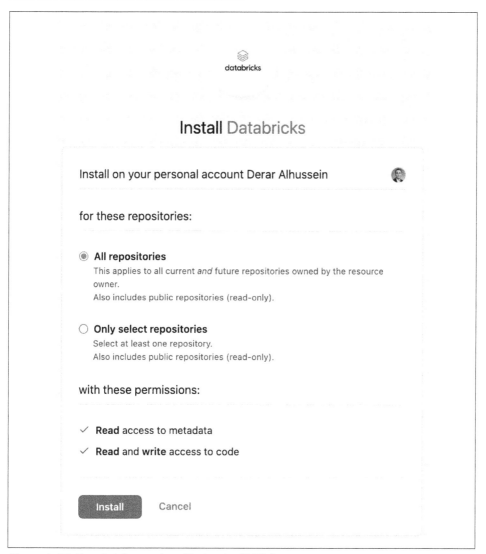

Figure 1-37. Databricks app installation in GitHub account

Creating Git Folders

For effective collaboration and version control, integrating a private GitHub repository with Databricks is essential. This process involves creating a Git folder within your Databricks workspace and linking it to your private repository. The following is a step-by-step guide to help you achieve this integration:

1. Creating a private GitHub repository: To begin, ensure you have a private GitHub repository set up. If you haven't done so yet, create a new one from your GitHub account and copy its URL.

2. Cloning the repository in Databricks: Now that you have your private repository ready, follow these steps to clone it into your Databricks workspace:

    a. Navigate to your workspace browser: In your Databricks workspace, navigate to the Workspace tab to access your Home directory.

    b. Create a Git folder: At the top of your directory, click the Create button and select "Git folder" from the drop-down menu, as illustrated in Figure 1-38.

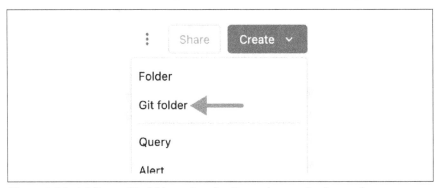

Figure 1-38. Adding a Git folder using the Create button in the workspace browser

This action will open a dialog box where you can specify the GitHub repository you want to clone, as shown in Figure 1-39.

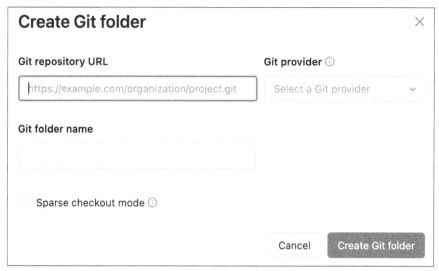

Create Git folder

×

Git repository URL

https://example.com/organization/project.git

Git provider ⓘ

Select a Git provider ⌄

Git folder name

Sparse checkout mode ⓘ

Cancel   **Create Git folder**

Figure 1-39. Git folder creation dialog

c. Paste the GitHub repository URL: In the Git folder creation dialog, paste the URL of your private repository. The interface will automatically detect the Git provider (e.g., GitHub) and fill in the repository name based on the URL provided.

d. Create the Git folder: After confirming the details, click the "Create Git folder" button to clone the repository.

Once the repository is cloned, you can navigate through its contents like any other folder. Git folders are easily recognized within the workspace browser by the current branch name displayed next to the folder name, as illustrated in Figure 1-40.

Figure 1-40. Branch name indicator in Git folders

Managing Git Branches

Branches are a fundamental aspect of Git, allowing multiple developers to work on different features or fixes simultaneously without interfering with the main codebase.

By default, your Git repository will open on the main branch. To create a new local branch (e.g., a development branch), follow these steps:

1. Open the Git dialog: Click the branch name indicator next to the folder name. This will open the Git dialog, as shown in Figure 1-41.

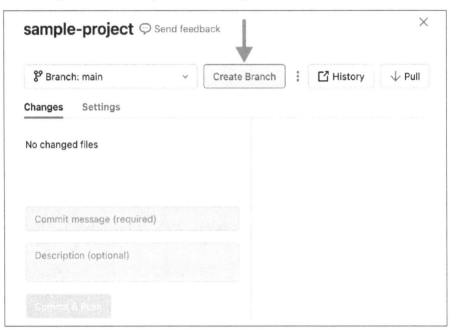

Figure 1-41. Git dialog in Databricks

2. Create the branch: Click the Create Branch button, specify the branch name (e.g., "dev" branch), and click Create.

This creates a local branch in the workspace and activates it immediately, allowing you to start working on your changes, just like you would on your machine. You can easily switch between branches at any time using the drop-down menu next to the Create Branch button.

With your development branch selected, you can begin working on your project by creating new notebooks or importing existing ones. Any edits you make to the source code are contained within this branch, which keeps the main branch stable and unaffected. Once your updates are ready and thoroughly tested, you can commit and push them to the remote repository.

Committing and Pushing Changes

Once you've made changes in your Git folder, you can commit and push these changes to the remote repository to ensure your work is saved and shared with others.

To commit your changes, follow these steps:

1. Open the Git dialog: Click the branch name indicator to open the Git dialog.

2. Review changes: The Git dialog will display all the modifications made in the current branch, as illustrated in Figure 1-42.

Figure 1-42. Committing and pushing changes using the Git dialog

3. Add a commit message: At the bottom of the dialog, write a descriptive commit message summarizing the changes and any other information your organization might require.

4. Commit & Push: Click the blue Commit & Push button. This will save your changes locally and then push them to the remote repository on GitHub.

After pushing your changes, you can verify the update on the GitHub website. Navigate to your private repository and check the development branch to ensure the changes have been successfully applied.

Pulling Changes from GitHub

To keep your local repository in sync with the remote repository, especially after merging branches or when working in collaboration with others, pulling new changes is a common operation.

Synchronizing with merged pull requests

As a fundamental principle of Git, changes made in one branch are isolated from other branches until explicitly merged. To verify this, switch to the main branch in your Git folder by selecting it from the branch drop-down in the Git dialog. You will notice that the changes made in the dev branch are not visible in the main branch until a pull request (PR) is created and merged.

Databricks Git folders do not support creating pull requests directly; this must be done through your Git provider. For GitHub, follow these steps:

1. Create a pull request: On GitHub, navigate to your *sample-project* repository and create a pull request to merge changes from the dev branch into the main branch.

2. Merge the pull request: Once the pull request is reviewed and approved, merge it into the main branch on GitHub.

Pulling changes

To pull changes from the remote main branch to your local repository in Git folder, follow these steps:

1. Open the Git dialog: Click the branch name indicator in your Git folder to open the Git dialog.

2. Initiate a pull: With the main branch selected, click the Pull button, as displayed in Figure 1-43.

This action will fetch and merge changes from the remote main branch into your local copy. After merging, you can review the updates in your folder to ensure the integration was successful. As a best practice, perform regular pulls to minimize conflicts, especially in collaborative development environments where multiple contributors are working on the same codebase.

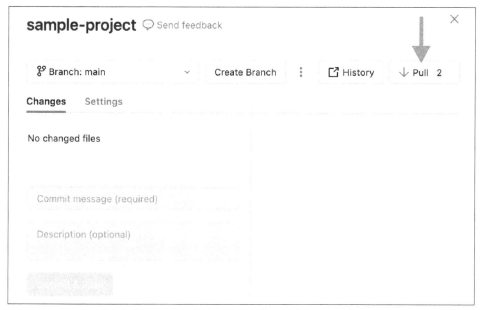

Figure 1-43. Pulling changes using the Git dialog

Conclusion

In conclusion, this chapter has provided an essential overview of the Databricks Data Intelligence Platform, covering its foundational architecture and offering practical guidance on working with clusters and notebooks. By mastering these essential components, you are now well-equipped to leverage the full potential of Databricks, which will be further explored in subsequent chapters.

Sample Exam Questions

Databricks certification exams primarily consist of multiple-choice questions with a single correct answer. The questions are categorized into two types: conceptual and code-based. Preparing for both types is critical for passing the certification exam.

Conceptual Questions

Conceptual questions focus on assessing your understanding of the core principles and features of Databricks. These questions typically ask you to recall definitions, describe functionality, or identify the role of different components within the Databricks environment.

Here is a sample conceptual question to give you a sense of what you might encounter:

Question 1. According to the Databricks lakehouse architecture, which of the following locations hosts the customer data?

A. Control plane

B. Databricks account

C. Customer's cloud account

D. Databricks Runtime

E. Workspace

This question tests your understanding of where Databricks stores customer data. The correct answer to this question is available in Appendix C.

Code-Based Questions

Code-based questions assess your ability to read, write, and debug code in the Databricks environment. These questions often present a block of code and ask you to either fill in missing portions of code, identify errors, or suggest modifications to ensure the code runs correctly.

Let's look at a sample code-based question:

Question 2. A data engineer has written the following code block within a cell in a SQL notebook, intending to list the files in the Databricks datasets directory:

```
files = dbutils.fs.ls("/databricks-datasets/")
print(files)
```

However, the code returns a syntax error.

What modification should be made to the code block to resolve this issue?

A. Replace `print(files)` with `display(files)`.

B. Use the following command instead:

```
files = %fs ls 'databricks-datasets'
print(files)
```

C. Use the following command instead:

```
files = %fs ls 'databricks-datasets'
display(files)
```

D. Add `%python` at the beginning of the cell.

E. Add `%run` at the beginning of the cell.

This question tests your ability to properly use the Databricks utility methods and understand how to display results in a notebook environment. The correct answer to this question can also be found in Appendix C.

CHAPTER 2

Managing Data with Delta Lake

Data lakehouses leverage specialized storage frameworks to enhance the functionality of traditional data lakes. Among these frameworks, Delta Lake stands out as a leading technology that powers the Databricks Lakehouse Platform. In this chapter, we'll explore the fundamental concepts of Delta Lake by first introducing its core principles and then diving into its practical usage. Following this, we'll focus on advanced topics in Delta Lake such as time travel, table optimization, and vacuum operations.

Introducing Delta Lake

Traditional data lakes often suffer from inefficiencies and encounter various challenges in processing big data. Delta Lake technology is an innovative solution designed to operate on top of data lakes to overcome these issues. To establish a clear understanding of Delta Lake, let's first study its definition as provided by its original creators at Databricks.

What Is Delta Lake?

> Delta Lake is an open-source storage layer that brings reliability to data lakes by adding a transactional storage layer on top of data stored in cloud storage.
>
> —Databricks

In the context of data lakehouses, a storage layer refers to the framework responsible for managing and organizing data stored within the data lake. It serves as an intermediary platform through which data is ingested, queried, and processed.

In other words, Delta Lake is not a storage medium or storage format. Common storage formats like Parquet or JSON define how data is physically stored in the lake. However, Delta Lake runs on top of such data formats to provide a robust solution that overcomes the challenges of data lakes.

While data lakes are excellent solutions for storing massive volumes of diverse data, they often encounter several challenges related to data inconsistency and performance issues. The primary factor behind these limitations is the absence of ACID transaction support in a data lake. ACID stands for atomicity, consistency, isolation, and durability, and represents fundamental rules that ensure operations on data are reliably executed, as in traditional databases. This absence led to issues such as partially committed data and corrupted files, ultimately affecting the overall reliability of the data stored in the lake.

What makes Delta Lake an innovative solution is its ability to overcome such challenges posed by traditional data lakes. Delta Lake provides ACID transaction guarantees for data manipulation operations in the lake. It offers transactional capabilities that enable performing data operations in an atomic and consistent manner. This ensures that there is no partially committed data; either all operations within a transaction are completed successfully or none of them is. These capabilities allow you to build reliable data lakes that ensure data integrity, consistency, and durability.

Delta Lake is optimized for cloud object storage. It seamlessly integrates with leading cloud storage platforms such as Amazon S3, Azure Data Lake Storage, and Google Cloud Storage.

On top of all this, Delta Lake is an open source library. Unlike proprietary solutions, Delta Lake's source code is freely available to you on GitHub (*https://oreil.ly/delta*).

To put it all together, we can visualize these concepts through an illustrative graph. In Figure 2-1, we highlight the key elements that constitute the Delta Lake technology.

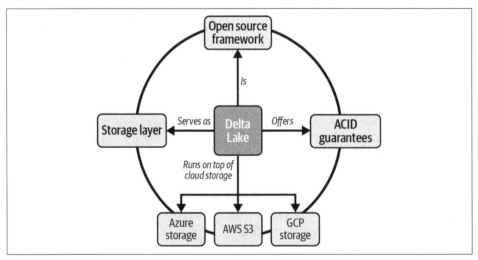

Figure 2-1. Delta Lake technology

Delta Lake Transaction Log

The Delta Lake library is deployed on the cluster as part of the Databricks Runtime. When you create a Delta Lake table within this ecosystem, the data is stored on the cloud storage in one or more data files in Parquet format. However, alongside these data files, Delta Lake creates a transaction log in JSON format, as illustrated in Figure 2-2.

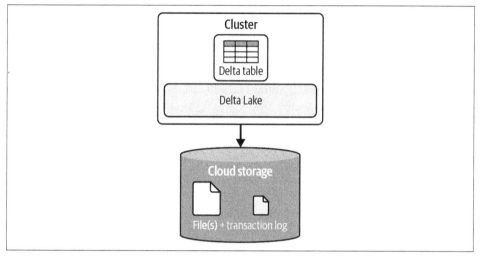

Figure 2-2. Delta Lake tables creation

The Delta Lake transaction log, often referred to as the Delta Log, is an ordered record of every transaction performed on the table since its creation. As a result, it functions as the source of truth for the table's state and history. So every time you query the table, Spark checks this transaction log to determine the most recent version of the data.

Each committed transaction is recorded in a JSON file. This file contains essential details about the operations performed, such as its type (insert, update, …, etc.) and any predicate used during these operations, including conditions and filters. Beyond simply tracking the operations executed, the log captures the names of all data files affected by these operations.

In the next section, we will see how these transactional capabilities are leveraged by Delta Lake to ensure ACID compliance during data retrieval and manipulation.

Understanding Delta Lake Functionality

Let's learn how Delta Lake functions by looking at a series of illustrative examples, each designed to provide a deeper understanding of its behavior in different scenarios. For instance, consider a situation where two users, Alice and Bob, interact with a

Delta Lake table. Alice represents a data producer, while Bob is a data consumer. Their interaction on the table can be described in four key scenarios: data writing and reading, data updating, concurrent writes and reads, and, lastly, failed write attempts. Let's discuss them in detail one by one.

Writing and reading scenario

In this first scenario, we will examine how data is written to and read from a Delta Lake table by Alice and Bob.

Write operation by Alice. Alice initiates this scenario by creating the Delta table and populating it with data, as illustrated in Figure 2-3. The Delta module stores the table, for example, in two data files (*part 1* and *part 2*), and saves them in a Parquet format within the table directory on the storage. Upon the completion of writing the data files, the Delta module adds a transaction log, labeled as 000.json, into the *_delta_log* subdirectory. This transaction log captures metadata information about the changes made to the Delta table. This includes the operation type, the name of the newly created data files, the transaction timestamp, and any other relevant information.

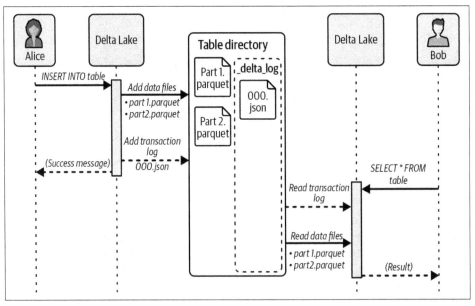

Figure 2-3. Writing and reading scenario

Read operation by Bob. Subsequently, Bob queries the Delta table through a SQL SELECT statement. However, before directly accessing the data files, the Delta module always begins by consulting the transaction log associated with the table. In this particular case, it starts by reading the 000.json transaction log located in the *_delta_log* subfolder. This log contains metadata information regarding the data files *part*

1.parquet and *part 2.parquet* that capture the changes made by Alice during the write operation. The Delta module proceeds by reading these two data files and returning the results to Bob.

So, Delta Lake follows a structured approach for managing and processing the data in the lake. It always uses the transaction log as a point of reference to interact with the data files of Delta Lake tables.

Updating scenario

In our second scenario, Alice makes an update to a record residing in file *part 1.parquet* of the Delta table, as illustrated in Figure 2-4. However, since Parquet files are immutable—meaning their contents cannot be changed after they are written—Delta Lake takes a unique approach to updates. Instead of directly modifying the record within the existing file, the Delta module makes a copy of the data from the original file and applies the necessary updates in a new data file, *part 3.parquet*. It then updates the log by writing a new transaction record (`001.json`). The new log file is now aware that the data file *part 1.parquet* is no longer relevant to the current state of the table.

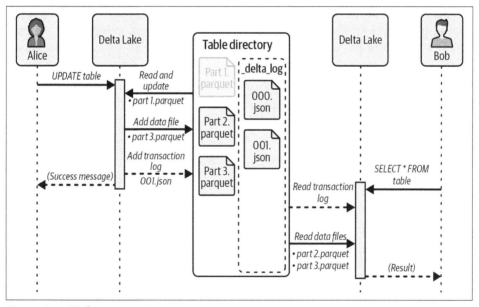

Figure 2-4. Updates scenario

When Bob attempts to read data from the table, the Delta module first consults the transaction log to determine the valid files for the current table version. In this instance, the log indicates that only the parquet files *part 2* and *part 3* are included in the latest version of the table. As a result, the Delta module confidently reads data from these two files and ignores the outdated file *part 1.parquet.*

So, Delta Lake follows the principle of immutability; once a file is written to the storage layer, it remains unchanged. The approach of handling updates through file copying and transaction log management ensures that the historical versions of data are preserved. This offers a comprehensive record of all modifications performed on the table. We will explore in the following section how to leverage these historical versions for tasks such as auditing, rollbacks, and time travel queries.

Concurrent writes and reads scenario

In this scenario, Alice and Bob are both interacting with the table simultaneously, as illustrated in Figure 2-5. Alice is inserting new data, initiating the creation of a new data file, *part 4.parquet.* Meanwhile, Bob is querying the table, where the Delta module starts by reading the transaction log to determine which Parquet files contain the relevant data.

At the time Bob executes the query, the transaction log includes information about the Parquet files *part 2* and *part 3* only, as the file *part 4.parquet* is not fully written yet. So, Bob's query reads the two latest files available that represent the current table state at that moment. Using this methodology, Delta Lake guarantees that you will always get the most recent version of the data. Your read operations will never have a deadlock state or conflicts with any ongoing operation on the table.

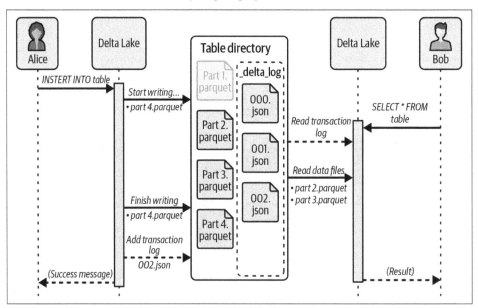

Figure 2-5. Concurrent writes and reads scenario

Finally, once Alice's query finishes writing the new data, the Delta module adds a new JSON file to the transaction log, named *002.json*.

In summary, Delta Lake's transaction log helps avoid conflicts between write and read operations on the table. So, even when write and read operations are occurring simultaneously, read operations can proceed without waiting for the writes to complete. This capability helps maintain the reliability and performance of data operations on Delta Lake tables.

Failed writes scenario

Here is our last scenario: imagine that Alice attempts again to insert new data into the Delta table, as illustrated in Figure 2-6. The Delta module begins writing the new data to the lake in a new file, *part 5.parquet*. However, an unexpected error occurs during this operation, resulting in the creation of an incomplete file. This failure prevents the Delta module from recording any information related to this incomplete file in the transaction log.

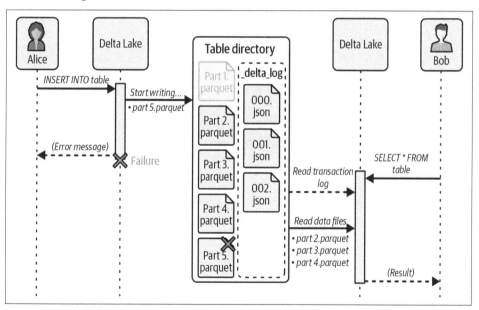

Figure 2-6. Failed writes scenario

Now, when Bob queries the table, the Delta module starts, as usual, by reading the transaction log. Since there is no information about the incomplete file *part 5.parquet* in the log, only the parquet files *part 2*, *part 3*, and *part 4* will be considered for the query output. Consequently, Bob's query is protected from accessing the incomplete or dirty data created by Alice's unsuccessful write operation.

In essence, Delta Lake guarantees the prevention of reading incomplete or inconsistent data. The transaction log serves as a reliable record of committed operations on the table. And in the event of a failed write, the absence of corresponding information in the log ensures that subsequent queries won't be affected by incomplete data. Later in this chapter, we will explore how uncommitted and unused data files in the table directory can be cleaned up using vacuum operations.

Delta Lake Advantages

Delta Lake's strength arises from its robust transaction log, which serves as the backbone of this innovative solution. This log empowers Delta Lake to deliver a range of features and advantages that can be summarized by the following key points:

Enabling ACID transactions
> The main advantage of the transaction log is that it enables Delta Lake to execute ACID transactions on traditional data lakes. This feature helps maintain data integrity and consistency when performing data operations, ensuring that they are processed reliably and efficiently.

Scalable metadata handling
> Another primary benefit of Delta Lake is the ability to handle table metadata efficiently. The table metadata, which represents information about the structure, organization, and properties of the table, is stored in the transaction log instead of a centralized metastore. This strategy enhances query performance when it comes to listing large directories and reading vast amounts of data. It also includes table statistics to accelerate operations.

Full audit logging
> Additionally, the transaction log serves as a comprehensive audit trail that captures every change occurring on the table. It tracks all modifications, additions, and deletions made to the data, along with the timestamps and user information associated with each operation. This allows you to trace the evolution of the data over time, which facilitates troubleshooting issues and ensures data governance.

Working with Delta Lake Tables

In this section, we dive into the practical aspects of Delta Lake. We'll walk through essential tasks such as creating Delta Lake tables, inserting data, updating tables with new information, and exploring the underlying directory structure. Through hands-on examples, you'll gain a comprehensive understanding of how Delta Lake works in your Databricks environment.

We will conduct these exercises within a new SQL notebook, named "2.1 - Delta Lake," which you can find on the book's GitHub repository (*https://github.com/derar-alhussein/oreilly-databricks-dea*).

In Databricks, tables are organized in a database within a catalog. For the sake of simplicity and ease of storage access, we will use the hive_metastore catalog, which is available by default in every Databricks workspace. A detailed discussion on data catalogs will be provided in the next chapter. For the present, let us proceed by executing the following command to set the active catalog in our notebook to hive_metastore:

```
USE CATALOG hive_metastore
```

This command configures the current notebook to use the hive_metastore catalog, ensuring that all subsequent operations on Delta Lake tables are executed under this catalog.

Creating Tables

Creating Delta Lake tables closely resembles the conventional method of creating tables in standard SQL. It starts with the CREATE TABLE keyword followed by the table name. Then, you provide the schema of the table by specifying the columns along with their corresponding data types. Consider the following example where we create an empty Delta Lake table named product_info:

```
CREATE TABLE product_info (
    product_id INT,
    product_name STRING,
    category STRING,
    price DOUBLE,
    quantity INT
)
USING DELTA;
```

In this example, product_info represents a table designed to store product-related details. It includes five columns: product_id of type integer, product_name and category of type string, price of type double, and quantity (integer representing available stock of each product).

It's worth mentioning that explicitly specifying USING DELTA identifies Delta Lake as the storage layer for the table, but this clause is optional. Even in its absence, the table will still be recognized as a Delta Lake table since DELTA is the default table format in Databricks.

Catalog Explorer

After creating the Delta Lake table named product_info using the provided SQL script, you can explore it via the Catalog Explorer interface, as shown in Figure 2-7. To open the Catalog Explorer, click the Catalog tab in the left sidebar of your Databricks workspace.

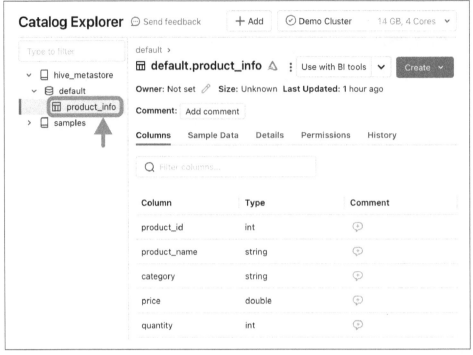

Figure 2-7. Catalog Explorer interface

In the interface, navigate to the default database in the left panel to find the product_info table. If you click it, you can examine the table's columns, review sample data entries, and explore additional information displayed on the right panel.

Inserting Data

In Delta Lake, data insertion can be easily achieved through the use of the standard SQL INSERT INTO statement, as defined by ANSI SQL. Like in standard SQL, you can use this statement to add a single line or multiple lines of data:

```
INSERT INTO product_info (product_id, product_name, category, price, quantity)
VALUES (1, 'Winter Jacket', 'Clothing', 79.95, 100);

INSERT INTO product_info (product_id, product_name, category, price, quantity)
VALUES
  (2, 'Microwave', 'Kitchen', 249.75, 30),
  (3, 'Board Game', 'Toys', 29.99, 75),
  (4, 'Smartcar', 'Electronics', 599.99, 50);
```

Each operation on the table represents an individual transaction influencing the table's state. In this context, each INSERT statement generates a separate data file within the table directory. So, after executing these two INSERT commands, two distinct data files will be added to the table directory. The first file contains the initial single record, while the second data file contains the three additional records that were inserted in the subsequent INSERT statement. This example simulates real-world scenarios where data is written to a table in several operations, such as data ingestion by multiple runs of scheduled jobs.

By executing the previous two INSERT commands, four records will be inserted into the table. But if you execute them in the same cell, the displayed result will indicate the successful insertion of just three records. This outcome occurs due to the default behavior in the notebook editor wherein only the result of the last command executed within the cell is typically displayed.

 To view the outcomes of individual SQL statements when having multiple commands in a single cell, select each specific SQL statement separately and press Shift+Ctrl+Enter to run the selected text. Alternatively, you can use separate cells for each SQL statement.

To access and verify the inserted data, simply query the table through the standard SQL SELECT statement:

```
SELECT * FROM product_info
```

Figure 2-8 displays the result of the SELECT query on the product_info table. It displays the four inserted records, confirming that the two transactions were successfully performed on the table.

1^2_3 product_id	^A_C product_name	^A_C category	1.2 price	1^2_3 quantity
2	Microwave	Kitchen	249.75	30
3	Board Game	Toys	29.99	75
4	Smartphone	Electronics	599.99	50
1	Winter Jacket	Clothing	79.95	100

Figure 2-8. The result of the SELECT statement from the product_info table

Like in SQL, you can also filter data based on conditions using the WHERE clause and aggregate information if needed with GROUP BY.

Exploring the Table Directory

As previously discussed, the execution of the two transactional operations on the table resulted in creating two small data files in the table directory. To validate this, we can use the DESCRIBE DETAIL command on our table. This command enables you to explore the metadata of Delta Lake tables. It provides essential information about the table, such as the numFiles field, indicating the number of data files in the current table version:

```
DESCRIBE DETAIL product_info
```

Figure 2-9 shows the output of the DESCRIBE DETAIL command on the product_info table. The numFiles column confirms that the table indeed has two data files resulting from our two INSERT operations.

$^{A^B}_C$ name	$^{A^B}_C$ location	1^2_3 numFiles	1^2_3 sizeInBytes
spark_catalog.default.product_info	dbfs:/user/hive/warehouse/product_info	2	338

Figure 2-9. The output of the DESCRIBE DETAIL command on the product_info table

Additionally, the previous command shows the location of the table, indicating the directory where the table files are stored on the storage. As indicated, the product_info table is stored under *dbfs:/user/hive/warehouse/product_info*.

 If you are working with Unity Catalog, be aware that tables will be stored in a different location marked by __unitystorage, which is fully managed by Unity Catalog. This means that certain commands, such as listing table contents, may not function correctly due to restricted access to this managed storage. Therefore, in the context of this book, it is advisable to switch to the Hive metastore using the command USE CATALOG hive_metastore.

To gain a deeper understanding of the table's file structure, you can use the %fs ls magic command that allows you to explore the contents of the table directory:

```
%fs ls 'dbfs:/user/hive/warehouse/product_info'
```

Figure 2-10 illustrates the result of executing the %fs command. It shows that the table directory indeed holds two data files, both in Parquet format.

	name	size	modificationTime
1	_delta_log/	0	1708652042000
2	part-00000-aa695b3d-e814-4d72-ad60-6034c09ef2e2-c000.snappy.parquet	1595	1708652049000
3	part-00000-d406ce78-0c67-4bc6-9ec5-57b7fc13d1f7-c000.snappy.parquet	1577	1708652048000

Figure 2-10. The output of the %fs command on the product_info table directory

Furthermore, the table directory contains the *_delta_log* subdirectory, which contains the transaction log files of the table.

Updating Delta Lake Tables

Now, considering update operations, let's explore a scenario where the task involves adjusting the price of product 3 (Board Game) by incrementing its price by $10:

```
UPDATE product_info
SET price = price + 10
WHERE product_id = 3
```

Examining the table directory after this update operation reveals an interesting observation: a new file addition (Figure 2-11).

	$^{A^B_C}$ name	$^{1^2_3}$ size	$^{1^2_3}$ modificationTime
1	_delta_log/	0	1708793922000
2	> part-00000-40ada852-ef55-4367-994a-eae08e0684d4-c000.snappy.parquet	1683	1708793936000
3	> part-00000-485c4e80-678f-4c03-9330-67159e215eb8-c000.snappy.parquet	1701	1708793940000
4	> part-00000-a21a2e7e-29b5-433a-a7ce-3d886f37e7dd-c000.snappy.parquet	1701	1708794052000

Figure 2-11. The output of the %fs command after the update operation

As previously mentioned, when updates occur, Delta Lake doesn't directly modify existing files but rather creates updated copies of them. Afterward, Delta Lake leverages the transaction log to indicate which files are valid in the current version of the table. To confirm this behavior, you can run the DESCRIBE DETAIL command again to display the table metadata following this update, as illustrated in Figure 2-12.

$^{A^B_C}$ name	$^{A^B_C}$ location	$^{1^2_3}$ numFiles	$^{1^2_3}$ sizeInBytes
spark_catalog.default.product_info	dbfs:/user/hive/warehouse/product_info	2	338

Figure 2-12. The output of the DESCRIBE DETAIL command after the update operation

The numFiles column shows that the count of the table's files is still 2, and not 3! These are the two files that represent the current table version, including the newly updated file resulting from the recent update operation. When querying the Delta table again, the query engine leverages the transaction logs to identify all the data files that are valid in the current version and exclude any outdated data files. If you query the table after this update operation, you can verify that the pricing information of product 3 has been successfully updated.

Starting from Databricks Runtime Version 14, adjustments have been made to the way update and delete operations are applied, affecting the associated data files in the table directory. This change is due to the introduction of deletion vectors in Delta Lake (*https://oreil.ly/CfOM5*).

Exploring Table History

In Delta Lake, the transaction log maintains the history of changes made to the tables. To access the history of a table, you can use the `DESCRIBE HISTORY` command:

```
DESCRIBE HISTORY product_info
```

Figure 2-13 illustrates the table history, revealing four distinct versions starting from the table creation at version 0. Moving forward, versions 1 and 2 indicate write operations on the table, representing our two insert commands, while version 3 indicates the update operation. All this information is captured within the transaction log of the table.

version	timestamp	userName	operation	operationParameters
3	2024-02-24T17:00:52.000+00:00	Derar Alhussein	UPDATE	> {"predicate":"[\"(product_id#2123
2	2024-02-24T16:59:01.000+00:00	Derar Alhussein	WRITE	> {"mode":"Append","statsOnLoad":"
1	2024-02-24T16:58:57.000+00:00	Derar Alhussein	WRITE	> {"mode":"Append","statsOnLoad":"
0	2024-02-24T16:58:42.000+00:00	Derar Alhussein	CREATE TABLE	> {"partitionBy":"[]","description":nu

Figure 2-13. The output of the `DESCRIBE HISTORY` command on the `product_info` table

The transaction log is located under the *_delta_log* folder in the table directory. You can navigate to this folder using the `%fs ls` command:

```
%fs ls 'dbfs:/user/hive/warehouse/product_info/_delta_log'
```

Figure 2-14 illustrates the contents of the *_delta_log* folder located within the `product_info` table directory. You can observe that it contains nothing but JSON files, along with their associated checksum[1] files (having the *.crc* extension). Each JSON file corresponds to a distinct version of the Delta Lake table. In the context of the `product_info` table, we observe four JSON files, corresponding precisely to the four table versions examined previously through the `DESCRIBE HISTORY` command.

---

1 A checksum is a unique value computed from the contents of a file using an algorithm. It serves as a sort of digital fingerprint that helps determine if any changes or corruption have occurred in the associated file. In other words, a checksum ensures data integrity of the associated file.

^A_C name	$^{12}_3$ size	$^{12}_3$ modificationTime
00000000000000000000.crc	2220	1708793932000
00000000000000000000.json	1224	1708793922000
00000000000000000001.crc	2926	1708793940000
00000000000000000001.json	1282	1708793937000
00000000000000000002.crc	3619	1708793942000
00000000000000000002.json	1274	1708793941000
00000000000000000003.crc	3632	1708794054000
00000000000000000003.json	1927	1708794052000

Figure 2-14. The output of the %fs command on the _delta_log folder

To gain a deeper understanding of the transaction log, we can use the %fs head command to explore the content of one of those JSON files. In particular, we can examine the latest JSON file that represents version 3 of the table:

```
%fs head
'dbfs:/user/hive/warehouse/product_info/_delta_log/00000000000000000003.json'
{ "commitInfo":{"operation": "UPDATE", "timestamp": 1708794052735,
               "userName": "Derar Alhussein", ...}
}
{ "add":{"path": "part-00000-a21a2e7e-29b5-433a-c000.snappy.parquet",
         "modificationTime": 1708794052000, ...}
}
{ "remove":{"path": "part-00000-485c4e80-678f-4c03-c000.snappy.parquet",
            "deletionTimestamp": 1708794052717, ...}
}
```

The output of the %fs head command shows that the JSON file contains structured JSON data about our update operation. The add element specifies the new data file appended to the table, while the remove element specifies the data file marked for soft deletion—in other words, it's no longer part of the latest table version.

Exploring Delta Time Travel

Time travel is a feature in Delta Lake that allows you to retrieve previous versions of data in Delta Lake tables. The key aspect of Delta Lake time travel is the automatic versioning of the table. This versioning provides an audit trail of all the changes that have happened on the table. Whenever a change is made to the data, Delta Lake captures and stores this change as a new version. Each version represents the state of the table at a specific point in time.

To explore the historical versions of a Delta table, you can leverage the DESCRIBE HISTORY command in SQL. This command provides a detailed log of all the operations performed on the table, including information such as the timestamp of the operation, the type of operation (insert, update, delete, etc.), and any additional metadata associated with the change.

Here's an example of how you might use the `DESCRIBE HISTORY` command:

```
DESCRIBE HISTORY <table_name>;
```

This command returns a result set containing the operations performed on the specified table in reverse chronological order, along with relevant details for each operation.

Let's review again the history of the `product_info` table:

```
DESCRIBE HISTORY product_info
```

Figure 2-15 displays the table history, illustrating how Delta Lake's versioning system automatically assigns a unique version number and timestamp to every operation performed on a table.

1²₃ version	🗓 timestamp	ᴬᵇc userName	ᴬᵇc operation	⅏ operationParameters
3	2024-02-24T17:00:52.000+00:00	Derar Alhussein	UPDATE	> {"predicate":"[\"(product_id#2123
2	2024-02-24T16:59:01.000+00:00	Derar Alhussein	WRITE	> {"mode":"Append","statsOnLoad":{
1	2024-02-24T16:58:57.000+00:00	Derar Alhussein	WRITE	> {"mode":"Append","statsOnLoad":{
0	2024-02-24T16:58:42.000+00:00	Derar Alhussein	CREATE TABLE	> {"partitionBy":"[]","description":nu

Figure 2-15. The output of the `DESCRIBE HISTORY` command on the `product_info` table

Our table has currently four distinct versions:

Version 0
> This is the initial version of the table, representing its state at creation. Since the table was created empty, this version captures only the initial schema and metadata of the table.

Versions 1 and 2
> These versions indicate write operations on the table, representing our two insert commands.

Version 3
> This version indicates the update operation on the table, which represents the latest state of the table. Additionally, note that this update operation includes the predicate used to match records in the `operationParameters` column.

Querying Older Versions

To query older versions of a table, Delta Lake offers two distinct approaches, using either the timestamp or the version number.

Querying by timestamp

The first method allows you to retrieve the table's state as it existed at a specific point in time. This involves specifying the desired timestamp in the SELECT statement using the TIMESTAMP AS OF keyword:

```
SELECT * FROM <table_name> TIMESTAMP AS OF <timestamp>
```

Querying by version number

The second method involves using the version number associated with each operation on the table, as illustrated in the table history in Figure 2-16.

1^2_3 version	⬚ timestamp	^A_c userName	^A_c operation	⬙ operationParameters
3	2024-02-24T17:00:52.000+00:00	Derar Alhussein	UPDATE	> {"predicate":"[\"(product_id#2123
2	2024-02-24T16:59:01.000+00:00	Derar Alhussein	WRITE	> {"mode":"Append","statsOnLoad":"
1	2024-02-24T16:58:57.000+00:00	Derar Alhussein	WRITE	> {"mode":"Append","statsOnLoad":"
0	2024-02-24T16:58:42.000+00:00	Derar Alhussein	CREATE TABLE	> {"partitionBy":"[]","description":nu

Figure 2-16. The output of the DESCRIBE HISTORY command on the product_info table

You can use the VERSION AS OF keyword to travel back in time to a specific version of the table:

```
SELECT * FROM <table_name> VERSION AS OF <version>
```

Consider a scenario where we need to retrieve the product data exactly as it existed before the update operation, identified as version 2 in our product_info table. We can simply use the following query:

```
SELECT * FROM product_info VERSION AS OF 2
```

Alternatively, you can use its short syntax represented by @v followed by the version number:

```
SELECT * FROM product_info@v2
```

Figure 2-17 shows the result of querying version 2 of our table.

1^2_3 product_id	^A_c product_name	^A_c category	1.2 price	1^2_3 quantity
2	Microwave	Kitchen	249.75	30
3	Board Game	Toys	29.99	75
4	Smartphone	Electronics	599.99	50
1	Winter Jacket	Clothing	79.95	100

Figure 2-17. The result of querying version 2 of the product_info table

So, Delta Lake's time travel enables you to independently investigate different versions of the data without impacting the current state of the table. This feature is possible thanks to those extra data files that had been marked as removed in our transaction log.

Rolling Back to Previous Versions

Delta Lake time travel is particularly useful in scenarios where undesired data changes need to be rolled back to a previous state. For instance, in case of bad writes or unintended data modifications, you can easily undo these changes by reverting to a previous version of the table.

Delta Lake offers the RESTORE TABLE command that allows you to roll back the table to a specific timestamp or version number:

```
RESTORE TABLE <table_name> TO TIMESTAMP AS OF <timestamp>

RESTORE TABLE <table_name> TO VERSION AS OF <version>
```

Imagine a scenario where data has been accidentally deleted from our product_info table and we need to restore it.

```
DELETE FROM product_info
```

Upon executing the DELETE command, it removes all four records currently in the table. You can easily confirm this by querying the table again. In addition, we can review the table history to see that the delete operation has been recorded as a new table version, labeled as version 4 (Figure 2-18).

¹²₃ version	🕓 timestamp	ᴬᴮc userName	ᴬᴮc operation	⿻ operationParameters
4	2024-02-25T00:09:54.000+00:00	Derar Alhussein	DELETE	> {"predicate":"[\"true\"]"}
3	2024-02-24T17:00:52.000+00:00	Derar Alhussein	UPDATE	> {"predicate":"[\"(product_
2	2024-02-24T16:59:01.000+00:00	Derar Alhussein	WRITE	> {"mode":"Append","statsC
1	2024-02-24T16:58:57.000+00:00	Derar Alhussein	WRITE	> {"mode":"Append","statsC
0	2024-02-24T16:58:42.000+00:00	Derar Alhussein	CREATE TABLE	> {"partitionBy":"[]","descrip

Figure 2-18. The output of the DESCRIBE HISTORY command after running the DELETE command

To roll back the table to a previous version that existed before the deletion occurred, specifically version 3, we can use the RESTORE TABLE command:

```
RESTORE TABLE product_info TO VERSION AS OF 3
```

Figure 2-19 displays the output of the restoration operation. It shows that two files have been restored, confirming the data has been successfully restored to its original state. The `product_info` table again contains the complete dataset, as it did before the deletion took place. You can easily confirm this by querying the table again.

$_{123}$ table_size_after_restore	$_{123}$ num_of_files_after_restore	$_{123}$ num_removed_files	$_{123}$ num_restored_files
3384	2	0	2

Figure 2-19. The output of the `RESTORE TABLE` command on the `product_info` table

We can also examine what really happened at our table by exploring its history:

```
DESCRIBE HISTORY product_info
```

Figure 2-20 displays the table history after the restoration operation. It shows that this operation has been recorded as a new table version, labeled version 5.

$_{123}$ version	$\overset{\boxdot}{\Box}$ timestamp	$_A{}^B{}_C$ userName	$_A{}^B{}_C$ operation	⅋ operationParameters
5	2024-02-25T00:33:33.000+00:00	Derar Alhussein	RESTORE	> {"version":"3","timestamp'
4	2024-02-25T00:09:54.000+00:00	Derar Alhussein	DELETE	> {"predicate":"[\"true\"]"}
3	2024-02-24T17:00:52.000+00:00	Derar Alhussein	UPDATE	> {"predicate":"[\"(product_
2	2024-02-24T16:59:01.000+00:00	Derar Alhussein	WRITE	> {"mode":"Append","statsC
1	2024-02-24T16:58:57.000+00:00	Derar Alhussein	WRITE	> {"mode":"Append","statsC
0	2024-02-24T16:58:42.000+00:00	Derar Alhussein	CREATE TABLE	> {"partitionBy":"[]","descrip

Figure 2-20. The output of the `DESCRIBE HISTORY` command after the restoration operation

In summary, Delta Lake's time travel brings a new level of flexibility to data management within Delta tables. It provides you with the capability to travel back in time to specific versions of your tables and restore them to a previous state if needed.

Optimizing Delta Lake Tables

Delta Lake provides an advanced feature for optimizing table performance through compacting small data files into larger ones. This optimization is particularly significant as it enhances the speed of read queries from a Delta Lake table. You trigger compaction by executing the `OPTIMIZE` command:

```
OPTIMIZE <table_name>
```

Say you have a table that has accumulated many small files due to frequent write operations. By running the `OPTIMIZE` command, these small files can be compacted into one or more larger files. This concept is illustrated in an example in Figure 2-21, where the optimization process results in two consolidated data files instead of six small files.

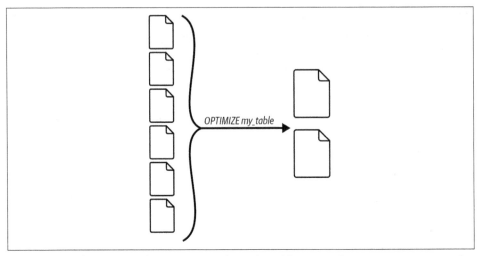

Figure 2-21. The process of optimizing Delta Lake tables using the OPTIMIZE command

Table optimization improves the overall performance of the table by minimizing overhead associated with file management and enhancing the efficiency of data retrieval operations.

Z-Order Indexing

A notable extension of the OPTIMIZE command is the ability to leverage Z-Order indexing. Z-Order indexing involves the reorganization and co-location of column information within the same set of files. To perform Z-Order indexing, you simply add the ZORDER BY keyword to the OPTIMIZE command. This should be followed by specifying one or more column names on which the indexing will be applied:

```
OPTIMIZE <table_name>
ZORDER BY <column_names>
```

For instance, recalling our previous example in Figure 2-21, let's consider the data files containing a numerical column such as ID that ranges between 1 and 100. Applying Z-Order indexing to this column during the optimization process results in different content written to the two compacted files. In this case, Z-Order indexing will aim to have the first compacted file contain values ranging from 1 to 50, while the subsequent file contains values from 51 to 100, as illustrated in Figure 2-22.

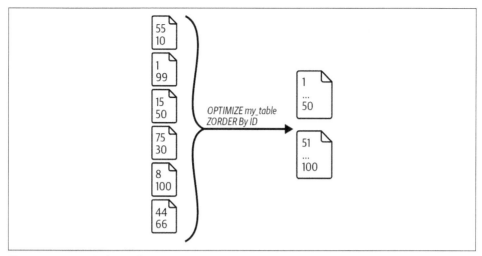

Figure 2-22. Z-Order indexing

This strategic arrangement of data enables data skipping in Delta Lake, which helps avoid unnecessary file scans during query processing. In the provided example, if a query targets an ID, such as 25, Delta Lake can quickly determine that ID #25 resides in the first compacted file. Consequently, it can confidently ignore scanning the second file altogether, resulting in significant time savings.

Let's now optimize our `product_info` table that currently has two small data files, as indicated in the `numFiles` field of the table metadata (Figure 2-23):

```
DESCRIBE DETAIL product_info
```

$^{A^B}_C$ name	$^{A^B}_C$ location	$^{1^2}_3$ numFiles	$^{1^2}_3$ sizeInBytes
spark_catalog.default.product_info	dbfs:/user/hive/warehouse/product_info	2	3384

Figure 2-23. The output of the DESCRIBE DETAIL command before optimization

We can use the `OPTIMIZE` command to combine these files toward an optimal size:

```
OPTIMIZE product_info
ZORDER BY product_id
```

Figure 2-24 shows the output of the `OPTIMIZE` command. The `numFilesRemoved` in the metrics column indicates that two small data files have been soft deleted, while the `numFilesAdded` metric indicates that a new optimized file is added, compacting those two files.

A^B_C path	$\&$ metrics
dbfs:/user/hive/warehouse/product_info >	{"numFilesAdded":1,"numFilesRemoved":2,"filesAdded":{"min":1745,"max":174...

Figure 2-24. The output of the OPTIMIZE command

In addition, we have added the Z-Order indexing with our OPTIMIZE command. As an example, we apply Z-Order indexing to the product_id column. However, with such a small dataset, the benefits of Z-Order indexing may not be as significant, and its impact may not be noticeable.

To confirm the result of the optimization process, let's review again the details of our table:

```
DESCRIBE DETAIL product_info
```

Indeed, as illustrated in Figure 2-25, the current table version consists of only one consolidated data file, indicating the success of the optimization operation.

A^B_C name	⋮ ⩴	A^B_C location	1^2_3 numFiles	1^2_3 sizeInBytes
spark_catalog.default.product_info		dbfs:/user/hive/warehouse/product_info	1	1745

Figure 2-25. The output of the DESCRIBE DETAIL command after optimization

In addition, we can check how the OPTIMIZE operation has been recorded in our table history:

```
DESCRIBE HISTORY product_info
```

As expected and illustrated in Figure 2-26, the OPTIMIZE command created another version of our table. This means that version 6 is the most recent version of the table.

1^2_3 version	⌸ timestamp	A^B_C userName	A^B_C operation	$\&$ operationParameters
6	2024-02-25T02:44:34.000+00:00	Derar Alhussein	OPTIMIZE	> {"predicate":"[]","zOrderBy":"[\"product_id\"]"
5	2024-02-25T00:33:33.000+00:00	Derar Alhussein	RESTORE	> {"version":"3","timestamp":null}
4	2024-02-25T00:09:54.000+00:00	Derar Alhussein	DELETE	> {"predicate":"[\"true\"]"}
3	2024-02-24T17:00:52.000+00:00	Derar Alhussein	UPDATE	> {"predicate":"[\"(product_id#2123 = 3)\"]"}
2	2024-02-24T16:59:01.000+00:00	Derar Alhussein	WRITE	> {"mode":"Append","statsOnLoad":"false","part
1	2024-02-24T16:58:57.000+00:00	Derar Alhussein	WRITE	> {"mode":"Append","statsOnLoad":"false","part
0	2024-02-24T16:58:42.000+00:00	Derar Alhussein	CREATE TABLE	> {"partitionBy":"[]","description":null,"isManage

Figure 2-26. The output of the DESCRIBE HISTORY command after the optimization operation

Lastly, let us explore the data files in our table directory:

```
%fs ls 'dbfs:/user/hive/warehouse/product_info'
```

In Figure 2-27, we can see that there are four data files in the table directory. However, it is important to remember that our current table version references only one file following the optimization operation. This means that other data files in the directory are unused files, and we can simply clean them up. In the next section, we will learn how to achieve this task with vacuuming.

Aᴮ꜀ name	1²₃ size	1²₃ modificationTime
_delta_log/	0	1708793922000
> part-00000-40ada852-ef55-4367-994a-eae08e0684d4-c000.snappy.parquet	1683	1708793936000
> part-00000-485c4e80-678f-4c03-9330-67159e215eb8-c000.snappy.parquet	1701	1708793940000
> part-00000-82ca5e99-c61f-44b7-80d4-d66f3e3f72b8-c000.snappy.parquet	1745	1708829074000
> part-00000-a21a2e7e-29b5-433a-a7ce-3d886f37e7dd-c000.snappy.parquet	1701	1708794052000

Figure 2-27. The output of the %fs command on the product_info table directory after optimization

In essence, Delta Lake's OPTIMIZE command, coupled with Z-Order indexing, offers a powerful mechanism to optimize table performance. It enhances the speed of read queries by compacting small files and intelligently organizing their column information.

Vacuuming

Delta Lake's vacuuming provides an efficient mechanism for managing unused data files within a Delta table. As data evolves over time, there might be scenarios where certain files become obsolete, either due to uncommitted changes or because they are no longer part of the latest state of the table. The VACUUM command in Delta Lake enables you to clean up these unwanted files, ensuring efficient storage management that saves storage space and cost.

Here's an example of how you might use the VACUUM command:

```
VACUUM <table_name> [RETAIN num HOURS]
```

The process involves specifying a retention period threshold for the files, so the command will automatically remove all files older than this threshold. The default retention period is set to seven days, meaning that the vacuum operation will prevent you from deleting files less than seven days old. This is a safety measure to ensure that no active or ongoing operations are still referencing any of the files to be deleted.

It's important to note that running the VACUUM command comes with a trade-off. Once the operation is executed and files older than the specified retention period are deleted, you lose the ability to time travel back to a version older than that period. This is because the associated data files are no longer available. Therefore, it is crucial to carefully consider the retention period based on your data retention policies and data storage requirements.

Vacuuming in Action

Let's optimize the storage and tidy up the file structure of our `product_info` table. Before we start, let us first explore the data files in our table directory:

```
%fs ls 'dbfs:/user/hive/warehouse/product_info'
```

As shown in Figure 2-28, there are currently four data files in the table directory.

$^{A}_{C}$ name	$^{1}_{3}$ size	$^{1}_{3}$ modificationTime
_delta_log/	0	1708793922000
> part-00000-40ada852-ef55-4367-994a-eae08e0684d4-c000.snappy.parquet	1683	1708793936000
> part-00000-485c4e80-678f-4c03-9330-67159e215eb8-c000.snappy.parquet	1701	1708793940000
> part-00000-82ca5e99-c61f-44b7-80d4-d66f3e3f72b8-c000.snappy.parquet	1745	1708829074000
> part-00000-a21a2e7e-29b5-433a-a7ce-3d886f37e7dd-c000.snappy.parquet	1701	1708794052000

Figure 2-28. The output of the %fs command on the `product_info` table directory before vacuuming

Remember, our current table version references only one file following the optimization operation detailed in the previous section. This means that other data files in the directory are unused files, and we can simply clean them up using the VACUUM command:

```
VACUUM product_info
```

However, upon executing the command, you realize that the files are still present in the table directory. This is because, by default, VACUUM retains files for a period of seven days to ensure ongoing operations can still access them if needed.

To overcome this default behavior, we attempt to specify a retention period of zero hours to retain only the current version of the data:

```
VACUUM product_info RETAIN 0 HOURS

IllegalArgumentException: requirement failed: Are you sure you would like
to vacuum files with such a low retention period? If you have writers that are
currently writing to this table, there is a risk that you may corrupt
the state of your Delta table.
```

However, this command throws an exception since the retention period is low, compared to the default retention period of seven days. As a workaround solution, and for demonstration purposes only, we can temporarily disable the retention duration check in Delta Lake. It's important to note that this approach is not recommended for production environments (*https://oreil.ly/6Z59C*) due to potential data integrity issues.

```
SET spark.databricks.delta.retentionDurationCheck.enabled = false
```

With the retention duration check disabled, we can now proceed and rerun our VACUUM command with a 0 HOURS retention period. To confirm its output, let's explore the table directory:

```
%fs ls 'dbfs:/user/hive/warehouse/product_info'
```

Indeed, as illustrated in Figure 2-29, the operation this time successfully removed the old data files from the table directory.

$^A{}^B_C$ name	1^2_3 size	1^2_3 modificationTime
_delta_log/	0	1708793922000
part-00000-82ca5e99-c61f-44b7-80d4-d66f3e3f72b8-c000.snappy.parquet	1745	1708829074000

Figure 2-29. The output of the %fs command on the product_info table directory after vacuuming

While the cleanup operation enhances storage efficiency, it comes at the cost of losing access to older data versions for time travel queries. Attempting to query an old table version results in a "file not found" exception, since the corresponding data files have been deleted during the previous VACUUM operation:

```
SELECT * FROM product_info@v1

FileReadException: Error while reading file
part-00000-40ada852-ef55-4367-994a-eae08e0684d4-c000.snappy.parquet.
File referenced in the transaction log cannot be found.
Caused by: FileNotFoundException: Operation failed: "The specified path
does not exist.", 404, GET, PathNotFound, "The specified path does not exist.
```

Dropping Delta Lake Tables

In the final step of managing Delta Lake tables within the lakehouse architecture, we can drop the table and permanently erase its associated data. Similar to SQL syntax, we use the DROP TABLE command for this purpose:

```
DROP TABLE product_info
```

Upon executing this command, the table, along with its data, will be deleted from the lakehouse environment. To confirm this action, you can attempt to query the table again, only to find that it is no longer found in the database. Furthermore, the directory containing the table's files is also completely removed:

```
%fs ls 'dbfs:/user/hive/warehouse/product_info'

FileNotFoundException: No such file or directory
                       dbfs:/user/hive/warehouse/product_info
```

Thus, the VACUUM command provides a mechanism for optimizing storage by removing unnecessary data files of Delta Lake tables. However, it's crucial to understand the impacts of file retention duration and consider the trade-offs between storage efficiency and historical data accessibility.

Conclusion

Throughout this chapter, we've explored how Delta Lake works, demonstrating its essential role in transforming traditional data lakes into reliable lakehouses. By mastering Delta Lake, you can significantly enhance your data workflows and enable more robust analytics. The knowledge gained from this chapter will serve as a foundation for fully leveraging Delta Lake's potential in subsequent discussions and use cases.

Sample Exam Questions

Conceptual Question

1. Which of the following statements best describes the time travel feature in Delta Lake?

A. It compacts old small files into larger ones to improve query performance and optimize storage usage.

B. It partitions the table based on datetime columns, ensuring that historical data retrieval is optimized.

C. It uses Z-Order indexing to reorganize datetime column information within the same set of files, enhancing the performance of range queries.

D. It generates periodic backups of the data to ensure that all information can be easily restored in the event of system failure.

E. It allows users to query Delta Lake tables at a specific point in time, providing views of previous states of the data.

Code-Based Question

2. A data engineer is investigating a Delta Lake table named customer_orders, which has experienced slow performance for the past week. The engineer has found that it contains too many small files, potentially contributing to these performance issues.

To enhance the query performance for this table, which command should the data engineer execute?

A. ZORDER BY customer_orders

B. OPTIMIZE customer_orders

C. VACUUM customer_orders

D. VACUUM customer_orders RETAIN 0 HOURS

E. RESTORE TABLE customer_orders TO TIMESTAMP AS OF current_timestamp() - INTERVAL '7' DAYS

The correct answers to these questions are listed in Appendix C.

Mastering Relational Entities in Databricks

Relational entities, particularly databases, tables, and views, are essential components for organizing and managing structured data in Databricks. Understanding how these entities interact with the metastore and storage locations is crucial for efficient querying and data management. In this chapter, we will cover in detail how these entities function within the Databricks environment and understand their relationship with the underlying storage.

Understanding Relational Entities

This section provides a detailed understanding of relational entities in Databricks, covering databases, tables, and views, with a focus on their interactions with both the metastore and storage systems.

Databases in Databricks

In Databricks, a database essentially corresponds to a schema in a data catalog. This means that when you create a database, you're essentially defining a logical structure where tables, views, and functions can be organized. This collection of database objects is called a *schema*. You have the flexibility to create a database using either the CREATE DATABASE or CREATE SCHEMA syntax, as they are functionally equivalent.

Every Databricks workspace includes a local data catalog, called hive_metastore, that all clusters can access to persist object metadata. The Hive metastore serves as a repository for metadata, storing essential information about data structures such as databases, tables, and partitions. This metadata includes details like table definitions, data formats, and storage locations.

Default database

By default, a `database` named "default" is provided in the `hive_metastore` catalog. When you create tables without explicitly specifying a database name, they are created under the default database. The data for these tables is stored in the default directory for Hive, typically located at */user/hive/warehouse* on the DBFS, as illustrated in Figure 3-1.

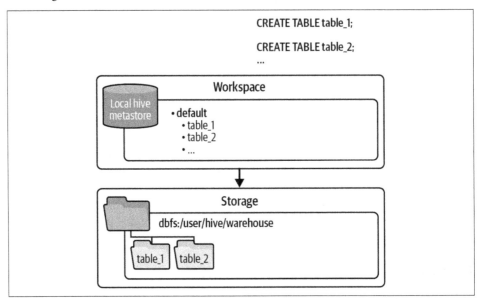

Figure 3-1. Creating tables under the default database

Creating databases

Apart from the `default` database, you can create additional databases using the `CREATE DATABASE` or `CREATE SCHEMA` syntax. These databases are also stored in the Hive metastore, with their corresponding folders under the default Hive directory in */user/hive/warehouse*. These database folders are distinguished by the *.db* extension to differentiate them from table directories, as illustrated in Figure 3-2.

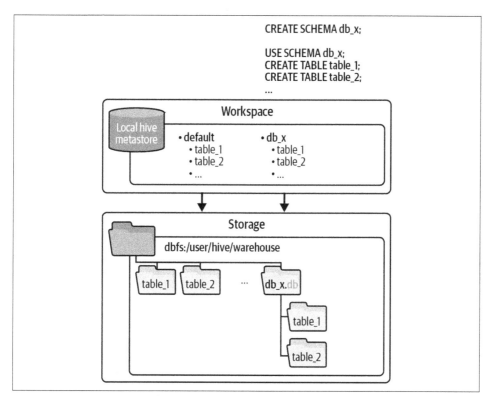

Figure 3-2. Creating an additional database and tables within this database

Custom-location databases

Moreover, you can create databases outside of the default Hive directory by specifying a custom location using the LOCATION keyword in the CREATE SCHEMA syntax. In this case, the database definition still resides in the Hive metastore, but the database folder is located in the specified custom path. Tables created within these custom databases will have their data stored in the respective database folder within the custom location, as illustrated in Figure 3-3.

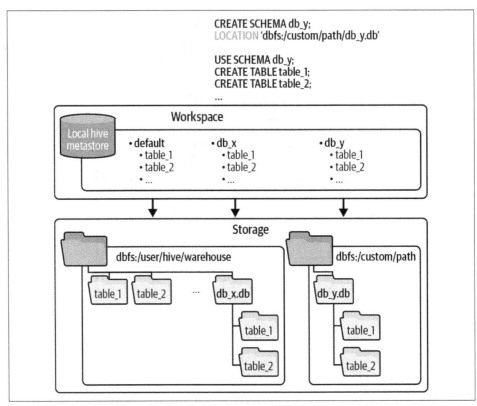

Figure 3-3. Creating a database in a custom location

Tables in Databricks

In Databricks, there are two types of tables: managed tables and external tables. Understanding the distinction between them is essential for effectively managing your data. Table 3-1 summarizes the key differences between these two types of tables.

Table 3-1. Comparison of managed and external tables in Delta Lake

Managed table	External table

Created within its own database directory:
 	
`CREATE TABLE table_name`
	Created outside the database directory (in a path specified by the LOCATION keyword):
	
	`CREATE TABLE table_name`
	`LOCATION <path>`

Dropping the table deletes both the metadata and the underlying data files of the table.	Dropping the table only removes the metadata of the table. It does not delete its underlying data files.

Let's dive deeper to gain a comprehensive understanding of these two types of tables.

Managed tables

A managed table is the default type in Databricks, where the table and its associated data are managed by the metastore, typically the Hive metastore or Unity Catalog. When you create a managed table, the table data is stored in a location controlled by the metastore. This means that the metastore owns both the metadata and the table data, enabling it to manage the complete lifecycle of the table. This integrated management simplifies data lifecycle management tasks, such as table deletion and maintenance.

So, when you drop a managed table, not only is its metadata removed from the metastore, but the underlying data files associated with the table are also deleted from storage. This approach ensures that the data remains consistent with the table definition throughout its lifecycle. However, it's essential to exercise caution when dropping managed tables, as the associated data will be permanently removed.

External tables

In contrast to managed tables, an external table in Databricks is a table where only its metadata is managed by the metastore, while the data files themselves reside outside the database directory. When creating an external table, you specify the location of the data files using the LOCATION keyword:

```
CREATE TABLE table_name
LOCATION <path>
```

Since the metastore does not own the underlying data files, dropping an external table only removes the metadata associated with the table, leaving its data files intact. This distinction is crucial, as it enables you to manage the actual data files of the table separately from its metadata. This is particularly useful when working with data that is stored in external locations outside the DBFS, like in S3 buckets or Azure storage containers.

To better understand external tables, let's revisit our diagram. Figure 3-4 illustrates creating an external table in the default database. We simply use the CREATE TABLE statement with the LOCATION keyword. The definition of this external table will be in the Hive metastore under the default database, while the actual data files will reside in the specified external location.

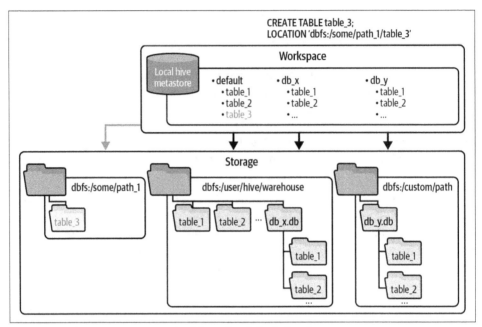

Figure 3-4. Creating an external table in the default database

Similarly, we can create an external table in any database. Figure 3-5 illustrates creating an external table in our database db_x. First, we specify the database name via the USE DATABASE or USE SCHEMA keyword. Then, we create the table with the LOCATION keyword, indicating the path where the external table data should be stored. This path could be the same as the previous one used for default.table_3 table or a different location, depending on our requirements. And again, the table definition will be stored in the Hive metastore, while the data files will be located in the given external location.

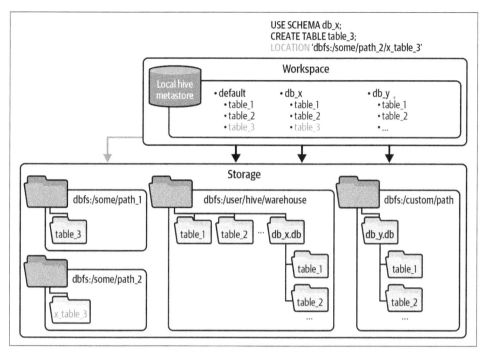

USE SCHEMA db_x;
CREATE TABLE table_3;
LOCATION 'dbfs:/some/path_2/x_table_3'

Figure 3-5. Creating an external table in the new database db_x

Even if the database was created in a custom location outside of the default Hive directory, we can still create external tables within it. Figure 3-6 illustrates this scenario by using our custom-location database db_y. Once again, we specify the database using the USE SCHEMA keyword and create the external table with the LOCATION keyword. In this scenario, let's assume we choose the same path as in the previous example. As before, the table definition will be stored in the metastore, while the data files will be located in the specified external location.

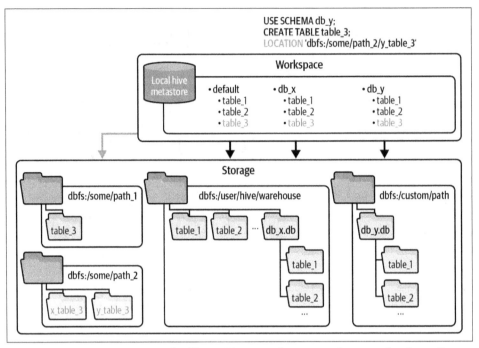

Figure 3-6. Creating an external table, `table_3`, in the custom-location database `db_y`

In summary, Databricks provides two types of tables: managed tables and external tables. Depending on the use case and data requirements, choosing the appropriate table type ensures efficient data organization, storage, and maintenance. Opting for managed tables ensures integrated management, while choosing external tables provides greater flexibility and control when managing your tables.

Putting Relational Entities into Practice

Let's now put theory into practice. In this section, we will use a new SQL notebook titled "3.1 - Databases and Tables" to create managed and external tables in various database types. In addition, we will explore the differences in behavior when dropping each type of table.

Working in the Default Schema

Before we start, let's explore the Catalog Explorer, where we can access the Hive metastore for our Databricks workspace. To open the Catalog Explorer, click the Catalog tab in the left sidebar of your Databricks workspace.

By default, under the `hive_metastore` catalog, there's a database named `default`, as illustrated in Figure 3-7. We'll begin by creating some tables within this default database.

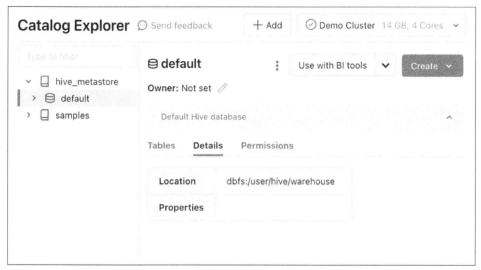

Figure 3-7. Catalog Explorer showing the `default` *database in* `hive_metastore`

Creating managed tables

First, we create a managed table named `managed_default` and populate it with data:

```
USE CATALOG hive_metastore;

CREATE TABLE managed_default
 (country STRING, code STRING, dial_code STRING);

INSERT INTO managed_default
VALUES ('France', 'Fr', '+33')
```

Since we're not specifying the `LOCATION` keyword, this table is considered managed in this database. Checking back in the Catalog Explorer, we can confirm that the `managed_default` table has been created under the default database. Alternatively, without leaving the working notebook, you can directly access the catalog by clicking the catalog icon located in the sidebar of the notebook editor (Figure 3-8).

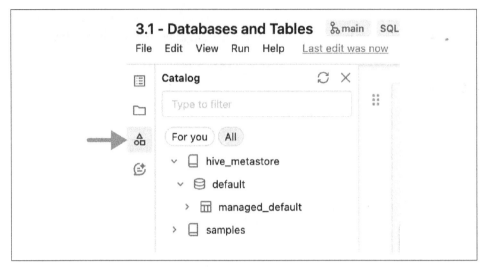

Figure 3-8. The catalog in the notebook editor showing the `managed_default` *table*

Executing the DESCRIBE EXTENDED command on our table provides advanced meta-data information, as illustrated in Figure 3-9.

```
DESCRIBE EXTENDED managed_default
```

ᴬᴮᴄ col_name	ᴬᴮᴄ data_type	ᴬᴮᴄ comment
Created By	Spark 3.4.1	
Type	MANAGED	
Location	dbfs:/user/hive/warehouse/managed_default	
Provider	delta	
Owner	root	

Figure 3-9. The output of the DESCRIBE EXTENDED *command on the* `managed_default` *table*

Among this metadata information, we focus on three key elements:

- The type of table, which is indeed MANAGED
- The location, which shows that our table resides in the default Hive metastore under *dbfs:/user/hive/warehouse*
- The provider, which confirms that this is a Delta Lake table

Creating external tables

Next, we create an external table within the default database. To achieve this, we simply add the LOCATION keyword followed by the desired storage path. In our case, we'll store this table under the */mnt/demo* directory through the DBFS:

```
CREATE TABLE external_default
 (country STRING, code STRING, dial_code STRING)
LOCATION 'dbfs:/mnt/demo/external_default';

INSERT INTO external_default
VALUES ('France', 'Fr', '+33')
```

After creating and inserting data into this external table, you can use the Catalog Explorer to verify the presence of the table in the Hive metastore. In addition, running DESCRIBE EXTENDED on the external table confirms its external nature and its storage location under */mnt/demo*, as illustrated in Figure 3-10.

```
DESCRIBE EXTENDED external_default
```

ᴬᴮ_C col_name	ᴬᴮ_C data_type	ᴬᴮ_C comment
Created By	Spark 3.4.1	
Type	EXTERNAL	
Location	dbfs:/mnt/demo/external_default	
Provider	delta	
Owner	root	

Figure 3-10. The output of the DESCRIBE EXTENDED command on the external_ default table

Dropping tables

If you want to remove tables from the database, you can simply drop them using the DROP TABLE command. However, it is important to note that the behavior differs for managed and external tables. Let's discuss the consequences of this action on each table type. We start by running the DROP TABLE command on our managed table:

```
DROP TABLE managed_default
```

When you drop a table, it deletes its metadata from the metastore. This means that the table's definition, including its schema, column names, data types, and other relevant information, is no longer stored in the metastore. We can confirm this by trying to query the table, which will result in a "table not found" error:

```
SELECT * FROM managed_default

[TABLE_OR_VIEW_NOT_FOUND] The table or view `managed_default` cannot be found.
Verify the spelling and correctness of the schema and catalog.
```

Dropping the managed table not only removes its metadata from the metastore, but also deletes all associated data files from the storage. This is confirmed by "a file not found" exception received upon checking the table directory:

```
%fs ls 'dbfs:/user/hive/warehouse/managed_default'
```

```
FileNotFoundException:
No such file or directory dbfs:/user/hive/warehouse/managed_default
```

However, when the external table is dropped, we see different behavior:

```
DROP TABLE external_default
```

Dropping the external table also removes its entry from the metastore. We can confirm this by trying to query the table, which should result in a "table not found" error. However, since the underlying data is stored outside the database directory, the data files remain intact. We can easily confirm that the data files of the table still persist by checking the table directory:

```
%fs ls 'dbfs:/mnt/demo/external_default'
```

Figure 3-11 confirms that the data files of the external table continue to exist in the table directory even after the table has been dropped.

ᴬᴮc name	1²3 size	1²3 modificationTime
_delta_log/	0	1708878942000
part-00000-dbbee599-e747-44d9-a277-4efdc7eefd55-c000.snappy.parquet	1045	1708878945000

Figure 3-11. The output of the %fs command on the external_default table directory

In Databricks, you can directly access a Delta table by querying its directory using the following SELECT statement:

```
SELECT * FROM DELTA.`dbfs:/mnt/demo/external_default`
```

Figure 3-12 shows the result of directly querying the table directory, confirming that the data of this external table remains unaffected by dropping the table from the metastore.

Figure 3-12. The result of directly querying the external_default table directory

You can manually remove the table directory and its content by the running the
dbutils.fs.rm function in Python:

```
%python
dbutils.fs.rm('dbfs:/mnt/demo/external_default', True)
```

Working in a New Schema

In addition to the default database, we can also create additional databases and manage tables within those databases. Let's walk through the process step-by-step.

Creating a new database

You can create a new database using either the CREATE SCHEMA or CREATE DATABASE
syntax, which are interchangeable:

```
CREATE SCHEMA new_default
```

Once the database is created, you can inspect its metadata using the DESCRIBE DATABASE EXTENDED command. This command provides information about the database, such as its location in the underlying storage:

```
DESCRIBE DATABASE EXTENDED new_default
```

As illustrated in Figure 3-13, the new database is stored under the default Hive directory with a *.db* extension to distinguish it from other table folders in the directory.

ᴬᵇ𝒸 **database_description_item**	ᴬᵇ𝒸 **database_description_value**
Namespace Name	new_default
Comment	
Location	dbfs:/user/hive/warehouse/new_default.db

*Figure 3-13. The output of the DESCRIBE DATABASE EXTENDED command on the
new_default schema*

Creating tables in the new database

Let's now create managed tables and external tables within our newly created database. To create tables within a database, you need first to set it as the current schema by specifying its name through the USE DATABASE keyword:

```
USE DATABASE new_default;

-- create a managed table
CREATE TABLE managed_new_default
  (country STRING, code STRING, dial_code STRING);
```

```
INSERT INTO managed_new_default
VALUES ('France', 'Fr', '+33');
-----------------------------------
-- Create an external table
CREATE TABLE external_new_default
 (country STRING, code STRING, dial_code STRING)
LOCATION 'dbfs:/mnt/demo/external_new_default';

INSERT INTO external_new_default
VALUES ('France', 'Fr', '+33');
```

In the Catalog Explorer, you can locate the new schema and confirm that the two tables have been successfully created within this database. Alternatively, you can just refresh the catalog in the notebook editor to show the new objects, as shown in Figure 3-14.

Figure 3-14. Refreshing the catalog in the notebook editor shows the `new_default` schema and its tables

By running `DESCRIBE EXTENDED` on each of these tables, we can see that the first table is indeed a managed table created in its database folder under the default Hive directory (Figure 3-15). Meanwhile, the second table, where we use the `LOCATION` keyword, has been defined as an external table under the */mnt/demo* location (Figure 3-16).

```
DESCRIBE EXTENDED managed_new_default
```

^A_C col_name	^A_C data_type
Type	MANAGED
Location	dbfs:/user/hive/warehouse/new_default.db/managed_new_default
Provider	delta

Figure 3-15. Metadata of the managed_new_default *table*

```
DESCRIBE EXTENDED external_new_default
```

^A_C col_name	^A_C data_type
Type	EXTERNAL
Location	dbfs:/mnt/demo/external_new_default
Provider	delta

Figure 3-16. Metadata of the external_new_default *table*

Dropping tables

Let's proceed to drop the newly created tables:

```
DROP TABLE managed_new_default;
DROP TABLE external_new_default;
```

Dropping the tables removes their entries from the Hive metastore. You can easily confirm this in the Catalog Explorer. Moreover, this action on the managed table results in the removal of its directory and associated data files from the storage:

```
%fs ls 'dbfs:/user/hive/warehouse/new_default.db/managed_new_default'

FileNotFoundException: No such file or directory
dbfs:/user/hive/warehouse/new_default.db/managed_new_default
```

However, as expected, in the case of the external table, although the table itself is dropped from the database, the directory and its data files persist in the specified external location (Figure 3-17).

```
%fs ls 'dbfs:/mnt/demo/external_new_default'
```

^A_C name	$^{12}_3$ size	$^{12}_3$ modificationTime
_delta_log/	0	1708886523000
part-00000-ed0309f1-7be6-49ee-a88f-5aeaa4176a75-c000.snappy.parquet	1074	1708886525000

Figure 3-17. The output of the %fs *command on the* external_new_default *table directory*

Working In a Custom-Location Schema

In our last scenario, we will create a database in a custom location outside of the default Hive directory.

Creating the database

To achieve this, we begin by using the CREATE SCHEMA statement, and we add the LOCATION keyword followed by the desired storage path, in our case *dbfs:/Shared/schemas*:

```
CREATE SCHEMA custom
LOCATION 'dbfs:/Shared/schemas/custom.db'
```

You can inspect the Catalog Explorer to confirm that the database has been created within the Hive metastore. Upon closer examination, using the DESCRIBE DATABASE EXTENDED command, we confirm that the database was situated in the custom location we specified during its creation (Figure 3-18):

```
DESCRIBE DATABASE EXTENDED custom
```

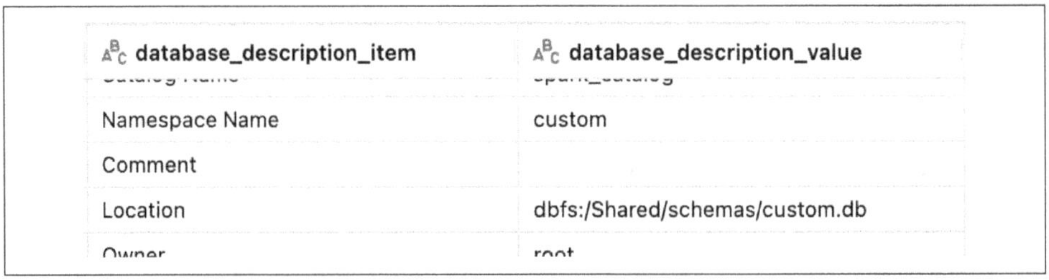

Aᴮc database_description_item	Aᴮc database_description_value
Namespace Name	custom
Comment	
Location	dbfs:/Shared/schemas/custom.db
Owner	root

Figure 3-18. The output of the DESCRIBE DATABASE EXTENDED command on the custom schema

Creating tables

We proceed to use this database to create tables and populate them with data. Again, we create both managed and external tables:

```
USE DATABASE custom;

-- Create a managed table
CREATE TABLE managed_custom
 (country STRING, code STRING, dial_code STRING);

INSERT INTO managed_custom
VALUES ('France', 'Fr', '+33');
-----------------------------------
-- Create an external table
CREATE TABLE external_custom
 (country STRING, code STRING, dial_code STRING)
LOCATION 'dbfs:/mnt/demo/external_custom';
```

```
INSERT INTO external_custom
VALUES ('France', 'Fr', '+33');
```

You can inspect the Catalog Explorer to confirm that the two tables have been successfully created within our new database. In addition, by running DESCRIBE EXTENDED on each of these tables, we can confirm that the managed_custom table is indeed a managed table, since it is created in its database folder located in the custom location (Figure 3-19). Meanwhile, the external_custom table is an external table because its location was specified during table creation (Figure 3-20).

```
DESCRIBE EXTENDED managed_custom
```

ᴬᵇᴄ col_name	ᴬᵇᴄ data_type
Type	MANAGED
Location	dbfs:/Shared/schemas/custom.db/managed_custom
Provider	delta

Figure 3-19. Metadata of the managed_custom table

```
DESCRIBE EXTENDED external_custom
```

ᴬᵇᴄ col_name	ᴬᵇᴄ data_type
Type	EXTERNAL
Location	dbfs:/mnt/demo/external_custom
Provider	delta

Figure 3-20. Metadata of the external_custom table

Dropping tables

Let's proceed to drop the newly created tables:

```
DROP TABLE managed_custom;
DROP TABLE external_custom;
```

Once more, dropping the tables removes both of their entries from the Hive metastore. You can easily confirm this in the Catalog Explorer. Dropping the managed table still removes its directory and associated data files from the database directory located in the custom location:

```
%fs ls 'dbfs:/Shared/schemas/custom.db/managed_custom'
```

FileNotFoundException:
No such file or directory dbfs:/Shared/schemas/custom.db/managed_custom

However, as expected, in the case of an external table, the table's directory and data files remain intact in their external location (Figure 3-21).

```
%fs ls 'dbfs:/mnt/demo/external_custom'
```

A^B_C name	1^2_3 size	1^2_3 modificationTime
_delta_log/	0	1708908057000
part-00000-14b104ad-8a23-474d-99e0-87225bcc129a-c000.snappy.parquet	1074	1708908059000

Figure 3-21. The output of the %fs command on the external_custom table directory

Remember, you can manually remove the table directory and its content by running the dbutils.fs.rm function in Python.

Setting Up Delta Tables

We've explored the dynamics of managed and external tables, illustrating how they interact within the context of a different type of databases. With this understanding, we're equipped to dive into more advanced topics on Delta Lake tables in the following sections.

CTAS Statements

One of the key features of Delta Lake tables is their flexibility in creation. While traditional methods like the regular CREATE TABLE statements are available, Databricks also supports CTAS, or CREATE TABLE AS SELECT, statements. CTAS statements allow the creation and population of tables at the same time based on the results of a SELECT query. This means that with CTAS statements, you can create a new table from existing data sources:

```
CREATE TABLE table_2
AS SELECT * FROM table_1
```

This simple yet powerful syntax shows how CTAS statements work. In this example, we're creating table_2 by selecting all data from table_1. CTAS statements automatically infer schema information from the query results, eliminating the need for manual schema declaration.

CTAS statements in Databricks offer a convenient means to perform transformations on data during the creation of Delta tables. These transformations can include tasks such as renaming columns or selecting specific columns for inclusion in the target table. Let's illustrate this with an abstract example:

```
CREATE TABLE table_2
AS SELECT col_1, col_3 AS new_col_3 FROM table_1
```

In this example, the CTAS statement generates a new table named table_2, by selecting columns col_1 and col_3 from table_1. Additionally, the col_3 is renamed to new_col_3 in the resulting table.

Moreover, a range of options (*https://oreil.ly/mApQm*) can be added to the CREATE TABLE clause to customize table creation, allowing for precise control over table properties and storage configurations.

```
CREATE TABLE new_users
 COMMENT "Contains PII"
 PARTITIONED BY (city, birth_date)
 LOCATION '/some/path'
 AS SELECT id, name, email, birth_date, city FROM users
```

In the provided example, we illustrate several of these options:

Comment

The COMMENT clause enables you to provide a descriptive comment for the table, helping in the discovery and understanding of its contents. Here, we've added a comment indicating that the table contains personally identifiable information (PII), such as the user's name and email.

Partitioning

The underlying data of the table can be partitioned into subfolders. The PARTITIONED BY clause allows for data partitioning based on one or more columns. In this case, we're partitioning the table by city and birth_date.

Partitioning can significantly enhance the performance of large Delta tables by facilitating efficient data retrieval. However, it's important to note that for small to medium-sized tables, the benefits of partition may be negligible or outweighed by drawbacks. One significant drawback is the potential emergence of what is known as the "small files problem." This problem arises when data partitioning results in the creation of numerous small files, each containing a relatively small amount of data.

While partitioning aims to improve query performance by reducing the amount of data scanned, the presence of many small files can prevent file compaction and efficiency in data skipping. In general, partitioning should be selectively applied based on the size and nature of the data.

External location

> The location option enables the creation of external tables. Remember, the LOCATION keyword allows you to specify the storage location for the created table. This means that the data associated with the table will be stored in an external location specified by the provided path.

Comparing CREATE TABLE and CTAS

Table 3-2 summarizes the differences between regular CREATE TABLE statements and CTAS (CREATE TABLE AS SELECT) statements.

Table 3-2. Comparison of CREATE TABLE and CTAS statements

	CREATE TABLE statement	CTAS statement
	`CREATE TABLE table_2` `(col1 INT, col2 STRING, col3 DOUBLE)`	`CREATE TABLE table_2` `AS SELECT col1, col2, col3 FROM table_1`
Schema declaration	Requires manual schema declaration.	Does not allow manual schema declaration. It automatically infers the table schema.
Populating data	Creates an empty table; a data loading statement, such as INSERT INTO, is required to populate it.	The table is created with data as specified.

Let's dive deeper to gain a comprehensive understanding of these differences.

Schema declaration

Regular CREATE TABLE statements require manual schema declaration. For instance, you would explicitly specify the data types for each column, such as integer for column 1, string for column 2, and double for column 3. By contrast, CTAS statements automate schema declaration by inferring schema information directly from the results of the query.

Populating data

When using regular CREATE TABLE statements, an empty table is created, requiring an additional step to load data into it, such as using the INSERT INTO statement. By contrast, CTAS statements simplify this process by simultaneously creating the table and populating it with data from the output of the SELECT statement. In the upcoming module, we'll see CTAS statements in action, observing how they offer a more efficient and straightforward approach to table creation and data population compared to traditional CREATE TABLE statements.

Table Constraints

After creating a Delta Lake table, whether through a regular `CREATE TABLE` statement or a CTAS statement, you have the option to enhance its integrity by adding constraints. Databricks currently supports two types of table constraints:

- `NOT NULL` constraints
- `CHECK` constraints

```
ALTER TABLE table_name ADD CONSTRAINT <constraint_name> <constraint_detail>
```

When applying constraints to a Delta table, it's crucial to ensure that existing data in the table adheres to these constraints before defining them; otherwise, the statement will fail. Once a constraint is enforced, any new data that violates the constraint will result in a write failure.

For instance, let's consider the addition of a `CHECK` constraint to the `date` column of a Delta table. `CHECK` constraints resemble standard `WHERE` clauses used to filter datasets. They define conditions that incoming data must satisfy in order to be accepted into the table. For instance, suppose we want to ensure that dates in the `date` column fall within a specific range. We can add a `CHECK` constraint to enforce this condition:

```
ALTER TABLE my_table
ADD CONSTRAINT valid_date CHECK (date >= '2024-01-01' AND date <= '2024-12-31');
```

In this example, `valid_date` is the name of our constraint, and the condition ensures that the `date` column values fall within the specified range for the year 2024. Any attempt to insert or update data with dates outside this range will be rejected. This helps maintain data consistency and integrity within the Delta Lake table.

Cloning Delta Lake Tables

In Databricks, if you need to back up or duplicate your Delta Lake table, you have two efficient options: deep clone and shallow clone.

Deep cloning

Deep cloning involves copying both data and metadata from a source table to a target. Here's an example of how you might use the command:

```
CREATE TABLE table_clone
DEEP CLONE source_table
```

Simply, use the `CREATE TABLE` statement, specify the name of the new target table, and include the `DEEP CLONE` keyword followed by the name of the source table.

This copy process can occur incrementally, allowing you to synchronize changes from the source to the target location. Simply, execute CREATE OR REPLACE TABLE instead in order to create a new table version with the new changes:

```
CREATE OR REPLACE TABLE table_clone
DEEP CLONE source_table
```

It's important to note that because in deep cloning all the data must be copied over, this process may take quite a while, especially for large source tables.

Shallow cloning

On the other hand, the shallow clone provides a quicker way to create a copy of a table. It only copies the Delta transaction logs, meaning no data movement takes place during shallow cloning:

```
CREATE TABLE table_clone
SHALLOW CLONE source_table
```

Shallow cloning is an ideal option for scenarios where, for example, you need to test applying changes on a table without altering the current table's data. This makes it particularly useful in development environments where rapid iteration and experimentation are common.

Data integrity in cloning

Whether you choose deep cloning or shallow cloning, any modifications made to the cloned version of the table will be tracked and stored separately from the source. This ensures that changes made during testing or experimentation do not affect the integrity of the original source table.

Exploring Views

In Databricks, views serve as virtual tables without physical data. A view is nothing but a saved SQL query against actual tables, where this logical query is executed each time the view is queried.

Figure 3-22 illustrates an abstract example of creating a view on top of two tables by performing an inner join between them. Each time the view is queried, the join operation will be executed again against these tables.

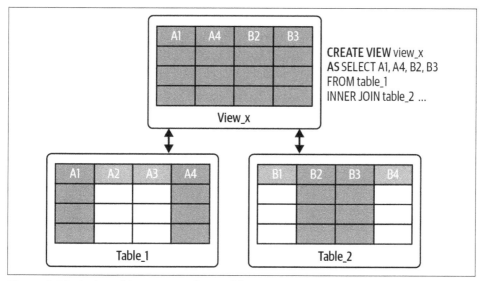

Figure 3-22. A view object on top of two tables

To demonstrate how views function within Databricks, we will use a new SQL note-book titled "3.2A - Views." We start by creating a table of data to be used in this dem-onstration, called `cars`. This table contains columns for the ID, model, brand, and release year of the cars.

```
USE CATALOG hive_metastore;

CREATE TABLE IF NOT EXISTS cars
(id INT, model STRING, brand STRING, year INT);

INSERT INTO cars
VALUES (1, 'Cybertruck', 'Tesla', 2024),
    (2, 'Model S', 'Tesla', 2023),
    (3, 'Model Y', 'Tesla', 2022),
    (4, 'Model X 75D', 'Tesla', 2017),
    (5, 'G-Class G63', 'Mercedes-Benz', 2024),
    (6, 'E-Class E200', 'Mercedes-Benz', 2023),
    (7, 'C-Class C300', 'Mercedes-Benz', 2016),
    (8, 'Everest', 'Ford', 2023),
    (9, 'Puma', 'Ford', 2021),
    (10, 'Focus', 'Ford', 2019)
```

After creating the table and inserting some data into it, you can verify its creation in the Catalog Explorer. Additionally, we can use the SHOW TABLES command to list all tables and views in the default database:

```
SHOW TABLES
```

Figure 3-23 displays the output of the SHOW TABLES command. As observed, we have a table named cars in the default database.

A^Bc database	A^Bc tableName	isTemporary
default	cars	false

Figure 3-23. The output of the SHOW TABLES command

View Types

There are three types of views available in Databricks: stored views, temporary views, and global temporary views. Let's explore these different types of views and how they function within the platform.

Stored views

Stored views, often referred to simply as *views*, are similar to traditional database views. They are database objects where their metadata is persisted in the database. To create a stored view, we use the CREATE VIEW statement followed by the AS keyword and the logical SQL query defining the view:

```
CREATE VIEW view_name
AS <query>
```

Let's create a stored view that displays only Tesla cars from our cars table. We use the CREATE VIEW statement, naming our view view_tesla_cars, and specify the logical query following the AS keyword. This query selects all records from the cars table where the brand is equal to Tesla:

```
CREATE VIEW view_tesla_cars
AS SELECT *
    FROM cars
    WHERE brand = 'Tesla';
```

Running the SHOW TABLES command again confirms that the view has been persisted in the default database and it is not a temporary object, as shown in the isTemporary column in Figure 3-24.

A^Bc database	A^Bc tableName	isTemporary
default	cars	false
default	view_tesla_cars	false

Figure 3-24. The output of the SHOW TABLES command after creating the view_tesla_cars view

Once created, you can query the stored view using a standard SELECT statement, treating it as if it were a table object:

```
SELECT * FROM view_tesla_cars;
```

Figure 3-25 displays the result of querying this view.

$1^2{}_3$ id		$_A{}^B{}_C$ model	$_A{}^B{}_C$ brand	$1^2{}_3$ year
	1	Cybertruck	Tesla	2024
	2	Model S	Tesla	2023
	3	Model Y	Tesla	2022
	4	Model X 75D	Tesla	2017

Figure 3-25. The result of querying the `view_tesla_cars` stored view

It's worth noting that this result is retrieved directly from the cars table. Remember, each time the view is queried, its underlying logical query is actually executed against the source table, in this case, the cars table.

Temporary views

The second type of views in Databricks is temporary views. Temporary views are bound to the Spark session and are automatically dropped when the session ends. They are handy for temporary data manipulations or analyses. To create a temporary view, you simply add the TEMPORARY, or TEMP, keyword to the CREATE VIEW command:

```
CREATE TEMP VIEW view_name
AS <query>
```

Let's create a temporary view called temp_view_cars_brands. This temporary view simply retrieves the unique list of brands from our cars table (Figure 3-26):

```
CREATE TEMP VIEW temp_view_cars_brands
AS  SELECT DISTINCT brand
    FROM cars;

SELECT * FROM temp_view_cars_brands;
```

	$_A{}^B{}_C$ brand
1	Mercedes-Benz
2	Tesla
3	Ford

Figure 3-26. The result of querying the `temp_view_cars_brands` temporary view

Running the SHOW TABLES command confirms the addition of the temporary view to the list, as illustrated in Figure 3-27. The isTemporary column indicates its temporary nature. In addition, since it's a temporary object, it is not persisted to any database, as indicated by having no database specified in the database column.

Aᴮc database	Aᴮc tableName	⅀ isTemporary
default	cars	false
default	view_tesla_cars	false
	temp_view_cars_brands	true

Figure 3-27. The output of the SHOW TABLES command after creating the temp_view_cars_brands temporary view

The lifespan of a temporary view is limited to the duration of the current Spark session. It's essential to note that a new Spark session is initiated in various scenarios within Databricks, such as the following:

- Opening a new notebook
- Detaching and reattaching a notebook to a cluster
- Restarting the Python interpreter due to a Python package installation
- Restarting the cluster itself

To confirm this, let's create a new notebook called "3.2B - Views (Session 2)," and observe the behavior of our created views within it. In this new Spark session, let's first run the SHOW TABLES command:

```
USE CATALOG hive_metastore;

SHOW TABLES;
```

Figure 3-28 displays the output of the SHOW TABLES command in the newly created Spark session. This result confirms the existence of the cars table, as expected. In addition, the stored view of Tesla cars also exists in this new notebook. However, the temporary view of the car brands does not exist in this new session.

Aᴮc database	Aᴮc tableName	⅀ isTemporary
default	cars	false
default	view_tesla_cars	false

Figure 3-28. The output of the SHOW TABLES command in a new Spark session

Global temporary views

Global temporary views behave similarly to other temporary views but are tied to the cluster instead of a specific session. This means that as long as the cluster is running, any notebook attached to it can access its global temporary views. To define a global temporary view, you add the GLOBAL TEMP keyword to the CREATE VIEW command:

```
CREATE GLOBAL TEMP VIEW view_name
AS <query>
```

In our original "3.2A - Views" notebook, let's create a global temporary view, called global_temp_view_recent_cars. This view retrieves all cars from our cars table released in 2022 or later, ordered in descending order:

```
CREATE GLOBAL TEMP VIEW global_temp_view_recent_cars
AS SELECT * FROM cars
   WHERE year >= 2022
   ORDER BY year DESC;
```

Global temporary views are stored in a cluster's temporary database, named global_temp. When querying a global temporary view in a SELECT statement, you need to specify the global_temp database qualifier:

```
SELECT * FROM global_temp.global_temp_view_recent_cars;
```

Figure 3-29 displays the result of querying our global temporary view, showing the latest entries from the cars table.

1^2_3 id	^A_c model	^A_c brand	1^2_3 year
1	Cybertruck	Tesla	2024
5	G-Class G63	Mercedes-Benz	2024
2	Model S	Tesla	2023
6	E-Class E200	Mercedes-Benz	2023
8	Everest	Ford	2023
3	Model Y	Tesla	2022

Figure 3-29. The result of querying the global temporary view

If you run the SHOW TABLES command, you will notice that our global temporary view is not listed among other objects. This occurs because, by default, the command only displays objects in the default database. Since the global temporary views are tied to the global_temp database, we need to use the command SHOW TABLES IN, explicitly specifying the database name global_temp:

```
SHOW TABLES IN global_temp;
```

In Figure 3-30, we can see the global_temp_view_recent_cars, which is indeed a temporary object tied to the global_temp database. Since our temp_view_cars_brands is not tied to any database, it's typically shown with every SHOW TABLES command.

Aᴮc database	Aᴮc tableName	✓= isTemporary
global_temp	global_temp_view_recent_cars	true
	temp_view_cars_brands	true

Figure 3-30. The output of the SHOW TABLES command in the global_temp database

Now, let's switch back to the second notebook, "3.2B - Views (Session 2)." In this new Spark session, we can explore the objects in the global_temp database (Figure 3-31).

Aᴮc database	Aᴮc tableName	✓= isTemporary
global_temp	global_temp_view_recent_cars	true

Figure 3-31. The output of the SHOW TABLES command in the global_temp database within the new Spark session

Since we are leveraging the same cluster, our global temporary view also exists in this new session. As long as the cluster is running, the global_temp database persists, and any notebook attached to the cluster can access its global temporary views. You can confirm this by querying the global temporary view to see the recent cars in this new session.

Comparison of View Types

Understanding the distinctions between the view types and their lifecycles is essential for effective data manipulation and collaboration within your Spark environment. Table 3-3 summarizes the differences between these three types of views.

Table 3-3. Comparison of view types

	(Stored) view	Temporary view	Global temporary view
Creation syntax	CREATE VIEW	CREATE **TEMP** VIEW	CREATE GLOBAL TEMP VIEW
Accessibility	Accessed across sessions/ clusters	Session-scoped	Cluster-scoped
Lifetime	Dropped only by DROP VIEW statement	Dropped when session ends	Dropped when cluster restarted or terminated

Creation syntax

There's a slight difference in the `CREATE VIEW` statements for temporary and global temporary views. For temporary views, we include the `TEMP` keyword, whereas for global temporary views, we add the `GLOBAL TEMP` keyword.

Accessibility

Stored views are similar to tables in that their definitions are stored in the metastore, but they don't contain a physical copy of the data they reference. Remember, a view essentially represents a SQL query. Since stored views are saved in the metastore, they can be accessed across multiple sessions and clusters.

Temporary views, in contrast, are accessible only within the current session. Global temporary views bridge the gap between stored and temporary views; they can be accessed across multiple sessions but are tied to the same cluster.

Lifetime

Lastly, when it comes to removing these views, different methods apply. Stored views are dropped using the `DROP VIEW` command, while temporary views are automatically dropped when the session ends. Similarly, global temporary views are automatically dropped, but this occurs when the cluster is restarted or terminated.

Dropping Views

Let's finally drop our stored view by running the `DROP VIEW` command, like in standard SQL:

```
DROP VIEW view_tesla_cars;
```

If you want to delete temporary views without waiting for the session to end or for the cluster to terminate, you can manually achieve this by using the `DROP VIEW` command as well:

```
DROP VIEW temp_view_cars_brands;
DROP VIEW global_temp.global_temp_view_recent_cars;
```

This allows you to manually clean up such resources when they are no longer needed.

Thus, views in Databricks serve as a powerful solution for organizing and manipulating data without the need to duplicate it physically. With three types of views, Databricks offers a variety of options to suit different use cases and requirements.

Conclusion

In conclusion, mastering relational entities such as databases, tables, and views is fundamental to effectively organizing and managing structured data in Databricks. By understanding their interactions with the metastore and storage locations, you can enhance your data querying and management efficiency. This chapter has provided a comprehensive overview of these entities, setting the stage for further exploration of advanced data management techniques within the Databricks environment.

Sample Exam Questions

Conceptual Question

1. A data engineer is tasked with cleaning up unused Delta tables from a production data catalog. When they drop a Delta table, they notice that this action not only removes the table entry from the catalog but also deletes the underlying data files. Which of the following best explains this behavior?

A. The Delta table was created using a deep clone, which causes both the source table and its data files to be removed when the cloned table is dropped.

B. The Delta table was created using a shallow clone, and shallow clones automatically delete the source table's data files when dropped.

C. The Delta table was created using an external location, so dropping it removes all associated data files.

D. The Delta table was registered as a managed table, and by default, managed tables delete both the metadata and data files when dropped.

E. The Delta table was defined as a stored view, and dropping a stored view automatically deletes the stored data files associated with that view.

Code-Based Question

2. A data engineer at a growing e-commerce company is tasked with creating an external Delta Lake table to store customer information. The table needs to be located in the directory *dbfs:/ecommerce/customers*.

Which of the following SQL statements correctly creates the external Delta Lake table?

A. ```
CREATE TABLE customers
(id INT, name STRING, email STRING)
EXTERNAL 'dbfs:/ecommerce/customers';
```
```

B. CREATE TABLE customers

   USING DELTA

   (id INT, name STRING, email STRING)

   AS EXTERNAL ('dbfs:/ecommerce/customers');

C. CREATE TABLE customers

   (id INT, name STRING, email STRING)

   LOCATION 'dbfs:/ecommerce/customers';

D. CREATE TABLE customers

   USING DELTA

   (id INT, name STRING, email STRING)

   LOCATION AS OF 'dbfs:/ecommerce/customers';

E. CREATE EXTERNAL TABLE customers

   (id INT, name STRING, email STRING)

   PATH = 'dbfs:/ecommerce/customers';

The correct answers to these questions are listed in Appendix C.

Transforming Data with Apache Spark

The Databricks platform provides numerous transformative capabilities powered by Apache Spark. In this chapter, we will navigate through various data transformations tasks such as querying data files, writing to tables with various strategies, and performing advanced ETL operations. Moreover, we will discover the potential of higher-order functions and user-defined functions (UDFs) in Spark SQL.

Querying Data Files

Querying files in Databricks is a fundamental aspect of data exploration and analysis. In this section, we will explore the process of querying file content using SQL-like syntax. The primary mechanism for this is the SELECT statement, which allows us to query files directly to extract the file content.

To initiate a file query, we use the SELECT * FROM syntax, followed by the file format and the path to the file, as illustrated in Figure 4-1. It's important to note that the filepath is specified between backticks (`` `</path/>` ``), and not single quotes ('</path/>'). This distinction is essential to prevent potential syntax errors and ensure the correct interpretation of the path.

A filepath in this context can refer to a single file, or it can incorporate a wildcard character to simultaneously read multiple files. Alternatively, the path can point to an entire directory, assuming that all files within that directory adhere to the same format and schema. This flexibility is particularly advantageous when dealing with large datasets spread across multiple files.

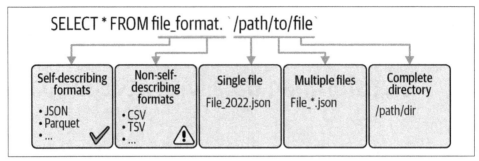

Figure 4-1. SELECT statement to query files

For example, when querying a JSON file located at `path/file.json`, the query would look like this:

```
SELECT * FROM json.`path/file.json`
```

We can demonstrate extracting data directly from files using a real-world dataset representing an online school environment. This dataset consists of three tables: students, enrollments, and courses, illustrated in the entity-relationship diagram shown in Figure 4-2.

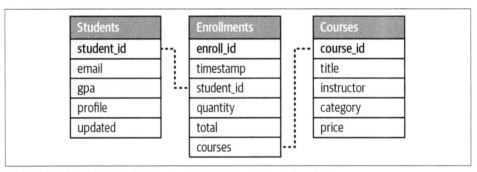

Figure 4-2. Entity-relationship diagram of the online school dataset

In this demonstration, we will use a new SQL notebook titled "4.1 - Querying Files." We begin by running a helper notebook, "School-Setup," which can be found within the *Include* subfolder in the book's GitHub repository. This helper notebook facilitates downloading the dataset to the Databricks file system and prepares the working environment accordingly:

```
%run ../Includes/School-Setup
```

Querying JSON Format

The student data in this dataset is formatted in JSON. Let's review the *students* folder situated in our dataset directory. The placeholder `dataset_school` referenced in the query is a variable defined within our "School-Setup" notebook. It points to the location where the dataset files are stored on the file system:

```python
%python
files = dbutils.fs.ls(f"{dataset_school}/students-json")
display(files)
```

Figure 4-3 shows that there are six JSON files in the *students* folder.

$\overset{B}{\underset{C}{A}}$ path	$\overset{B}{\underset{C}{A}}$ name	1^2_3 size	1^2_3 modificationTime
dbfs:/mnt/DE-Associate/datasets/school/students-json/export_001.json	export_001.json	82347	1709070937000
dbfs:/mnt/DE-Associate/datasets/school/students-json/export_002.json	export_002.json	82976	1709070937000
dbfs:/mnt/DE-Associate/datasets/school/students-json/export_003.json	export_003.json	82755	1709070937000
dbfs:/mnt/DE-Associate/datasets/school/students-json/export_004.json	export_004.json	82949	1709070937000
dbfs:/mnt/DE-Associate/datasets/school/students-json/export_005.json	export_005.json	82704	1709070937000
dbfs:/mnt/DE-Associate/datasets/school/students-json/export_006.json	export_006.json	55220	1709070937000

Figure 4-3. The content of the students-json directory

To read a single JSON file, the SELECT statement is used with the syntax SELECT * FROM json., and then the full path for the JSON file is specified between backticks. In SQL, we use the dataset.school placeholder with the $ character to reference the location where the dataset files are stored. This placeholder is configured in the "School-Setup" notebook:

```
SELECT * FROM json.`${dataset.school}/students-json/export_001.json`
```

The result in Figure 4-4 displays the extracted student data, including student ID, email, GPA score, profile information (in JSON format), and the last updated timestamp. As indicated, the preview display shows all 300 records from the source file.

	$\overset{B}{\underset{C}{A}}$ student_id	$\overset{B}{\underset{C}{A}}$ email	1.2 gpa	$\overset{B}{\underset{C}{A}}$ profile	$\overset{B}{\underset{C}{A}}$ updated
1	S00001	dabby2y@japanpost.jp	1.48	∨ {"first_name":"Dniren","last_name":"Abby","gender":"Female","address": {"street":"768 Mesta Terrace","city":"Annecy","country":"France"}}	2021-12-14T23:15:43.3
2	S00002	eabbysc1@github.com	3.02	∨ {"first_name":"Etti","last_name":"Abbys","gender":"Female","address": {"street":"1748 Vidon Plaza","city":"Varge Mondar","country":"Portugal"}}	2021-12-14T23:15:43.3
3	S00003	rabelovd1@wikispaces.com	3.31	∨ {"first_name":"Ronnie","last_name":"Abelov","gender":"Male","address": {"street":"363 Randy Park","city":"San Celestio","country":"Philippines"}}	2021-12-14T23:15:43.3
4	S00004	rabels9g@behance.net	1.89	∨ {"first_name":"Ray","last_name":"Abels","gender":"Female","address":	2021-12-14T23:15:43.3
↓	300 rows	0.40 seconds runtime			

Figure 4-4. The result of querying the students data in the export_001.json file

To query multiple files simultaneously, you can use the wildcard character (*) in the path. For instance, you can easily query all JSON files starting with the name export_:

```
SELECT * FROM json.`${dataset.school}/students-json/export_*.json`
```

Furthermore, you can query an entire directory of files, assuming a consistent format and schema across all files in the directory. In the following query, the directory path is specified instead of an individual file:

```
SELECT * FROM json.`${dataset.school}/students-json`
```

When dealing with multiple files, adding the `input_file_name` function becomes useful. This built-in Spark SQL function records the source data file for each record. This helps in troubleshooting data-related issues by precisely pinpointing their exact source:

```
SELECT *, input_file_name() source_file
FROM json.`${dataset.school}/students-json`;
```

Figure 4-5 displays, in addition to the original columns, a new column: `source_file`. This column provides supplementary information about the origin of each record in the dataset.

⫶a	$^{A^B_C}$ profile	$^{A^B_C}$ updated	$^{A^B_C}$ source_file
1.98	> {"first_name":"Gerek","last_name":"Peat","g...	> 2021-12-14T23:15...	dbfs:/mnt/DE-Associate/datasets/school/students-json/export_004.json
2.92	> {"first_name":"Dolores","last_name":"Pecha...	> 2021-12-14T23:15...	dbfs:/mnt/DE-Associate/datasets/school/students-json/export_004.json
2.65	> {"first_name":"Levi","last_name":"Peddar","...	> 2021-12-14T23:15...	dbfs:/mnt/DE-Associate/datasets/school/students-json/export_004.json
1.95	> {"first_name":"Susana","last_name":"Gonne...	> 2021-12-14T23:15...	dbfs:/mnt/DE-Associate/datasets/school/students-json/export_003.json
3.33	> {"first_name":"Ronna","last_name":"Gonnin...	> 2021-12-14T23:15...	dbfs:/mnt/DE-Associate/datasets/school/students-json/export_003.json
1.08	> {"first_name":"Reade","last_name":"Goode"...	> 2021-12-14T23:15...	dbfs:/mnt/DE-Associate/datasets/school/students-json/export_003.json

Figure 4-5. The result of adding the source file information to the extracted student data

Querying Using the text Format

When dealing with a variety of text-based files, including formats such as JSON, CSV, TSV, and TXT, Databricks provides the flexibility to handle them using the `text` format:

```
SELECT * FROM text.`path/file.txt`
```

This format allows you to extract the data as raw strings, which provide significant advantages, especially in scenarios where input data might be corrupted or contain anomalies. By extracting data as raw strings, you can leverage custom parsing logic to navigate and extract relevant values from the text-based files.

We can query our students' JSON data as raw text content using the `text` format:

```
SELECT * FROM text.`${dataset.school}/students-json`
```

Figure 4-6 displays the student data as raw string. Each line of the file is loaded as a record with one string column, named `value`.

AᴮC value

⌄ {"student_id":"S00301","email":"thomas.lane@gmail.com","gpa":1.06,"profile":"
{\"first_name\":\"Thomas\",\"last_name\":\"Lane\",\"gender\":\"Male\",\"address\":{\"street\":\"06 Boulevard Victor
Hugo\",\"city\":\"Paris\",\"country\":\"France\"}}","updated":"2021-12-14T23:15:43.375Z"}

⌄ {"student_id":"S00302","email":"ocolegatele@blogger.com","gpa":1.13,"profile":"
{\"first_name\":\"Odilia\",\"last_name\":\"Colegate\",\"gender\":\"Female\",\"address\":{\"street\":\"07 Sommers
Parkway\",\"city\":\"Lyon\",\"country\":\"France\"}}","updated":"2021-12-14T23:15:43.375Z"}

⌄ {"student_id":"S00303","email":"acolledged2@nbcnews.com","gpa":3.62,"profile":"
{\"first_name\":\"Andros\",\"last_name\":\"Colledge\",\"gender\":\"Male\",\"address\":{\"street\":\"342 Katie

Figure 4-6. The result of querying the student data in text *format*

With this result, you can easily apply custom parsing or transformation techniques to extract specific fields, correct anomalies, or reformat the data as needed for subsequent analysis.

Querying Using binaryFile Format

Moreover, there are scenarios where the binary representation of file content is essential, such as when working with images or unstructured data. In such cases, the binaryFile format is suited for this task:

```
SELECT * FROM binaryFile.`path/sample_image.png`
```

In the sample query provided, the binaryFile format is employed to query an image file (sample_image.png), allowing you to work directly with the binary representation of the file's content.

We can use the binaryFile format to extract the raw bytes and some metadata information of the student files:

```
SELECT * FROM binaryFile.`${dataset.school}/students-json`
```

As shown in Figure 4-7, the output of this query provides the following details about each source file:

- path provides the location of the source file on the storage.
- modificationTime gives the last modification time of the file.
- length indicates the size of the file.
- content represents the binary representation of the file.

AᴮC path	modificationTi...	length	content
dbfs:/mnt/DE-Associate/datasets/school/students-json/export_002.json	2024-02-27T21:4...	82976	eyJzdHVkZW50X2lkIjoiUzAwMzAwIiwiZW1haWwiOiJ0aG9tYX
dbfs:/mnt/DE-Associate/datasets/school/students-json/export_004.json	2024-02-27T21:4...	82949	eyJzdHVkZW50X2lkIjoiUzAwOTAxIiwiZW1haWwiOiJnbGVuY
dbfs:/mnt/DE-Associate/datasets/school/students-json/export_003.json	2024-02-27T21:4...	82755	eyJzdHVkZW50X2lkIjoiUzAwNjAxIiwiZW1haWwiOiJzZZ29ubn
dbfs:/mnt/DE-Associate/datasets/school/students-json/export_005.json	2024-02-27T21:4...	82704	eyJzdHVkZW50X2lkIjoiUzAxMiAxMiwiZW1haWwiOiJhcGGVkcn

Figure 4-7. The result of querying the student data in binary format

So, by using the binaryFile format, you can access both the content and metadata of files, offering a detailed view of your dataset.

In essence, Databricks enables you to efficiently handle a wide array of data types and query them directly. Whether dealing with a single file, multiple files, or an entire directory, a simple SELECT statement can be used to retrieve and analyze data.

Querying Non-Self-Describing Formats

The previous querying approach is particularly effective with self-describing file formats that possess a well-defined schema, such as JSON and Parquet. By nature, these formats offer a built-in structure that makes it easy to retrieve and interpret data using SELECT queries.

However, when dealing with non-self-describing formats like comma-separated-value (CSV), the SELECT statement may not be as informative. Unlike JSON and Parquet, CSV files lack a predefined schema, making the format less suitable for direct querying. In such cases, additional steps, such as defining a schema, may be necessary for effective data extraction and analysis.

Let's explore the result of reading the courses' data, which is provided in CSV format. Similar to previous examples, we can try using the SELECT statement, but this time with the csv format:

```
SELECT * FROM csv.`${dataset.school}/courses-csv`
```

As shown in Figure 4-8, the output of the query is not well-parsed. The header row is extracted as a table row, and all columns are loaded into a single column, _c0. This behavior is explained by the delimiter—the symbol used to separate columns in the file—which, in this case, is a semicolon rather than the standard comma.

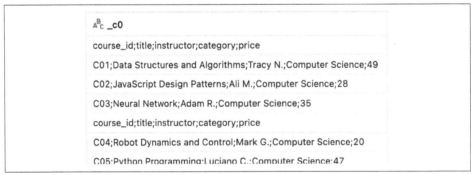

Figure 4-8. The result of querying the course data in csv format

This issue highlights a challenge with querying files without a well-defined schema, particularly in formats like CSV. In the upcoming sections, we will learn how to address this challenge.

Registering Tables from Files with CTAS

Using CTAS (CREATE TABLE AS SELECT) statements allows you to register tables from files, particularly when dealing with well-defined schema sources like Parquet files. This process is crucial for loading data into a lakehouse, allowing you to take full advantage of the Databricks platform's capabilities:

```
CREATE TABLE table_name
AS SELECT * FROM <file_format>.`/path/to/file`
```

CTAS statements simplify the process of creating Delta Lake tables by automatically inferring schema information from the query results. This eliminates the need for manual schema declaration.

In the following example, we create and populate the student data table using a CTAS statement. This ensures that the resulting table is a Delta Lake table:

```
CREATE TABLE students AS
SELECT * FROM json.`${dataset.school}/students-json`;

DESCRIBE EXTENDED students;
```

Figure 4-9 displays the metadata of our new table, students. The Provider value confirms the creation of a Delta Lake table. This means that the CTAS statement has extracted the data from the JSON files and loaded it into the students table in Delta format (i.e., in Parquet data files along with a Delta transaction log). Additionally, this table is identified as a managed table, as indicated by the Type value.

$^{AB}_{C}$ col_name	$^{AB}_{C}$ data_type	$^{AB}_{C}$ comment
email	string	null
gpa	double	null
profile	string	null
student_id	string	null
updated	string	null
Type	MANAGED	
Location	dbfs:/user/hive/warehouse/de_associate_school.db/students	
Provider	delta	

Figure 4-9. The output of the DESCRIBE EXTENDED command on the students table

Moreover, the schema has been automatically inferred from the query results, a feature common to CTAS statements. Remember, CTAS statements automatically infer schema information from the query results, making them a suitable choice for external data ingestion from sources with well-defined schemas, such as Parquet files.

However, it's important to note that CTAS statements come with certain limitations. One significant limitation is that CTAS statements do not support specifying additional file options. This becomes a challenge when trying to ingest data from CSV files or other formats that require specific configurations:

```
CREATE TABLE courses_unparsed AS
SELECT * FROM csv.`${dataset.school}/courses-csv`;

SELECT * FROM courses_unparsed;
```

Figure 4-10 shows that we have successfully created a Delta Lake table; however, the data is not well-parsed.

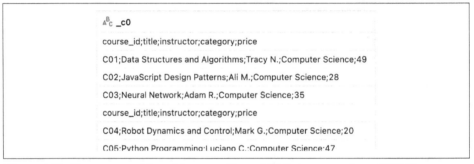

Figure 4-10. The output of the table created by a CTAS statement from CSV files

Typically, CSV files have delimiter or encoding options that need to be specified during the data loading process. In response to this requirement, we will now explore an alternative solution.

Registering Tables on Foreign Data Sources

In scenarios where additional file options are necessary, an alternative solution is to use the regular CREATE TABLE statement, but with the USING keyword. Unlike CTAS statements, this approach is particularly useful when dealing with formats that need specific configurations. The USING keyword provides increased flexibility by allowing you to specify the type of foreign data source, such as CSV format, as well as any additional files options, such as delimiter and header presence:

```
CREATE TABLE table_name
    (col_name1 col_type1, ...)
USING data_source
OPTIONS (key1 = val1, key2 = val2, ...)
LOCATION path
```

However, it's crucial to note that this method creates an external table, serving as a reference to the files without physically moving the data during table creation to Delta Lake.

Unlike CTAS statements, which automatically infer schema information, creating a table via the USING keyword requires you to provide the schema explicitly. So, this method offers more control over the schema definition.

Example 1: CSV

For instance, to deal with CSV files stored in an external location, the following example demonstrates the creation of a table using a CSV foreign source:

```
CREATE TABLE csv_external_table
(col_name1 col_type1, ...)
USING CSV
OPTIONS (header = "true",
        delimiter = ";")
LOCATION = '/path/to/csv/files'
```

This code sample creates an external table that points to CSV files located in the specified path. In addition, it configures the header option to indicate the presence of a header in the files, and the delimiter option is set to use a semicolon instead of the default comma separator.

Let's apply this method on our courses data:

```
1 CREATE TABLE courses_csv
2 (course_id STRING, title STRING, instructor STRING, category STRING, price
  DOUBLE)
3 USING CSV
4 OPTIONS (
5 header = "true",
6 delimiter = ";")
7 LOCATION "${dataset.school}/courses-csv"
```

In this example, the courses_csv table is created by specifying the CSV format as a foreign source (line 3), indicating the presence of a header in the files (line 5), defining the semicolon as the delimiter (line 6), and, lastly, specifying the location of the source files (line 7).

Once the table is created, querying it shows that we have the courses' data in a well-structured form (Figure 4-11).

```
SELECT * FROM courses_csv
```

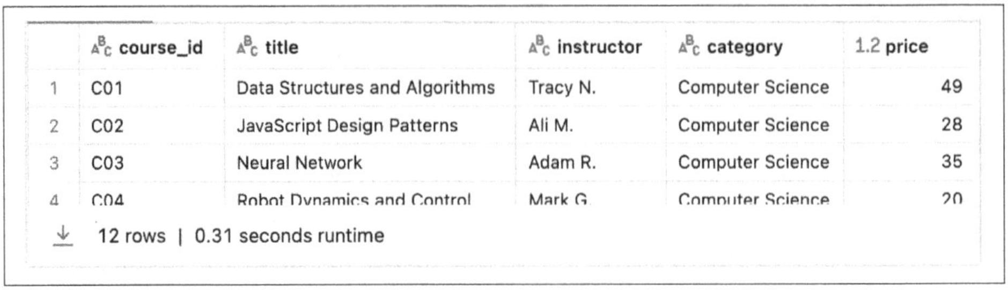

	Aᴮ꜀ course_id	Aᴮ꜀ title	Aᴮ꜀ instructor	Aᴮ꜀ category	1.2 price
1	C01	Data Structures and Algorithms	Tracy N.	Computer Science	49
2	C02	JavaScript Design Patterns	Ali M.	Computer Science	28
3	C03	Neural Network	Adam R.	Computer Science	35
4	C04	Robot Dynamics and Control	Mark G.	Computer Science	20

⬇ 12 rows | 0.31 seconds runtime

Figure 4-11. The result of querying the courses_csv table

It's essential to note that when working with CSV files as a data source, maintaining the column order becomes crucial, especially if additional data files will be added to the source directory. Spark relies on the specified order during table creation to load data and apply column names and data types correctly from CSV files. Therefore, any changes to the column order could impact the integrity of the data loading process.

Example 2: database

Another scenario where the CREATE TABLE statement with the USING keyword proves useful is when creating a table using a JDBC connection, which allows referencing data in an external SQL database. This approach enables you to establish a connection to an external database by defining necessary options such as the connection string, username, password, and specific database table containing the data.

Here is an example of creating an external table using a JDBC connection:

```
CREATE TABLE jdbc_external_table
USING JDBC
OPTIONS (
url = 'jdbc:mysql://your_database_server:port',
dbtable = 'your_database.table_name',
user = 'your_username',
password = 'your_password'
);
```

In this example, the following apply:

- The url option specifies the JDBC connection string to your external database.

- The dbtable option indicates the specific table within the external database.

- The user and password are credentials required for authentication.

This method facilitates seamless integration of data from external SQL databases into the lakehouse environment, allowing for cross-database analysis and reporting. By creating an external table using a JDBC connection, you can access and query data from the external database without physically moving or duplicating the data.

Limitation

It's crucial to be aware of the limitations associated with tables having foreign data sources—they are not Delta tables. This means that the performance benefits and features offered by Delta Lake, such as time travel and guaranteed access to the most recent version of the data, are not available for these tables. This limitation becomes especially noticeable when dealing with large database tables, potentially leading to performance issues.

Let's better understand the impact of not having a Delta table by exploring the consequences of working with an external table linked directly to CSV files. Before we start, let's review the table's type and storage details:

```
DESCRIBE EXTENDED courses_csv
```

Figure 4-12 reveals that the table is an external table, and this table is not a Delta table, as indicated in the Provider value. This means that no data conversion to Delta format occurred during table creation; instead, the table simply points to the CSV files stored in the external location.

ᴬᴮc col_name	ᴬᴮc data_type
Type	EXTERNAL
Provider	CSV
Location	dbfs:/mnt/DE-Associate-Book/datasets/school/courses-csv
Serde Library	org.apache.hadoop.hive.serde2.lazy.LazySimpleSerDe
InputFormat	org.apache.hadoop.mapred.SequenceFileInputFormat
OutputFormat	org.apache.hadoop.hive.ql.io.HiveSequenceFileOutputFormat
Storage Properties	[delimiter=;, header=true]

Figure 4-12. The output of the DESCRIBE EXTENDED command on the courses_csv table

Additionally, the Storage Properties value captures all metadata and options specified during table creation, ensuring that data in the location is always read with these specified options.

Impact of not having a Delta table

The absence of a Delta table introduces certain limitations and impacts. Unlike Delta Lake tables, which guarantee querying the most recent version of source data, tables registered against other data sources, like CSV, may represent outdated cached data. To illustrate this, we will add new data and observe the resulting behavior of the table. First, let's check the number of files in the `courses` directory:

```python
%python
files = dbutils.fs.ls(f"{dataset_school}/courses-csv")
display(files)
```

Figure 4-13 reveals that the directory currently contains four files.

$\text{A}^\text{B}_\text{C}$ path	$\text{A}^\text{B}_\text{C}$ name	1^2_3 size	1^2_3 modificationTime
dbfs:/mnt/DE-Associate-Book/datasets/school/courses-csv/export_001.csv	export_001.csv	214	1709073092000
dbfs:/mnt/DE-Associate-Book/datasets/school/courses-csv/export_002.csv	export_002.csv	223	1709073092000
dbfs:/mnt/DE-Associate-Book/datasets/school/courses-csv/export_003.csv	export_003.csv	213	1709073092000
dbfs:/mnt/DE-Associate-Book/datasets/school/courses-csv/export_004.csv	export_004.csv	218	1709073092000

Figure 4-13. The list of the files in the courses directory

Since each file contains three records, the table holds a total of twelve records, as shown in Figure 4-14.

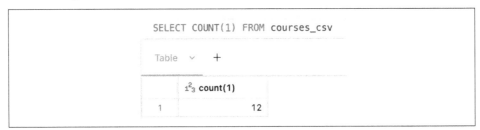

Figure 4-14. The number of records in the courses_csv table after adding the new file

Now, let's run the following Python command to duplicate and rename one of these files as `copy_001.csv`. This action simulates the ingestion of new CSV files by a source system:

```python
%python
dbutils.fs.cp(f"{dataset_school}/courses-csv/export_001.csv",
              f"{dataset_school}/courses-csv/copy_001.csv")
```

After this operation, exploring the courses directory confirms that the new file has been added (Figure 4-15).

A^B_C path	A^B_C name	1²₃ size	1²₃ modificationTime
1 dbfs:/mnt/DE-Associate-Book/datasets/school/courses-csv/copy_001.csv	copy_001.csv	214	1709128153000
2 dbfs:/mnt/DE-Associate-Book/datasets/school/courses-csv/export_001.csv	export_001.csv	214	1709073092000
3 dbfs:/mnt/DE-Associate-Book/datasets/school/courses-csv/export_002.csv	export_002.csv	223	1709073092000
4 dbfs:/mnt/DE-Associate-Book/datasets/school/courses-csv/export_003.csv	export_003.csv	213	1709073092000
5 dbfs:/mnt/DE-Associate-Book/datasets/school/courses-csv/export_004.csv	export_004.csv	218	1709073092000

Figure 4-15. The list of the files in the courses directory after adding the new file

Despite adding new data to the directory, we notice that the table does not immediately reflect the changes from 12 to 15 records, as shown in Figure 4-16.

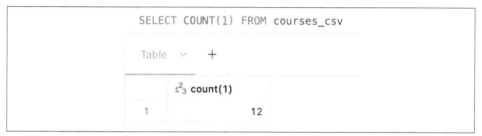

Figure 4-16. The number of records in the `courses_csv` table after adding the new file

Spark automatically caches the underlying data in local storage for better performance in subsequent queries. However, the external CSV file does not natively signal Spark to refresh this cached data. Consequently, the new data remains invisible until the cache is manually refreshed using the REFRESH TABLE command:

```
REFRESH TABLE courses_csv
```

However, this action invalidates the table cache, necessitating a rescan of the original data source to reload all data into memory. This process can be particularly time-consuming when dealing with large datasets.

Upon refreshing the table, querying it again retrieves the updated count, as illustrated in Figure 4-17. This confirms the need for manual cache refreshing when dealing with foreign data sources like CSV.

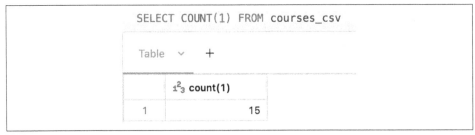

SELECT COUNT(1) FROM courses_csv

Table ⌄ +

	1^2_3 count(1)
1	15

Figure 4-17. The number of records in the courses_csv table after refreshing the table

This observation emphasizes the trade-offs and considerations associated with choosing between Delta tables and foreign data sources when working with Databricks.

Hybrid approach

To address this limitation and leverage the advantages of Delta Lake, a workaround involves creating a temporary view that refers to the foreign data source. Then, you can execute a CTAS statement on this temporary view to extract the data from the external source and load it into a Delta table. This hybrid approach allows you to combine the benefits of external tables with the performance and features of Delta Lake.

Here's an illustrative example of this process:

```
CREATE TEMP VIEW foreign_source_tmp_vw (col1 col1_type, ...)
  USING data_source
  OPTIONS (key1 = "val1", key2 = "val2", ..., path = "/path/to/files");

CREATE TABLE delta_table
AS SELECT * FROM foreign_source_tmp_vw
```

In this example, a temporary view is created referring to a foreign data source. Then, a Delta Lake table is created by executing a CTAS statement on the temporary view. This process moves the data into a Delta format (Parquet data files + transaction log in JSON format).

This approach highlights the flexibility of CTAS statements, as they can be employed not only to query files but also to query any object, such as a temporary view in this case.

In the same way, we can apply this approach on the course data, delivered in CSV format. We first create a temporary view and configure it to handle file options. Then, we execute a CTAS statement to make a copy of the data from the temporary view into a Delta table named courses:

```
CREATE TEMP VIEW courses_tmp_vw
  (course_id STRING, title STRING, instructor STRING, category STRING,
  price DOUBLE)
USING CSV
OPTIONS (
  path = "${dataset.school}/courses-csv/export_*.csv",
  header = "true",
  delimiter = ";"
);

CREATE TABLE courses AS
  SELECT * FROM courses_tmp_vw;
```

Figure 4-18 displays the metadata information of the courses table. It confirms that it is a Delta Lake table.

```
DESCRIBE EXTENDED courses
```

ᴬᴮ_C col_name	ᴬᴮ_C data_type
Type	MANAGED
Location	dbfs:/user/hive/warehouse/de_associate_school.db/courses
Provider	delta

Figure 4-18. The output of the DESCRIBE EXTENDED command on the courses table

Finally, querying the table confirms that it contains well-parsed data from the CSV files, as illustrated in Figure 4-19.

```
SELECT * FROM courses
```

ᴬᴮ_C course_id	ᴬᴮ_C title	ᴬᴮ_C instructor	ᴬᴮ_C category	1.2 price
C01	Data Structures and Algorithms	Tracy N.	Computer Science	49
C02	JavaScript Design Patterns	Ali M.	Computer Science	28
C03	Neural Network	Adam R.	Computer Science	35
C04	Robot Dynamics and Control	Mark G.	Computer Science	20

Figure 4-19. The result of querying the courses table

In the following sections of the book, we will regularly refer to this table whenever we need to access the courses data.

Writing to Tables

In this section, we cover the SQL syntax used for inserting and updating records in Delta Lake tables. We will continue using our online school dataset, consisting of three tables: students, enrollments, and courses, as illustrated in Figure 4-20.

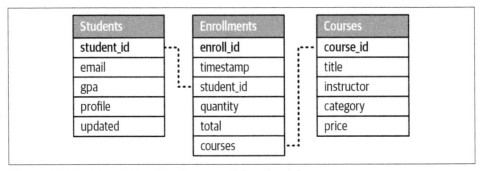

Figure 4-20. Entity-relationship diagram of the school dataset

In this demonstration, we will use a new SQL notebook titled "4.2 - Writing to Tables." We begin by running the "School-Setup" notebook to prepare our environment:

```
%run ../Includes/School-Setup
```

We initiate our exploration by using a CTAS statement to create the enrollments Delta table from Parquet files:

```
CREATE TABLE enrollments AS
SELECT * FROM parquet.`${dataset.school}/enrollments`
```

Once the table is created, we proceed to query its content:

```
SELECT * FROM enrollments
```

Figure 4-21 shows the query result. Since Parquet files have a well-defined schema, we observe that Delta Lake has accurately captured the schema and successfully extracted the data.

enroll_id	enroll_timestamp	student_id	quantity	total	courses
000003559	1657722056	S00001	1	7.2	> [{"course_id":"C09","discount_percent":70,"subtotal":7.2}]
000004243	1658786901	S00002	2	30.25	> [{"course_id":"C07","discount_percent":15,"subtotal":28.05},{"course_id...
000004321	1658934252	S00003	1	18	> [{"course_id":"C04","discount_percent":10,"subtotal":18}]
000004392	1659034513	S00004	1	26.65	> [{"course_id":"C08","discount_percent":35,"subtotal":26.65}]

Figure 4-21. The result of querying the enrollments table

Replacing Data

You can completely replace the content of a Delta Lake table either by overwriting the existing table or by other traditional methods like dropping and re-creating it. However, overwriting Delta tables offers several advantages over the approach of merely dropping and re-creating tables. Table 4-1 outlines these benefits.

Table 4-1. Comparison of dropping and re-creating table versus overwriting table methods

	Drop and recreate table	Overwrite table
Processing time	Time-consuming as it involves recursively listing directories and deleting large files.	Fast process since the updated data is just a new table version.
Leveraging Delta's time travel	Deletes the old versions of the table, making its historical data unavailable for retrieval.	Preserves the old table versions, allowing easy retrieval of historical data.
Concurrency	Concurrent queries are unable to access the table while the operation is ongoing.	Concurrent queries can continue reading the table seamlessly while the operation is in progress.
ACID guarantees	If the operation fails, the table cannot be reverted to its original state.	If the operation fails, the table will revert to its previous state.

In summary, the process of overwriting tables provides efficiency, reliability, and seamless integration with Delta's features such as time travel and ACID transactions. In Databricks, there are two methods to completely replace the content of Delta Lake tables:

- CREATE OR REPLACE TABLE statements
- INSERT OVERWRITE statements

1. CREATE OR REPLACE TABLE statement

The first method to achieve a complete table overwrite in Delta Lake is by using the CREATE OR REPLACE TABLE statement, also known as the CRAS (CREATE OR REPLACE AS SELECT) statement. This statement fully replaces the content of a table each time it executes:

```
CREATE OR REPLACE TABLE enrollments AS
SELECT * FROM parquet.`${dataset.school}/enrollments`
```

Upon executing this statement, the enrollments table will be overwritten with the newer data. To better understand what happened in the table, let's examine the table history:

```
DESCRIBE HISTORY enrollments
```

As illustrated in Figure 4-22, version 0 is nothing but a CTAS statement. Meanwhile, the `CREATE OR REPLACE` statement has generated a new table version. This new version reflects the updated state of the table after the overwrite operation.

₁²₃ version	🕒 timestamp	ᴬᵇᴄ userName	ᴬᵇᴄ operation	⚖ operationParameters
1	2024-02-28T17:5...	Derar Alhussein	CREATE OR REPLACE TABLE AS SELECT	⟩ {"partitionBy":"[]","description":null,"isManaged":"truℇ
0	2024-02-28T15:0...	Derar Alhussein	CREATE TABLE AS SELECT	⟩ {"partitionBy":"[]","description":null,"isManaged":"truℇ

Figure 4-22. The history log of the `enrollments` table

2. INSERT OVERWRITE

The second method for overwriting data in Delta Tables involves using the `INSERT OVERWRITE` statement:

```
INSERT OVERWRITE enrollments
SELECT * FROM parquet.`${dataset.school}/enrollments`
```

While this statement achieves a similar outcome to the `CREATE OR REPLACE TABLE` approach mentioned earlier, there are some key differences and nuances to consider. Unlike the `CREATE OR REPLACE TABLE` statement, which can create a new table if it doesn't exist, `INSERT OVERWRITE` can only overwrite an existing table. This means that the target table must already exist prior to performing the operation.

After executing the `INSERT OVERWRITE` statement, the table history is updated to reflect the overwrite operation:

```
DESCRIBE HISTORY enrollments
```

As displayed in Figure 4-23, Delta Lake records this operation as a new version, categorized as a standard `WRITE` operation. However, the mode of this operation is marked as `"Overwrite"` in the `operationParameters` field. This indicates that the existing data was replaced with the new records from the query.

₁²₃ version	🕒 timestamp	ᴬᵇᴄ userName	ᴬᵇᴄ operation	⚖ operationParameters
2	2024-02-28T17:5...	Derar Alhussein	WRITE	⟩ {"mode":"Overwrite","statsOnLoad":"false","partitionℇ
1	2024-02-28T17:5...	Derar Alhussein	CREATE OR REPLACE TABLE AS SELECT	⟩ {"partitionBy":"[]","description":null,"isManaged":"truℇ
0	2024-02-28T15:0...	Derar Alhussein	CREATE TABLE AS SELECT	⟩ {"partitionBy":"[]","description":null,"isManaged":"truℇ

Figure 4-23. The history log of the `enrollments` table after the `INSERT OVERWRITE` command

One significant advantage of using `INSERT OVERWRITE` is its ability to overwrite only the new records that match the current table schema. This prevents any risk of accidentally modifying the table structure. Thus, `INSERT OVERWRITE` is considered a more secure approach for overwriting existing tables.

When attempting to overwrite data using the INSERT OVERWRITE statement with a schema that differs from the existing table schema, a schema mismatch error will be generated. Let's consider an example where we attempt to add an extra column, containing the source file name, to our table:

```
INSERT OVERWRITE enrollments
SELECT *, input_file_name() FROM parquet.`${dataset.school}/enrollments`
```

AnalysisException: A schema mismatch detected when writing to the Delta table

The previous command results in an exception indicating a schema mismatch. This occurs because the schema of the new data being inserted does not match the existing schema of the enrollments table.

Delta Lake tables are by definition schema-on-write, which means that Delta Lake enforces schema consistency during write operations. Any attempt to write data with a schema that differs from the table's schema will be rejected to maintain data integrity. This behavior differs from the first method of the CREATE OR REPLACE TABLE statement, which replaces the entire table along with its schema.

Appending Data

One of the simplest methods to append records to Delta Lake tables is through the use of the INSERT INTO statement. This statement allows you to easily add new data to existing tables from the result of a SQL query. Let's explore how this process works with the following command:

```
INSERT INTO enrollments
SELECT * FROM parquet.`${dataset.school}/enrollments-new`
```

In our scenario, we use the INSERT INTO statement to add new records to the enrollments table. Note that we are not explicitly providing the corresponding column values to be added. Instead, we're using an input query to retrieve the new data from Parquet files located in a given directory. This query serves as the source of our new records, which we then insert into the designated table using the INSERT INTO clause.

By executing this INSERT INTO statement, we will insert 700 new records into our table. To confirm the success of our operation, we can perform a quick check to verify the updated number of records in the enrollments table. Figure 4-24 shows that the number of enrollments has indeed increased, now totaling 2850 records.

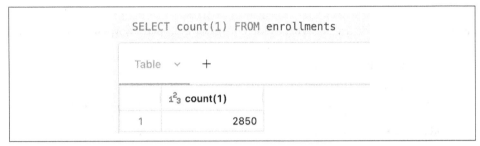

```
SELECT count(1) FROM enrollments

Table  ∨    +

        1²₃ count(1)

    1              2850
```

Figure 4-24. The number of records in the enrollments table after inserting new data

While the INSERT INTO statement provides a convenient means of appending records to tables, it lacks built-in mechanisms to prevent the insertion of duplicate data. This means that if the insertion query is executed multiple times, it will write the same records to the target table repeatedly, leading to the creation of duplicate entries.

To address this issue effectively, we turn to an alternative method: the MERGE INTO statement.

Merging Data

The MERGE INTO statement enables you to perform upsert operations—meaning you can insert new data and update existing records—and even delete records, all within a single statement. Let's explore how we can use this statement to update the student data in our online school dataset.

In this specific scenario, we aim to update student data with modified email addresses and add new students into the table. To accomplish this, we first create a temporary view containing the updated student data. This view will serve as the source from which we'll merge changes into our students table:

```
CREATE OR REPLACE TEMP VIEW students_updates AS
SELECT * FROM json.`${dataset.school}/students-json-new`;
```

The following merge operation is executed to merge the changes from the student_updates temporary view into the target students table, using the student ID as the key for matching records. Let's first look at the query, and then go into its details:

```
MERGE INTO students c
USING students_updates u
ON c. student_id = u. student_id
WHEN MATCHED AND c.email IS NULL AND u.email IS NOT NULL THEN
  UPDATE SET email = u.email, updated = u.updated
WHEN NOT MATCHED THEN INSERT *
```

Within this `MERGE INTO` statement, we define two primary actions based on the matching status of records:

Update action (`WHEN MATCHED` clause)
> When a match is found between the source and target records, an update action is performed. This action involves updating the email address and the last updated timestamp. Notice that we introduce additional conditions to this action. Specifically, we check if the email address in the current row is null while the corresponding record in the `student_updates` view contains a valid email address. For such records, we proceed by updating the email field and the last updated timestamp in the target table.

Insert action (`WHEN NOT MATCHED` clause)
> For records in the `student_updates` view that do not match any existing students based on the student ID, an insert action is triggered. This ensures that all new students are added into our target table.

Let's now proceed with the execution of this query. Figure 4-25 presents the metrics summarizing the outcomes of our merge operation.

$^{12}_3$ num_affected_rows	$^{12}_3$ num_updated_rows	$^{12}_3$ num_deleted_rows	$^{12}_3$ num_inserted_rows
301	100	0	201

Figure 4-25. The output of the `MERGE INTO` command on the `students` table

We observe that 100 records have been updated, reflecting the changes in email addresses and last updated timestamps. In addition, 201 new records have been inserted into the `students` table. No records have been deleted during this process since there was no delete action included in the query (`WHEN MATCHED [condition] THEN DELETE`).

One of the key advantages of the `MERGE INTO` statement is its ability to execute updates, inserts, and deletes within a single atomic transaction. This ensures data consistency and integrity by treating all operations as a single unit, thereby minimizing the risk of inconsistencies or partial changes on the table data.

Additionally, the merge operation serves as an excellent solution for preventing duplicates during record insertion. Let's consider another scenario where we have a set of new courses to be inserted, delivered in CSV format. To facilitate this, we'll establish a temporary view based on this new data:

```
CREATE OR REPLACE TEMP VIEW courses_updates
  (course_id STRING, title STRING, instructor STRING,
   category STRING, price DOUBLE)
USING CSV
```

```
OPTIONS (
  path = "${dataset.school}/courses-csv-new",
  header = "true",
  delimiter = ";"
);
```

Now, we can use the MERGE INTO statement to synchronize the courses table with the information sourced from the temporary view courses_updates.

In this scenario, we exclusively focus on the condition where there is no match. This implies that we'll only insert new data if it doesn't already exist in our target table, based on the unique key comprising both the course_id and the title fields. Among the new courses, our interest lies only in inserting those categorized under computer science. For this purpose, we'll specify that only records categorized under Computer Science are eligible for insertion by adding an additional criterion:

```
MERGE INTO courses c
USING courses_updates u
ON c.course_id = u.course_id AND c.title = u.title
WHEN NOT MATCHED AND u.category = 'Computer Science' THEN
  INSERT *
```

As displayed in Figure 4-26, the query execution resulted in the insertion of three new records, all belonging to the computer science category.

$^{1^2}_3$ num_affected_rows	$^{1^2}_3$ num_updated_rows	$^{1^2}_3$ num_deleted_rows	$^{1^2}_3$ num_inserted_rows
3	0	0	3

Figure 4-26. The output of the MERGE INTO command on the courses table

This operation is called insert-only merge, which demonstrates one of the primary advantages of the merge operation: its ability to prevent duplicate entries. To confirm this, let's rerun the previous query and see the resulting behavior.

As shown in Figure 4-27, the second execution of our merge statement didn't lead to the reinsertion of the records, as they already exist in the table.

$^{1^2}_3$ num_affected_rows	$^{1^2}_3$ num_updated_rows	$^{1^2}_3$ num_deleted_rows	$^{1^2}_3$ num_inserted_rows
0	0	0	0

Figure 4-27. The output of the second run of the MERGE INTO command on the courses table

In conclusion, while the INSERT INTO statement offers a straightforward method for appending records to tables, its drawback of duplicate record insertion necessitates the adoption of more robust strategies, such as the `MERGE INTO` statement. With `MERGE INTO`, you can effectively upsert data to avoid duplicates.

Performing Advanced ETL Transformations

In this section, we will explore advanced transformations available in Spark SQL, covering the capabilities it provides for handling nested and complex data structures. We will continue using our online school dataset, consisting of three tables: `students`, `enrollments`, and `courses`.

In this demonstration, we will use a new SQL notebook titled "4.3 - Advanced Transformations." We begin by running the "School-Setup" notebook to prepare our environment:

```
%run ../Includes/School-Setup
```

Dealing with Nested JSON Data

Let's first recall our student data:

```
SELECT * FROM students
```

Figure 4-28 displays the result of querying the `students` table created in the previous section. It shows a column containing the profile information of each student, represented as a nested JSON structure. Specifically, we notice the address information of the profile is stored as a JSON object as well, comprising street, city, and country details.

	1.2 **gpa**	A^B_C **profile**	A^B_C **stu**
a@aol...	1.95	⌄ {"first_name":"Susana","last_name":"Gonnely","gender":"Female","address": {"street":"760 Express Court","city":"Obrenovac","country":"Serbia"}}	S0060
:@nb...	3.33	⌄ {"first_name":"Ronna","last_name":"Gonning","gender":"Non-binary","address": {"street":"48 Grim Way","city":"Metsemotlhaba","country":"Botswana"}}	S0060
a.gov	1.08	⌄ {"first_name":"Reade","last_name":"Goode","gender":"Male","address": {"street":"975 Mendota Center","city":"Seabra","country":"Brazil"}}	S0060
n@sk...	1.97	⌄ {"first_name":"Row","last_name":"Goodier","gender":"Female","address":	S0060

Figure 4-28. The result of querying the `students` table

To check the data type of the `profile` column, we can use the `DESCRIBE` command, which helps in exploring the schema of the table:

```
DESCRIBE students
```

In Figure 4-29, we observe that the `profile` column is nothing but a string; it's a JSON string.

$^{A}_{C}$ col_name	$^{A}_{C}$ data_type	$^{A}_{C}$ comment
email	string	null
gpa	double	null
profile	string	null
student_id	string	null
updated	string	null

Figure 4-29. The output of the DESCRIBE command on the students table

Spark SQL facilitates interaction with such JSON data by using a colon syntax (:) to navigate through its nested structures. In this example, we access the first name within the profile column using the colon syntax. Similarly, we extract the nested value of the country from the address within the profile:

```
SELECT student_id, profile:first_name, profile:address:country
FROM students
```

The output in Figure 4-30 confirms that we have successfully extracted the profile details from the JSON string.

$^{A}_{C}$ student_id	$^{A}_{C}$ first_name	$^{A}_{C}$ country
S00601	Susana	Serbia
S00602	Ronna	Botswana
S00603	Reade	Brazil
S00604	Row	United Kingdom

Figure 4-30. The result of extracting the profile details using the colon syntax

Parsing JSON into Struct Type

Spark SQL goes further by providing functionality to parse JSON objects into struct types—a native Spark type with nested attributes. The from_json function is employed for this task, but it requires knowledge of the schema of the JSON object in advance:

```
SELECT from_json(profile, <schema>) FROM students;
```

In response to this requirement, we can use the schema_of_json function, which derives the schema from sample data of the JSON object, provided the fields are non-null. In the following example, we provide sample data of a student's profile to obtain the corresponding schema. This schema is then used in the from_json function to allow successful parsing of JSON objects into struct types. Note that we could also use

a SQL-style column-type declaration for the schema instead of inferring it. Additionally, we store the resulting records in a temporary view for further analysis:

```
CREATE OR REPLACE TEMP VIEW parsed_students AS
  SELECT student_id, from_json(profile, schema_of_json('{"first_name":"Sarah",
  "last_name":"Lundi", "gender":"Female", "address":{"street":"8 Greenbank Road",
  "city":"Ottawa", "country":"Canada"}}')) AS profile_struct
  FROM students;

SELECT * FROM parsed_students
```

Figure 4-31 shows the result of parsing the profile JSON objects into struct types. As
illustrated, the preview display allows us to expand and collapse the struct object,
offering a convenient way to explore its contents.

Figure 4-31. The result of parsing the profile JSON objects into struct types

Let's check again the data type of the profile column by running the DESCRIBE command on our view:

```
DESCRIBE parsed_students
```

Figure 4-32 confirms that the column profile_struct is indeed of a struct type, and
its inner address field is of a struct type as well.

Aᴮ𝒸 col_name	Aᴮ𝒸 data_type
student_id	string
profile_struct	struct<address:struct<city:string,country:string,street:string>,first_name:string,gender:string,last_name:string>

Figure 4-32. The output of the DESCRIBE command on the parsed_students table

Interacting with Struct Types

When working with struct types, a notable aspect is the ability to interact with nested objects using standard period or dot (.) syntax, compared to the colon syntax used for JSON strings. This makes the code more intuitive and aligns with Spark's native representation.

```
SELECT student_id, profile_struct.first_name, profile_struct.address.country
FROM parsed_students
```

The output in Figure 4-33 confirms that we have successfully extracted the profile details from the struct type object using the dot syntax.

$^{AB}_C$ student_id	$^{AB}_C$ first_name	$^{AB}_C$ country
S00601	Susana	Serbia
S00602	Ronna	Botswana
S00603	Reade	Brazil
S00604	Row	United Kingdom

Figure 4-33. The result of extracting the profile details using the dot syntax

Flattening Struct Types

Once a JSON string is converted to a struct type, Spark SQL introduces a powerful feature—the ability to use the star (*) operation to flatten fields and create separate columns:

```
CREATE OR REPLACE TEMP VIEW students_final AS
  SELECT student_id, profile_struct.*
  FROM parsed_students;

SELECT * FROM students_final
```

The output in Figure 4-34 confirms that this transformation resulted in distinct columns for the first name, last name, gender, and address elements of the profile field.

In summary, Spark SQL's advanced transformations empower you to handle nested and complex data structures with ease, providing functionalities for parsing JSON objects into struct types and performing operations on them.

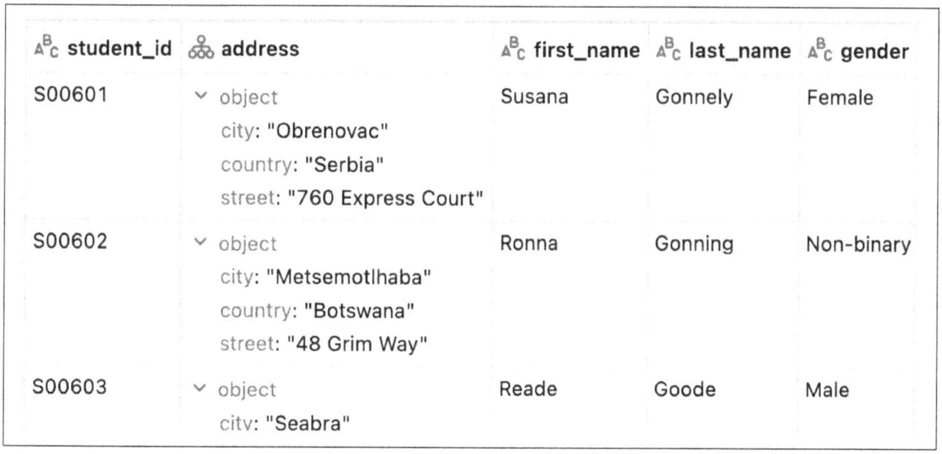

$_A^B{}_C$ student_id	$_⊗$ address	$_A^B{}_C$ first_name	$_A^B{}_C$ last_name	$_A^B{}_C$ gender
S00601	⌄ object city: "Obrenovac" country: "Serbia" street: "760 Express Court"	Susana	Gonnely	Female
S00602	⌄ object city: "Metsemotlhaba" country: "Botswana" street: "48 Grim Way"	Ronna	Gonning	Non-binary
S00603	⌄ object city: "Seabra"	Reade	Goode	Male

Figure 4-34. The result of the star operation flattens the profile's fields into separate columns

Leveraging the explode Function

In this section, we shift our focus to the `enrollments` table and explore an advanced feature in Spark SQL—the `explode` function. Let's begin by reviewing some fields within our table:

```
SELECT enroll_id, student_id, courses
FROM enrollments
```

Figure 4-35 shows that the `courses` column is an array of structs.

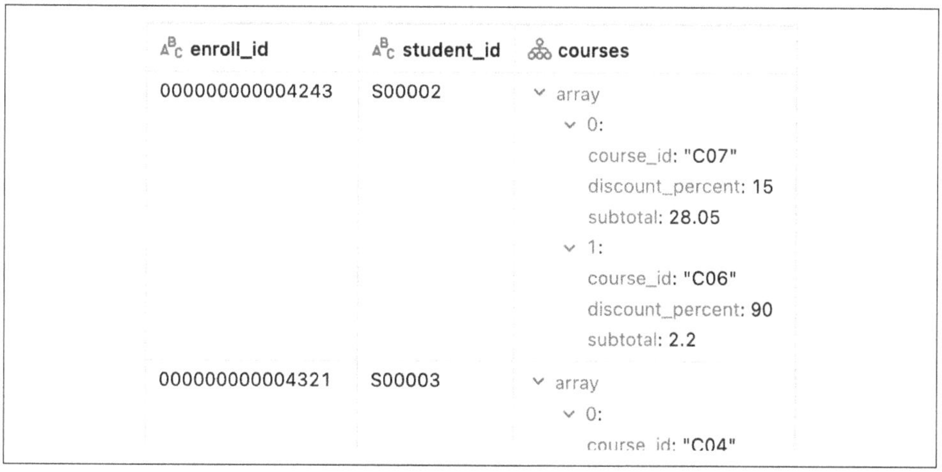

$_A^B{}_C$ enroll_id	$_A^B{}_C$ student_id	$_⊗$ courses

000000000004243	S00002	⌄ array
		  ⌄ 0:
		    course_id: "C07"
		    discount_percent: 15
		    subtotal: 28.05
		  ⌄ 1:
		    course_id: "C06"
		    discount_percent: 90
		    subtotal: 2.2

000000000004321	S00003	⌄ array
		  ⌄ 0:
		    course_id: "C04"

Figure 4-35. The result of querying the `enrollments` table

Spark SQL provides dedicated functions for efficiently handling arrays, like the `explode` function. This function allows us to transform an array into individual rows, each representing an element from the array:

```
SELECT enroll_id, student_id, explode(courses) AS course
FROM enrollments
```

Figure 4-36 displays the results of applying the `explode` function to the `courses` array. Each course element now occupies its own row, with the other information such as student ID and enrollment ID being duplicated for each course.

$^{AB}_{C}$ enroll_id	$^{AB}_{C}$ student_id	ᯓ course
000000000003559	S00001	> {"course_id":"C09","discount_percent":70,"subtotal":7.2}
000000000004243	S00002	> {"course_id":"C07","discount_percent":15,"subtotal":28.05}
000000000004243	S00002	> {"course_id":"C06","discount_percent":90,"subtotal":2.2}
000000000004321	S00003	> {"course_id":"C04","discount_percent":10,"subtotal":18}

Figure 4-36. The result of applying the `explode` function to the courses column

This layout is particularly useful when examining course-level patterns or performing operations such as aggregations and joins with other tables.

Aggregating Unique Values

Moving forward, we explore another interesting function—the `collect_set` function. This function is an aggregation function that returns an array of unique values for a given field. It can even deal with fields within arrays. In this example, the `courses_set` column is formed as an array of arrays:

```
SELECT student_id,
  collect_set(enroll_id) AS enrollments_set,
  collect_set(courses.course_id) AS courses_set
FROM enrollments
GROUP BY student_id
```

Figure 4-37 displays the resulting aggregations.

$^{AB}_{C}$ student_id	ᯓ enrollments_set	ᯓ courses_set
S00001	> ["000000000005191","000000000003559","000000000005067"]	> [["C09"],["C03","C12"],["C08","C02"]]
S00002	> ["000000000005192","000000000004550","000000000004243"]	> [["C04","C06"],["C02","C06","C01"],["C07","C06"]]
S00003	> ["000000000004321","000000000004575","000000000005193"]	> [["C09","C06"],["C04","C10"],["C04"]]
S00004	> ["000000000004392","000000000005022","000000000005194"]	> [["C09","C10"],["C08","C10"],["C08"]]

Figure 4-37. The result of applying the `collect_set` function

In the `courses_set` column, we notice that, for instance, the course with identifier C06 appears in multiple elements in the array of student S00002. To avoid such an issue, we can flatten this nested array and retain only the distinct values. This can be achieved in a two-step process. First, we apply the `flatten` function to flatten the array, and then, we use the `array_distinct` function to retain only the unique values:

```
SELECT student_id,
  collect_set(courses.course_id) As before_flatten,
  array_distinct(flatten(collect_set(courses.course_id))) AS after_flatten
FROM enrollments
GROUP BY student_id
```

Figure 4-38 offers a before-and-after perspective, showcasing the original state of the data and the result achieved after applying the `flatten` and `array_distinct` functions.

A^Bc student_id	⅋ before_flatten	⅋ after_flatten
S00001	> [["C09"],["C03","C12"],["C08","C02"]]	> ["C09","C03","C12","C08","C02"]
S00002	> [["C04","C06"],["C02","C06","C01"],["C07","C06"]]	> ["C04","C06","C02","C01","C07"]
S00003	> [["C09","C06"],["C04","C10"],["C04"]]	> ["C09","C06","C04","C10"]
S00004	> [["C09","C10"],["C08","C10"],["C08"]]	> ["C09","C10","C08"]

Figure 4-38. The result of flattening the array

In practice, the `flatten` function is employed to transform the nested array into a flat structure. Following this, the `array_distinct` function is applied to eliminate any duplicate values. This confirms, for example, that our course identifier C06 of student S00002 is now represented only once in the resulting array.

Mastering Join Operations in Spark SQL

Spark SQL also supports join operations to facilitate blending data from different tables. It offers a variety of standard join operations, including inner, outer, left, right, anti, cross, and semi joins. In the following example, we'll focus on an inner join operation, where we combine the result of an explode operation with the `courses` lookup table to extract the course's details, such as course titles and instructor names.

The first step in this operation involves performing an explode operation on our dataset to transform array elements into individual rows. Subsequently, we desire to enrich this exploded data with additional information from the `courses` lookup table. To achieve this, we execute an inner join based on the common key, in this case, the `course_id`.

The syntax used for joining data in Spark SQL follows the conventions of standard SQL. We specify the type of join we want (inner, outer, left, right, etc.), the tables we are joining, and the conditions for the join. In this example, an inner join is applied based on matching the `course_id` key. This ensures that only matching records from both tables are retained in the final result set. Lastly, we store the enriched data in a temporary view named enrollments_enriched:

```
CREATE OR REPLACE VIEW enrollments_enriched AS
SELECT *
FROM (
  SELECT *, explode(courses) AS course
  FROM enrollments) e
INNER JOIN courses c
ON e.course.course_id = c.course_id;


SELECT * FROM enrollments_enriched
```

Figure 4-39 displays the result of this join operation, incorporating information from both the exploded data and the courses lookup table. For each course, we can now easily access its details like the title, instructor name, and category.

ᴬᴮ꜀ enroll_id	₁²₃ enroll_time...	ᴬᴮ꜀ student_id	₁²₃ quantity	1.2 total	ᴬᴮ꜀ title	ᴬᴮ꜀ instructor	ᴬᴮ꜀ cat₁
000003559	1657722056	S00001	1	7.2	Advanced Data Structures	Pierre B.	Compu
000004243	1658786901	S00002	2	30.25	Machine Learning	Andriy R.	Compu
000004243	1658786901	S00002	2	30.25	Deep Learning	François R.	Compu
000004321	1658934262	S00003	1	18	Robot Dynamics and ...	Mark G.	Compu

Figure 4-39. The result of joining enrollments with courses

Exploring Set Operations in Spark SQL

Similar to relational databases, Spark SQL supports various set operations such as union, intersect, and except/minus. Let's explore these set operations by applying them to our enrollments table, which currently holds 2,150 records, alongside a temporary view that will introduce 700 new records. To begin, we'll create the view under the name enrollments_updates:

```
CREATE OR REPLACE TEMP VIEW enrollments_updates
AS SELECT * FROM parquet.`${dataset.school}/enrollments-new`;
```

Union operation

The union operation in Spark SQL enables the combination of two datasets by stacking them vertically, with two variants available: UNION and UNION ALL. While UNION (or UNION DISTINCT) returns only distinct rows, UNION ALL includes all rows from both datasets, preserving duplicates. In the following example, we demonstrate the UNION ALL operation by combining the old and new data of the enrollments table. This results in a unified dataset that includes all records from both sources, including duplicates:

```
SELECT * FROM enrollments
UNION ALL
SELECT * FROM enrollments_updates
```

Figure 4-40 displays 3,550 records as a result of this union operation, which includes duplicate entries. This provides a comprehensive view that incorporates both old and new records.

	A^B_C enroll_id	1^2_3 enroll_timestamp	A^B_C student_id	1^2_3 quantity	1.2 total
1	000000000003559	1657722056	S00001	1	7.2
2	000000000004243	1658786901	S00002	2	30.25
3	000000000004321	1658934252	S00003	1	18
4	000000000004392	1659034513	S00004	1	26.65
⤓	3,550 rows	1.00 second runtime			

Figure 4-40. The result of the union operation

Intersect operation

The intersect operation, on the other hand, returns the common rows found in both datasets. This operation is useful when identifying overlaps between two datasets. In the following scenario, the INTERSECT command is applied to find rows that exist in both the enrollments table and the enrollments_updates view:

```
SELECT * FROM enrollments
INTERSECT
SELECT * FROM enrollments_updates
```

Figure 4-41 reveals that there are 700 records present in both sources. This stems from the insertion of these 700 records into the enrollments table, which we performed during the "Appending Data" on page 129 section.

	A^B_C enroll_id	1^2_3 enroll_timestamp	A^B_C student_id	1^2_3 quantity	1.2 total
1	000000000005801	1658000449	S00529	1	14
2	000000000006275	1658882475	S00852	1	31.35
3	000000000005775	1657922261	S00986	1	22.4
4	000000000006197	1658772555	S00726	1	2.05
⤓	700 rows	0.96 seconds runtime			

Figure 4-41. The result of the intersect operation

Minus operation

An interesting use case of set operations involves leveraging the MINUS operation to obtain records exclusive to one dataset. For instance, if we execute enrollments minus enrollments_updates, we effectively retrieve only the data from the original enrollments table that does not overlap with the 700 new records present in the enrollments_updates view:

```
SELECT * FROM enrollments
MINUS
SELECT * FROM enrollments_updates
```

Figure 4-42 displays the entries exclusive to the enrollments table after excluding the 700 shared records. The minus operation is particularly useful for isolating records of interest, allowing you to focus only on them. In the provided example, this allows you to focus on the enrollments' data before the last insert operation performed on the table.

ᴬᴮc enroll_id	¹²₃ enroll_timestamp	ᴬᴮc student_id	¹²₃ quantity	1.2 total
1 000000000004035	1658485056	S00241	2	33.15
2 000000000004016	1658437625	S00274	3	28
3 000000000004270	1658846414	S00416	2	14.2
4 000000000003927	1658313331	S00550	3	56.6

⬇ 2,150 rows | 1.16 seconds runtime

Figure 4-42. The result of the minus operation

In conclusion, the set operations available in Spark SQL enable you to perform a range of tasks including combining, comparing, and isolating datasets.

Changing Data Perspectives

In addition to its support for set operations, Spark SQL supports creating pivot tables for transforming data perspectives using the PIVOT clause. This provides a means to generate aggregated values based on specific column values. This transformation results in a pivot table, wherein the aggregated values become multiple columns. Let's explore the PIVOT clause with a practical example, where we aggregate and flatten the enrollment information for each student.

Before analyzing the query syntax, let's first execute the query and examine its output:

```
1 SELECT * FROM (
2 SELECT student_id, course.course_id AS course_id, course.subtotal AS subtotal
3  FROM enrollments_enriched
4 )
5 PIVOT (
6 sum(subtotal) FOR course_id IN (
7   'C01', 'C02', 'C03', 'C04', 'C05', 'C06',
8   'C07', 'C08', 'C09', 'C10', 'C11', 'C12')
9 )
```

Figure 4-43 displays the resulting pivot table that illustrates the aggregated sum of subtotal amounts per course for each student.

A_C student_id	1.2 C01	1.2 C02	1.2 C03	1.2 C04	1.2 C05	1.2 C06
S00682	null	5.6	null	11	null	
S00209	null	null	null	1	null	
S00801	null	2.8	null	null	null	
S00023	null	5.6	null	null	null	
S00249	null	22.4	null	null	21.15	
S00443	null	null	null	null	30.55	

Figure 4-43. The enrollments pivot table

The query syntax for generating the pivot table involves the following steps:

1. Selecting its input data from a table or subquery (lines 1–4).
2. Calling the pivot clause (lines 5–9), which consists of three key components:

   a. Aggregation function: The sum(subtotal) specifies the aggregation function to be applied, along with the column to be aggregated.

   b. FOR subclause: This subclause defines the pivot column, course_id, which is the basis for creating multiple columns in the output.

   c. IN operator: The IN operator lists the distinct values of the pivot column. In our case, it lists the distinct course IDs (from C01 to C12), each presented as separate columns in the pivot table.

In essence, the PIVOT clause in Spark SQL empowers you to reshape and aggregate data dynamically. This capability is essential for many analytical and machine learning tasks.

Working with Higher-Order Functions

Higher-order functions in Databricks provide a powerful toolset for working with complex data types, such as arrays. In this section, we'll cover two essential functions: FILTER and TRANSFORM.

In this demonstration, we will use a new SQL notebook titled "4.4 - Higher-Order Functions." To ensure our environment is properly configured, we start by executing the "School-Setup" notebook, maintaining our focus on using the online school dataset:

```
%run ../Includes/School-Setup
```

Let's first review our student enrollment data, illustrated in Figure 4-44:

```
SELECT * FROM enrollments
```

A^B_C enroll_id	1²₃ enroll_tim...	A^B_C student_id	1²₃ quantity	1.2 total	░ courses
000000000004243	1658786901	S00002	2	30.25	⌄ array
					⌄ 0:
					course_id: "C07"
					discount_percent: 15
					subtotal: 28.05
					⌄ 1:
					course_id: "C06"
					discount_percent: 90
					subtotal: 2.2
000000000004321	1658934252	S00003	1	18	⌄ array
					⌄ 0:
					course_id: "C04"
					discount percent: 10

Figure 4-44. The result of querying the enrollments table

The query result demonstrates that the courses column is of complex data type, specifically an array of struct objects. To effectively work with such hierarchical data, it is essential to use higher-order functions.

Filter Function

The FILTER function is a fundamental higher-order function that enables the extraction of specific elements from an array based on a given lambda function.

In the following example, we create a new column named highly_discounted_ courses to identify courses that were purchased with a significant discount. This column is populated by filtering the courses field to only include courses with a discount percentage of 60% or higher:

```
SELECT
enroll_id,
courses,
FILTER (courses,
        course -> course.discount_percent >= 60) AS highly_discounted_courses
FROM enrollments
```

Figure 4-45 displays the filtered data, where the column highly_discounted_ courses contains only the courses with a discount percentage of 60% or higher.

A‌B‌C enroll_id	⚬ courses	⚬ highly_discounted_courses
000000000004475	⌄ array	⌄ array
	⌄ 0:	⌄ 0:
	course_id: "C09"	course_id: "C07"
	discount_percent: 35	discount_percent: 90
	subtotal: 15.6	subtotal: 3.3
	⌄ 1:	
	course_id: "C07"	
	discount_percent: 90	
	subtotal: 3.3	
000000000004206	> [{"course_id":"C09","discount_percent":95,"su...	> [{"course_id":"C09","discount_percent":95,"sub
000000000004037	> [{"course_id":"C09","discount_percent":5,"sub...	> []
000000000004032	> [{"course_id":"C09","discount_percent":35,"su...	> []
000000000003574	> [{"course_id":"C02","discount_percent":85,"su...	> [{"course_id":"C02","discount_percent":85,"sub
000000000004459	> [{"course_id":"C01","discount_percent":60,"su...	> [{"course_id":"C01","discount_percent":60,"sub

Figure 4-45. The result of applying the FILTER function on the courses column

However, we observe that the column has several empty arrays. To resolve this, we can use a WHERE clause to display only non-empty array values. However, because a derived column generally cannot be referenced directly within a WHERE clause, using a subquery is essential to achieve the desired outcome:

```
SELECT enroll_id, highly_discounted_courses
FROM (
 SELECT
   enroll_id,
   courses,
   FILTER (courses,
       course -> course.discount_percent >= 60) AS highly_discounted_courses
 FROM enrollments)
WHERE size(highly_discounted_courses) > 0;
```

By using this subquery that applies the WHERE clause to the size of the returned column, you can successfully eliminate all empty arrays.

Transform Function

The TRANSFORM function is another essential higher-order function that facilitates the application of a transformation to each item in an array, extracting the transformed values. In our example, we apply a 20% tax to the subtotal value for each course in the courses array:

```
SELECT
enroll_id,
courses,
TRANSFORM (
  courses,
  course -> ROUND(course.subtotal * 1.2, 2) ) AS courses_after_tax
FROM enrollments;
```

Figure 4-46 displays the result of applying the TRANSFORM function, which adds a new column, courses_after_tax, containing an array of transformed values for each element in the courses array. The transformation, in this case, involves calculating a 20% tax on the subtotal value and then rounding the result.

A^Bc enroll_id	courses	courses_after_tax
000000000003650	∨ array	∨ array
	> 0: {"course_id": "C08", "discount_percent": 25, "subtotal": 30.75}	0: 36.9
	> 1: {"course_id": "C09", "discount_percent": 95, "subtotal": 1.2}	1: 1.44
	> 2: {"course_id": "C12", "discount_percent": 80, "subtotal": 6}	2: 7.2
000000000003910	> [{"course_id":"C09","discount_percent":25,"subtotal":18}]	> [21.6]
000000000003525	> [{"course_id":"C07","discount_percent":50,"subtotal":16.5},{"course...	> [19.8,2.64]
000000000004370	> [{"course_id":"C08","discount_percent":65,"subtotal":14.35},{"cour...	> [17,22,50.16]

Figure 4-46. The result of applying the TRANSFORM function on the courses *column*

Clearly, the transform function extracts only the transformed values by default. Instead, we can create a struct object containing multiple elements. This struct object contains two fields: the course ID for the original course, and subtotal_with_tax reflecting the subtotal amount after applying the tax:

```
SELECT
enroll_id,
courses,
TRANSFORM (
  courses,
  course -> (course.course_id,
             ROUND(course.subtotal * 1.2, 2) AS subtotal_with_tax)
) AS courses_after_tax
FROM enrollments;
```

Figure 4-47 displays the result of generating struct objects with the TRANSFORM function. This allows for more structured and detailed representation of the transformed data.

A^Bc enroll_id	courses	courses_after_tax
000003650	∨ array	∨ array
	> 0: {"course_id": "C08", "discount_percent": 25, "subtotal": 30.75}	> 0: {"course_id": "C08", "subtotal_with_tax": 36.9}
	> 1: {"course_id": "C09", "discount_percent": 95, "subtotal": 1.2}	> 1: {"course_id": "C09", "subtotal_with_tax": 1.44}
	> 2: {"course_id": "C12", "discount_percent": 80, "subtotal": 6}	> 2: {"course_id": "C12", "subtotal_with_tax": 7.2}
000003910	> [{"course_id":"C09","discount_percent":25,"subtotal":18}]	> [{"course_id":"C09","subtotal_with_tax":21.6}]
000003525	> [{"course_id":"C07","discount_percent":50,"subtotal":16.5},{"cours...	> [{"course_id":"C07","subtotal_with_tax":19.8},{"course_
000004370	> [{"course_id":"C08","discount_percent":65,"subtotal":14.35},{"cour...	> [{"course_id":"C08","subtotal_with_tax":17.22},{"course

Figure 4-47. The result of generating struct types with the TRANSFORM function

In summary, higher-order functions in Databricks, like FILTER and TRANSFORM, empower you to manipulate and extract specific information from complex data structures.

Developing SQL UDFs

SQL user-defined functions (UDFs) are a powerful way to encapsulate custom logic with a SQL-like syntax, making it reusable across different SQL queries. Unlike external UDFs written in Scala, Java, Python, or R, which appear as black boxes to the Spark Optimizer, SQL UDFs leverage Spark SQL directly. This typically provides better performance when applying custom logic to large datasets.

In this section, we'll explore the creation and usage of SQL UDFs in a new SQL notebook titled "4.5 - SQL UDFs." As we will continue using our online school dataset, we begin by running the "School-Setup" notebook to prepare our environment:

```
%run ../Includes/School-Setup
```

Creating UDFs

To create a SQL UDF, you need to specify a function name, optional parameters, the return type, and the custom logic. In the following example, we create a UDF named `gpa_to_percentage` for converting students' grade point average (GPA) scores into percentage equivalents. The UDF accepts a GPA score as a parameter of type `DOUBLE` and returns the percentage score as `integer`. The conversion logic assumes a GPA scale of 4.0, which is then translated into a percentage scale by multiplying it by 25. Additionally, the calculated percentage is rounded to the nearest integer using the `round` function and then cast to an integer data type:

```
CREATE OR REPLACE FUNCTION gpa_to_percentage(gpa DOUBLE)
RETURNS INT

RETURN cast(round(gpa * 25) AS INT)
```

Applying UDFs

Once the UDF is created, you can use it in any SQL query like a native function. In the following example, we apply the `gpa_to_percentage` UDF on the `gpa` column within the `students` table:

```
SELECT student_id, gpa, gpa_to_percentage(gpa) AS percentage_score
FROM students
```

Figure 4-48 confirms that our function has been successfully applied. The column `percentage_score` accurately provides the equivalent percentage score for each student's GPA.

A^B_C student_id	1.2 gpa	1²₃ percentage_score
S00612	2.9	73
S00613	3.46	87
S00614	1.42	36
S00615	1.88	47

Figure 4-48. The result of applying the `gpa_to_percentage` *UDF*

Understanding UDFs

SQL UDFs are permanent objects stored in the database, allowing them to be used across different Spark sessions and notebooks. The DESCRIBE FUNCTION command provides basic information about the UDF, such as the database, input parameters, and return type:

```
DESCRIBE FUNCTION gpa_to_percentage
```

As shown in Figure 4-49, the function belongs to the de_associate_school database, created in the "School-Setup" notebook. It accepts the gpa as an input of type DOUBLE and returns an integer.

A^B_C function_desc
Function: spark_catalog.de_associate_school.gpa_to_percentage
Type: SCALAR
Input: gpa DOUBLE
Returns: INT

Figure 4-49. The output of `DESCRIBE FUNCTION` *command on the* `gpa_to_percentage` *UDF*

Furthermore, the DESCRIBE FUNCTION EXTENDED command offers more details, including the SQL logic used in the function:

```
DESCRIBE FUNCTION EXTENDED gpa_to_percentage
```

Figure 4-50 displays some of the extended metadata information about our UDF. Specifically, the Body field reveals the SQL logic implemented within the function.

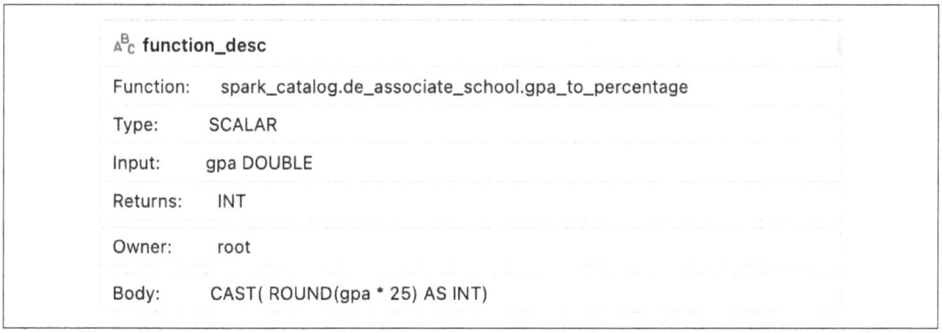

$^{AB}_C$ function_desc	
Function:	spark_catalog.de_associate_school.gpa_to_percentage
Type:	SCALAR
Input:	gpa DOUBLE
Returns:	INT
Owner:	root
Body:	CAST(ROUND(gpa * 25) AS INT)

Figure 4-50. The output of the DESCRIBE FUNCTION EXTENDED command on the gpa_to_percentage UDF

Complex Logic UDFs

SQL UDFs can incorporate complex logic, such as using standard SQL CASE WHEN statements to evaluate multiple conditions. In the following example, we define a UDF that takes a student's GPA and returns its corresponding letter grade based on the grading scale in Table 4-2.

Table 4-2. Grading scale

GPA (4.0 scale)	Grade letter
3.50–4.0	A
2.75–3.44	B
2.0–2.74	C
Below 2.0	F

To map GPA scores to their corresponding letter grades, we use a CASE WHEN statement within a function named get_letter_grade:

```
CREATE OR REPLACE FUNCTION get_letter_grade(gpa DOUBLE)
RETURNS STRING
RETURN CASE
        WHEN gpa >= 3.5 THEN "A"
        WHEN gpa >= 2.75 AND gpa < 3.5 THEN "B"
        WHEN gpa >= 2 AND gpa < 2.75 THEN "C"
        ELSE "F"
    END
```

We can now apply this complex UDF to our dataset:

```
SELECT student_id, gpa, get_letter_grade(gpa) AS letter_grade
FROM students
```

Figure 4-51 confirms that we have successfully applied our UDF. As expected, the column letter_grade gives us the corresponding letter grade to each student's GPA.

A^B_0 student_id	1.2 gpa	A^B_C letter_grade
S00606	1.42	F
S00607	3.14	B
S00608	2.49	C
S00609	3.56	A
S00610	3.34	B

Figure 4-51. The result of applying the `get_letter_grade` UDF

Thus, SQL UDFs in Databricks offer flexibility, reusability, and the ability to incorporate complex logic. All this, while benefiting from Spark's optimization for parallel execution.

Dropping UDFs

Finally, you can remove UDFs when they are no longer needed by using the DROP FUNCTION command:

```
DROP FUNCTION gpa_to_percentage;
DROP FUNCTION get_letter_grade;
```

After executing these commands, both UDFs will be completely removed from the database.

Conclusion

In conclusion, this chapter has highlighted key techniques for transforming data efficiently on the Databricks platform using Apache Spark. We've explored methods for querying and writing data, implemented advanced ETL operations, and leveraged the flexibility of higher-order functions and UDFs. With these tools, you are now equipped to perform robust data transformations that are both powerful and adaptable to diverse data processing needs.

Sample Exam Questions

Conceptual Question

1. A data engineer is tasked with replacing the content of a Delta table in a data pipeline. During a team meeting, they discuss the best approach for overwriting the table without disrupting ongoing analyses while ensuring optimal performance. The team considers two commands: INSERT OVERWRITE and CREATE OR REPLACE TABLE.

Given this scenario, which of the following factors should the data engineer consider when justifying the use of the INSERT OVERWRITE command over CREATE OR REPLACE TABLE?

A. The INSERT OVERWRITE operation is a more dynamic technique that ensures schema evolution when overwriting the table.

B. The INSERT OVERWRITE operation is a safer approach for overwriting the table without changing its schema.

C. The INSERT OVERWRITE operation can automatically optimize the table's layout for better query performance after the overwrite.

D. All of the above reasons explain why INSERT OVERWRITE is recommended over CREATE OR REPLACE TABLE.

E. None of the above! Both commands operate the same way.

Code-Based Question

2. A data engineer at a financial services company is tasked with creating a reusable SQL user-defined function (UDF). This function will calculate interest based on dynamic inputs across various datasets. The engineer needs to decide which code block would be appropriate for this task.

Which of the following code blocks should the data engineer use to create the SQL UDF?

A. CREATE FUNCTION calc_interest(amount DOUBLE, rate DOUBLE)
   RETURNS cast(amount * rate AS DOUBLE);

B. CREATE UDF calc_interest(amount DOUBLE, rate DOUBLE)
   RETURN amount * rate;

C. CREATE UDF calc_interest(amount DOUBLE, rate DOUBLE)
   RETURNS DOUBLE
   RETURN amount * rate;

D. CREATE FUNCTION calc_interest(amount DOUBLE, rate DOUBLE)
   RETURNS DOUBLE
   RETURN amount * rate;

E. DEF calc_interest(amount DOUBLE, rate DOUBLE)
   RETURN cast(amount * rate AS DOUBLE);

The correct answers to these questions are listed in Appendix C.

Processing Incremental Data

In the previous chapters, we explored the fundamentals of processing data in groups or batches at once. However, when data is generated continuously, traditional batch processing approaches tend to become insufficient. In this chapter, we will explore the concepts and techniques for processing streaming data, including Spark Structured Streaming and incremental data ingestion from files. Moreover, we will discuss the concept of medallion architecture and how to build it under the stream processing model.

Streaming Data with Apache Spark

Apache Spark provides robust support for processing streaming data, enabling you to efficiently perform real-time analytics. At the heart of this process is the concept of a data stream, which is the focus of processing. To effectively work with streaming data in Spark, let's first understand what a data stream is and its characteristics.

What Is a Data Stream?

A data stream represents an unbounded flow of data, often originating from various sources such as sensors, log files, or social media platforms. As new data is generated, it is appended to the stream, making it a dynamic and constantly changing dataset. Examples of data streams include the following:

Social media feeds
   Continuous streams of posts, each containing text, user information, and time-stamps, that can be processed and analyzed to track trends, sentiments, or user behavior.

Sensor readings

> Temperature and humidity readings, or other metrics, from a network of sensors in a smart building, used to optimize energy consumption.

Log data

> A stream of log messages from a server, containing system events and error messages, used to monitor system performance or detect security threats.

Processing data streams present a unique set of challenges due to their dynamic and ever-growing nature. To handle such continuous flows of information, there are typically two primary approaches:

Recompute

> In this classical approach, each time new data arrives, the entire dataset is reprocessed to incorporate the new information. While this method ensures accuracy, it can be computationally intensive and time-consuming, especially for large datasets.

Incremental processing

> Alternatively, incremental processing involves developing custom logic to identify and capture only the new data that has been added since the last update. This approach reduces processing overhead by focusing solely on the changes, thereby improving efficiency.

One powerful tool for incremental processing of data streams is Spark Structured Streaming, which is part of Apache Spark.

Spark Structured Streaming

Spark Structured Streaming is a scalable stream processing engine that revolutionizes the way data streams are processed and queried. It enables querying of infinite data sources, automatically detecting new data as it arrives and persisting results incrementally into target data sinks, as illustrated in Figure 5-1. A sink is often a durable storage system such as files or tables that serves as the destination for the processed data.

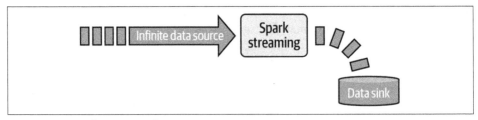

Figure 5-1. Spark Structured Streaming

In Structured Streaming, the key idea is to handle live data streams as unbounded, continuously growing tables, where each incoming data item is appended as a new row, as illustrated in Figure 5-2. This design allows you to apply familiar SQL and DataFrame operations on streaming data in the same way you would with batch data. By unifying batch and streaming operations, Structured Streaming eliminates the need for separate technology stacks and facilitates the migration of your existing batch Spark jobs to streaming jobs.

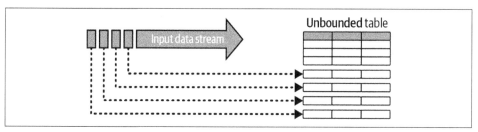

Figure 5-2. Fundamental concept of Spark Structured Streaming (image adapted from https://spark.apache.org)

The append-only requirement of streaming sources

One fundamental prerequisite for a data source to be considered valid for streaming is that it must adhere to the append-only requirement in Structured Streaming. This condition implies that data can only be added to the source, and existing data cannot be modified. If a data source allows data to be updated, deleted, or overwritten, it is then considered no longer streamable.

Therefore, it is essential to ensure that your data sources conform to this requirement in order to take advantage of the benefits of streaming data processing.

Delta Lake as streaming source

Spark Structured Streaming seamlessly integrates with various data sources, including directories of files, messaging systems like Kafka, and Delta Lake tables as well. Delta Lake is well-integrated with Spark Structured Streaming using the DataStreamReader and DataStreamWriter APIs in PySpark.

DataStreamReader. In Python, the spark.readStream method allows you to query a Delta Lake table as a streaming source. This functionality enables processing both existing data in the table and any new data that arrives subsequently. The result is a "streaming" DataFrame, which allows for applying transformations just like one would on a static DataFrame:

```
streamDF = spark.readStream.table("source_table")
```

DataStreamWriter. Once the necessary transformations have been applied, the results of the streaming DataFrame can be persisted using its writeStream method:

```
streamDF.writeStream.table("target_table")
```

This method enables configuring various output options to store the processed data into durable storage. Let's explore the following example, where we have two Delta Lake tables, Table_1 and Table_2. The goal is to continuously stream data from Table_1 to Table_2, appending new records into Table_2 every two minutes, as illustrated in Figure 5-3.

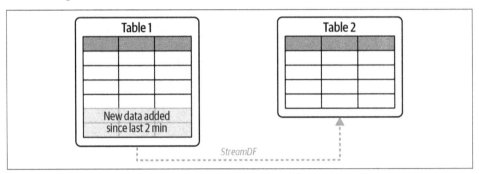

Figure 5-3. Streaming data between two Delta Lake tables

To achieve this, we use the following Python code. This code sets up a Structured Streaming job in Spark that continuously monitors Table_1 for new data, processes it at regular intervals of two minutes, and appends the new records to Table_2:

```
streamDF = spark.readStream
                .table("Table_1")

streamDF.writeStream
        .trigger(processingTime="2 minutes")
        .outputMode("append")
        .option("checkpointLocation", "/path")
        .table("Table_2")
```

In this code snippet, we start by defining a streaming DataFrame streamDF against the Delta table Table_1 using the spark.readStream method. Whenever a new version of the table is written, a new *micro-batch* containing the new data will come in through this readStream.

Next, we use the writeStream method to define the streaming write operation on the streamDF. Here, we specify the processing trigger interval using the trigger function, indicating that Spark should check for new data every two minutes. This means that the streaming job will be triggered at regular intervals of two minutes to process any new incoming data in the source.

We then set the output mode to "append" using the `outputMode` function. This mode ensures that only newly received records since the last trigger will be appended to the output sink, which in this case is the Delta table `Table_2`.

Additionally, we specify the checkpoint location using the `checkpointLocation` option. Spark uses checkpoints to store metadata about the streaming job, including the current state and progress. By providing a checkpoint location, Spark can recover the streaming job from failures and maintain its state across restarts.

Streaming Query Configurations

Now, let's examine the configurations of DataStreamWriter in detail.

Trigger Intervals

When setting up a streaming write operation, the trigger method defines how often the system should process incoming data. This timing mechanism is referred to as the trigger interval. There are two primary trigger modes: continuous and triggered, as illustrated in Table 5-1.

Table 5-1. Trigger intervals of DataStreamWriter

Mode	Usage	Behavior
Continuous	`.trigger(processingTime= "5 minutes")`	Processes data at fixed intervals (e.g., every 5 minutes). Default interval: 500ms.
Triggered	`#deprecated` `.trigger(once=True)`	Processes all available data in a single micro-batch, then stops automatically.
	`.trigger(availableNow=True)`	Processes all available data in multiple micro-batches, then stops automatically.

Let's dive deeper to gain a comprehensive understanding of these two modes.

Continuous mode: Near-real-time processing. In this mode, the streaming query will continuously run to process data in micro-batches at regular intervals. By default, if no specific trigger interval is provided, the data will be processed every half a second. This is equivalent to using the option `processingTime="500ms"`. Alternatively, you have the flexibility to specify another fixed interval according to your requirements. For instance, you might opt to process the data at a specified interval, such as every five minutes, by using the option `processingTime="5 minutes"`. This mode ensures a continuous flow of data, enabling near-real-time data processing.

Triggered mode: Incremental batch processing. In contrast to continuous mode, the triggered mode offers a batch-oriented approach known as incremental batch processing. In this mode, the streaming query processes all available data since the last trigger and then stops automatically. This mode is suited for scenarios where data arrival is not constant, eliminating the need for continuously running resources. Under the triggered mode, two options are available: Once and availableNow:

Trigger.Once

With this option, the stream processes the currently available data, all at once, in a single micro-batch. However, this can introduce challenges related to scalability when dealing with large volumes of data, as it may lead to out-of-memory (OOM) errors.

Trigger.availableNow

Similarly, the availableNow option also facilitates batch processing of all currently available data. However, it addresses scalability concerns by allowing data to be processed in multiple micro-batches until completion. This option offers flexibility in handling large data batches while ensuring efficient resource utilization.

> Since Databricks Runtime 11.3 LTS, the Trigger.Once setting has been deprecated. However, it's possible that you may encounter references to it in the current exam version or in older documentation. Databricks now recommends using Trigger.AvailableNow for all incremental batch processing workloads.

Output Modes

When writing streaming data, you can specify the output mode to define how the data is written to the target. There are primarily two output modes available: append mode and complete mode, as illustrated in Table 5-2.

Table 5-2. Output modes of DataStreamWriter

Mode	Usage	Behavior
Append (default)	.outputMode("append")	Only newly received rows are appended to the target table with each batch.
Complete	.outputMode("complete")	The target table is overwritten with each batch.

Append mode. Append mode is the default output mode if no specific mode is provided. It appends only new rows that have been received since the last trigger to the target table. This mode is suitable for scenarios where the target sink needs to maintain a continuously growing dataset based on the incoming streaming data.

Complete mode. Complete mode recomputes and rewrites the entire results to the sink every time a write is triggered. It replaces the entire contents of the output sink with the latest computed results with each batch. This mode is commonly used for updating summary tables with the latest aggregates.

Checkpointing

Checkpointing is a mechanism for saving the progress information of the streaming query. The checkpoints are stored in a reliable storage system, such as the DBFS or cloud storage like Amazon S3 or Azure Storage. This approach ensures that if the streaming job crashes or needs to be restarted, it can resume processing from the last checkpointed state rather than starting from scratch.

One important aspect to note about checkpoints in Apache Spark is that they cannot be shared between multiple streaming jobs. Each streaming write operation requires its own separate checkpoint location. This separation ensures that each streaming application maintains its own processing guarantees and doesn't interfere with or rely on the checkpoints of other jobs.

Structured Streaming Guarantees

Spark Structured Streaming offers, primarily, two guarantees to ensure end-to-end reliable and fault-tolerant stream processing: fault recovery and exactly-once semantics.

Fault recovery

In case of failures, such as node crashes or network issues, the streaming engine is capable of resuming processing from where it left off. This is achieved through the combination of checkpointing and a mechanism called write-ahead logs. They enable capturing the offset range corresponding to the data being processed during every trigger, which makes it possible to recover from failures without any data loss.

It's important to note that this guarantee mainly depends on the repeatability of the data sources. Data sources such as cloud-based object storage or pub/sub messaging services are typically repeatable, meaning that the same data can be read multiple times if needed. This allows the streaming engine to restart or reprocess the data under any failure condition.

Exactly-once semantics

Structured Streaming also guarantees that each record in the stream will be processed exactly once, even in the event of failures and retries. This is ensured by the implementation of idempotent streaming sinks. Idempotency means that if multiple writes occur for the same entities, no duplicates will be written to the sink. It relies on the offset of the entities as a unique identifier to recognize any duplicates and ignore them.

In essence, by accurately tracking offsets from replayable sources and leveraging idempotent sinks, Structured Streaming ensures reliable end-to-end processing, without any risk of data loss or duplication, even in the presence of failures.

Unsupported operations

As discussed earlier, infinite data sources are viewed as unbounded tables in Structured Streaming. While most operations are identical to those of batch processing, there are certain operations that are not supported due to the nature of streaming data. Operations such as sorting and deduplication introduce complexities in a streaming context and may not be directly applicable or feasible.

While a full discussion of these limitations is beyond the scope of this Associate-level certification, it's essential to know that there are alternative mechanisms to address similar requirements. For example, you can use advanced streaming techniques like windowing and watermarking for performing such operations over specific time windows. A detailed understanding of these techniques is typically expected at a more advanced level, particularly for the Databricks Data Engineer Professional certification.

Implementing Structured Streaming

Let's delve into the practical implementation of Spark Structured Streaming for enabling incremental data processing. We will continue using our online school dataset, consisting of three tables: students, enrollments, and courses, as illustrated in Figure 5-4.

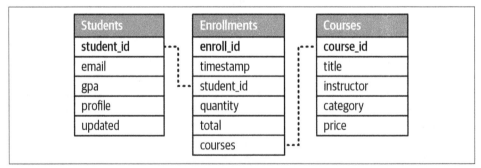

Figure 5-4. Entity-relationship diagram of the online school dataset

In this demonstration, we will use a new Python notebook titled "5.1 - Structured Streaming." We begin by running the "School-Setup" helper notebook to prepare our environment:

```
%run ../Includes/School-Setup
```

Structured Streaming provides high-level APIs in both SQL and Python for manipulating streaming data. However, regardless of the chosen language, the initial step always involves using the `spark.readStream` method from the PySpark API. This is the reason behind our utilization of a Python notebook in this context. The `spark.readStream` method allows you to query a Delta table as a streaming source and create a streaming DataFrame accordingly:

```
stream_df = spark.readStream.table("courses")
```

Once the streaming DataFrame is created, you can apply a wide range of transformations and operations to manipulate and analyze the streaming data. These transformations can be expressed in either SQL or Python syntax.

Streaming Data Manipulations in SQL

To begin manipulating streaming data using SQL, it is essential to convert the streaming DataFrame into a format that SQL can interpret and query. This can be achieved by registering a temporary view from the streaming DataFrame using the `createOrReplaceTempView` function:

```
stream_df.createOrReplaceTempView("courses_streaming_tmp_vw")
```

Creating a temporary view against a streaming DataFrame results in a `streaming` temporary view. This allows you to apply most SQL transformations on streaming data just like you would with static data. You can query this streaming temporary view using a standard `SELECT` statement, as shown here:

```
%sql
SELECT * FROM courses_streaming_tmp_vw
```

This query does not behave like a typical SQL query. Instead of executing once and returning a set of results, it initiates a continuous stream that runs indefinitely. As new data arrives in the source, it appears in the query results in near real time. To facilitate performance monitoring of such streams, Databricks Notebooks provide an interactive dashboard associated with the streaming query, as illustrated in Figure 5-5.

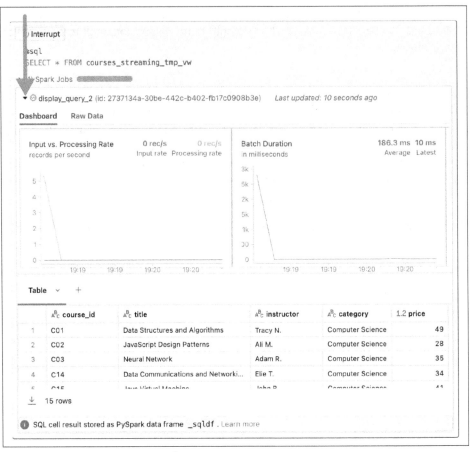

Figure 5-5. Streaming query results

In practice, we don't typically display the results of streaming queries in a notebook unless there is a need to inspect them during development. To stop an active streaming query, you can simply click Interrupt at the top of the cell.

Applying transformations

On a streaming temporary view, you can apply various transformations and operations. For instance, you can perform aggregations such as as counting occurrences within the streaming data:

```
%sql
SELECT instructor, count(course_id) AS total_courses
FROM courses_streaming_tmp_vw
GROUP BY instructor
```

Because we are querying a streaming object, this aggregation becomes a *stateful* streaming query that executes continuously and updates dynamically to reflect any changes in the source. Figure 5-6 displays the output of this streaming query.

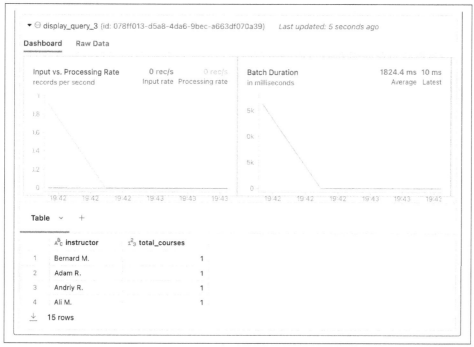

Figure 5-6. Streaming aggregation results

It's important to understand that at this stage, none of the records is stored anywhere; they are simply being displayed in the current notebook environment. In the following discussion, we will explore how to persist them to a durable storage. However, before proceeding, let us stop this active streaming query.

Remember, when working with streaming data, certain SQL operations are not directly supported. For example, attempting to sort our streaming data based on a given column will lead to an error:

```
%sql
SELECT *
FROM courses_streaming_tmp_vw
ORDER BY instructor

AnalysisException: Sorting is not supported on streaming DataFrames/Datasets,
unless it is on aggregated DataFrame/Dataset in Complete output mode; line 3 pos 1;
```

Executing this command results in an exception, clearly indicating that the sorting operation is not supported on all streaming datasets. As mentioned earlier, more advanced techniques like windowing and watermarking can be used to overcome such limitations. However, they are considered beyond the scope of this book.

Persisting streaming data

Persisting streaming data to a durable storage involves returning our logic back to the PySpark DataFrame API. For this, we begin by defining a new temporary view to encapsulate our desired output:

```sql
%sql
CREATE OR REPLACE TEMP VIEW instructor_counts_tmp_vw AS (
  SELECT instructor, count(course_id) AS total_courses
  FROM courses_streaming_tmp_vw
  GROUP BY instructor
)
```

With this SQL statement, we are creating another temporary view to hold the aggregated data. It's considered a "streaming" temporary view since it is derived from a query against a streaming object, specifically against our `courses_streaming_tmp_vw` view.

Once the streaming temporary view is created, we can access the output data using the PySpark DataFrame API. In the following snippet, the `spark.table` function loads the data from our streaming temporary view into a *streaming* DataFrame:

```
result_stream_df = spark.table("instructor_counts_tmp_vw")
```

It's essential to understand that Spark differentiates between streaming and static DataFrames. Consequently, when loading data from a streaming object, it's interpreted as a streaming DataFrame, while loading data from a static object yields a static DataFrame. This highlights the importance of using `spark.readStream` from the beginning (instead of `spark.read`) to support later incremental writing.

Now that we have our streaming DataFrame in place, we can proceed to persist the results to a Delta table using the `writeStream` method. This method enables configuring the output with several parameters, such as trigger intervals, output modes, and specifying a checkpoint location:

```
(result_stream_df.writeStream
                .trigger(processingTime='3 seconds')
                .outputMode("complete")
                .option("checkpointLocation",
                    "dbfs:/mnt/DEA-Book/checkpoints/instructor_counts")
                .table("instructor_counts")
)
```

In this configuration, the trigger interval is set to three seconds, meaning the stream will attempt an update every three seconds by checking the source for new data. The output mode is specified as "complete," indicating that the entire target table should be overwritten with the new calculations during each trigger interval. Additionally, the checkpoint location is provided to track the progress of the stream processing. Lastly, the target table is set to `instructor_counts`.

Executing this command initiates a streaming query, continuously updating the target table as new data arrives. Figure 5-7 visualizes this process through its interactive dashboard.

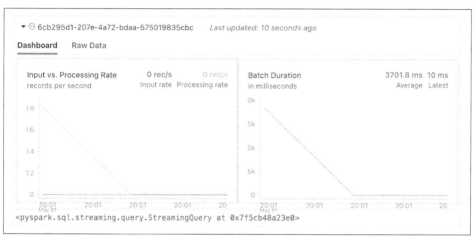

Figure 5-7. Streaming write operation

From this dashboard, we can observe a noticeable spike, indicating that our data has been processed. Subsequently, we can proceed to query the target table to validate the results:

```
%sql
SELECT * FROM instructor_counts
```

It's important to note that directly querying the target table does not trigger a streaming query. It's simply a normal, static table, rather than a streaming DataFrame.

Figure 5-8 displays the result of querying the `instructor_counts` table, confirming that the data has been written successfully. This result shows that each instructor currently teaches only one course.

_ᴮᴄ instructor	₁²₃ total_courses
Bernard M.	1
Tiffany M.	1
Andriy R.	1
Daniel M.	1
Pierre B.	1
Chris N.	1
Julia S.	1
John B.	1

Figure 5-8. The result of querying the `instructor_counts` *table*

Meanwhile, the streaming write query remains active, waiting for new data to arrive in the source. To illustrate this, let us add new data to our source table, the `courses` table:

```sql
%sql
INSERT INTO courses
values ("C16", "Generative AI", "Pierre B.", "Computer Science", 25),
       ("C17", "Embedded Systems", "Julia S.", "Computer Science", 30),
       ("C18", "Virtual Reality", "Bernard M.", "Computer Science", 35)
```

Upon executing this command, you can observe the processing of this batch of data using the dashboard of our streaming query, as shown in Figure 5-9.

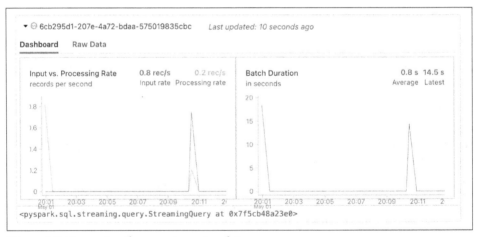

Figure 5-9. Processing the new streaming data

Subsequently querying our target table reveals updated course counts for each instructor. As illustrated in Figure 5-10, some instructors' course counts have increased as more records are processed.

$^{A^B}_C$ instructor	$^{1^2}_3$ total_courses
Bernard M.	2
Tiffany M.	1
Andriy R.	1
Daniel M.	1
Pierre B.	2
Chris N.	1
Julia S.	2
John B.	1

Figure 5-10. The result of querying the instructor_counts *table after processing the new data*

Now, let's explore another scenario to demonstrate incremental batch processing. However, before proceeding, let's stop our previous streaming write query. In a development environment, it is a good practice to stop active streams to prevent them from running indefinitely. Failing to do so can lead to unnecessary costs and resource consumption, as the cluster will not be able to auto-terminate if the process remains active.

In our next scenario, we will introduce a set of courses taught by new instructors and incorporate them into our source table:

```
%sql
INSERT INTO courses
values ("C19", "Compiler Design", "Sophie B.", "Computer Science", 25),
       ("C20", "Signal Processing", "Sam M.", "Computer Science", 30),
       ("C21", "Operating Systems", "Mark H.", "Computer Science", 35)
```

In this scenario, we will modify the trigger method to change our query from a continuous mode, executed every three seconds, to a triggered mode. We accomplish this using the availableNow trigger option:

```
(result_stream_df.writeStream
                .trigger(availableNow=True)
                .outputMode("complete")
                .option("checkpointLocation",
                    "dbfs:/mnt/DEA-Book/checkpoints/instructor_counts")
                .table("instructor_counts")
                .awaitTermination()
)
```

With the `availableNow` trigger option, the query will process all newly available data at the time of the read and automatically stop upon completion. In this case, we can optionally use the `awaitTermination` method to halt execution of other cells in the notebooks until the incremental batch write finishes successfully.

By running this command, you can observe that the streaming query was operated in a batch mode. It stopped automatically after processing the three recently added records. To confirm this, you can query the target table again to see that there are now 18 instructors instead of the previous 15.

Streaming Data Manipulations in Python

Manipulating streaming data in Python syntax is straightforward; there is no need for any temporary object or view. You can apply your data processing directly on the streaming DataFrame using the PySpark DataFrame API:

```
import pyspark.sql.functions as F

output_stream_df = (stream_df.groupBy("instructor")
                    .agg(F.count("course_id").alias("total_courses")))
```

In this snippet, we are performing the same aggregation operation previously executed using SQL syntax, but now using PySpark. We group our `stream_df` based on the `instructor` column and apply the count aggregation function to the `course_id` column. It's worth mentioning that streaming DataFrames, like static DataFrames, are immutable. This means that when you apply transformations to a DataFrame, it always creates a new DataFrame and leaves the original unchanged. In our case, this creates a new streaming DataFrame named `output_stream_df`.

At this point, the output streaming DataFrame has been created, but the stream itself is not yet active. This means that Spark hasn't started processing the input data. To activate the stream, we need to perform an action, such as writing or displaying the data. In Databricks notebooks, you can call the display function on a streaming Data-Frame to display the streaming data, as illustrated in Figure 5-11:

```
display(output_stream_df)
```

Figure 5-11. Displaying the streaming DataFrame

We can now stop this data stream and examine how to persist the results.

To persist these results to durable storage, we simply use the writeStream method directly on the streaming DataFrame:

```
(output_stream_df.writeStream
                 .trigger(availableNow=True)
                 .outputMode("complete")
                 .option("checkpointLocation",
                   "dbfs:/mnt/DEA-Book/checkpoints/instructor_counts_py")
                 .table("instructor_counts_py")
                 .awaitTermination()
)
```

It's essential to note that we are using a different checkpoint location for this new streaming query. Remember, each stream requires its own separate checkpoint location to ensure processing guarantees.

Once the streaming write is completed, you can query the resulting table directly:

```
%sql
SELECT * FROM instructor_counts_py
```

Alternatively, you can use the PySpark DataFrame API to query the table. This can be achieved using the `spark.read` method:

```
instructor_counts_df = spark.read.table("instructor_counts_py")

display(instructor_counts_df)
```

In this code snippet, the `spark.read` method is used to create a static DataFrame against our table. Then, the display function is invoked to show the queried data, as shown in Figure 5-12.

^A_C instructor	$^1_3$ total_courses
Bernard M.	2
Tiffany M.	1
Andriy R.	1
Daniel M.	1
Pierre B.	2
Chris N.	1
Julia S.	2
John B.	1

Figure 5-12. The result of querying the `instructor_count_py` table

In conclusion, Spark Structured Streaming provides a powerful and flexible solution for handling streaming data processing tasks. By using either Spark SQL or PySpark DataFrame APIs, you can perform a variety of data manipulations on streaming data sources, including Delta Lake. This enables you to build end-to-end reliable data pipelines for a wide range of use cases, from real-time analytics to incremental data ingestion, as you are about to see.

Incremental Data Ingestion

Data ingestion is a crucial step in data engineering pipelines, particularly when dealing with files stored in cloud storage. In this section, we will explore the different techniques of incrementally loading data from files into Delta Lake. Our focus will be on two primary methods: the `COPY INTO` command and Auto Loader.

Introducing Data Ingestion

Data ingestion, as used in this book, refers to the process of loading data from files into Delta Lake tables. One of the significant challenges in data ingestion is the need to avoid reprocessing the same files multiple times. In a traditional data pipeline, each time the pipeline is run, it would reprocess all the files, including those that have already been ingested previously. This approach can be computationally expensive, time-consuming, and can lead to additional deduplication work, especially when dealing with large datasets, and this is where incremental data ingestion comes into play.

Incremental data ingestion involves loading only files newly received since the last data ingestion cycle. This approach ensures that data pipelines are optimized by avoiding the reprocessing of previously ingested files, thereby reducing the processing time and resources required. Databricks offers two efficient mechanisms for the incremental processing of newly arrived files in a storage location: the COPY INTO SQL command and Auto Loader. Let us examine these methods in detail and learn how to implement them effectively.

COPY INTO Command

The COPY INTO command is a SQL statement that facilitates the loading of data from a specified file location into a Delta table. This command operates in an idempotent and incremental manner, meaning that each execution will only process new files from the source location, while previously ingested files are ignored.

The syntax for the COPY INTO command is straightforward and is structured as follows:

```
1 COPY INTO my_table
2 FROM '/path/to/files'
3 FILEFORMAT = <format>
4 FORMAT_OPTIONS (<format options>)
5 COPY_OPTIONS (<copy options>)
```

The command structure specifies the target table (line 1), the source file location (line 2), the format of the source files such as CSV or Parquet (line 3), any pertinent file options (line 4), and additional options to control the ingestion operation (line 5).

For instance:

```
COPY INTO my_table
FROM '/path/to/files'
FILEFORMAT = CSV
FORMAT_OPTIONS ('delimiter' = '|',
               'header' = 'true')
COPY_OPTIONS ('mergeSchema' = 'true')
```

In this example, the command is configured to ingest data into a Delta Lake table, named `my_table`, from a given source location. This location contains CSV files characterized by having headers and a specific delimiter, |. Furthermore, the `COPY_OPTIONS` parameter is leveraged to facilitate schema evolution in response to modifications in the structure of the incoming data.

Auto Loader

The second method for loading data incrementally from files in Databricks is Auto Loader. It leverages Structured Streaming in Spark to efficiently process new data files as they become available in a storage location. Notably, Auto Loader offers scalability by allowing for handling billions of files and supporting real-time ingestion rates of millions of files per hour.

Built upon Spark's Structured Streaming framework, Auto Loader employs check-pointing to track the ingestion process and store metadata information about the discovered files. This ensures that data files are processed exactly once by Auto Loader. Moreover, in the event of a failure, Auto Loader seamlessly resumes processing from the point of interruption.

Implementation

As an integral part of Spark's Structured Streaming, you can work with Auto Loader by using the `readStream` and `writeStream` methods:

```
spark.readStream
      .format("cloudFiles")
      .option("cloudFiles.format", <source_format>)
      .load('/path/to/files')
    .writeStream
      .option("checkpointLocation", <checkpoint_directory>)
      .table(<table_name>)
```

Auto Loader introduces a specific format of DataStreamReader named `cloudFiles`. The `cloudFiles.format` option is employed to specify the format of the source files. Then, the load function is used to indicate the location of the source files, where Auto Loader detects and queues new arrivals for ingestion. Subsequently, data is written into a target table using the DataStreamWriter, with the `checkpointLocation` parameter indicating where checkpointing information should be stored.

Schema management

Auto Loader offers a convenient feature that enables automatic schema detection for loaded data, allowing you to create tables without explicitly defining the data schema. Moreover, if new columns are added, the table schema can evolve accordingly. However, to avoid inference costs during each stream startup, the inferred schema can be stored for subsequent use. This is achieved by specifying a location where Auto Loader can store the schema using the cloudFiles.schemaLocation option.

Note that the schema inference behavior of Auto Loader varies depending on the file format. For formats with typed schemas, such as Parquet, Auto Loader extracts the predefined schemas from the files. On the other hand, for formats that don't encode data types, like JSON and CSV, Auto Loader infers all columns as strings by default. To enable inferring column data types from such sources, you can set the option cloudFiles.inferColumnTypes to true:

```
spark.readStream
        .format("cloudFiles")
        .option("cloudFiles.format", <source_format>)
        .option("cloudFiles.inferColumnTypes", "true")
        .option("cloudFiles.schemaLocation", <schema_directory>)
        .load('/path/to/files')
    .writeStream
        .option("checkpointLocation", <checkpoint_directory>)
        .option("mergeSchema", "true")
        .table(<table_name>)
```

It's worth mentioning that the designated schema location can be identical to the checkpoint location for simplicity and convenience; they will not conflict.

Comparison of Ingestion Mechanisms

When deciding between the COPY INTO command and Auto Loader for your data ingestion tasks, it's important to consider two key factors, which are summarized in Table 5-3.

Table 5-3. Comparison of the incremental data ingestion mechanisms

	COPY INTO	Auto Loader
File volume	Thousands of files	Millions of files
Efficiency	Less efficient at scale	Efficient at scale

File volume

The COPY INTO command is ideal for scenarios where the volume of incoming files is relatively small, typically on the order of thousands. It offers simplicity and straight-forward execution, making it well-suited for smaller-scale data ingestion tasks. On the other hand, Auto Loader is suited for scenarios where the volume of incoming files is on the order of millions or more over time.

Efficiency

Auto Loader has the capability to split processing into multiple batches, thereby ena-bling faster and more efficient data ingestion compared to the COPY INTO command.

This attribute makes Auto Loader an ideal choice for environments characterized by high data velocity and volume.

As a general best practice, Databricks recommends using Auto Loader when ingesting data from cloud object storage.

Auto Loader in Action

Let's walk through the practical implementation of Auto Loader for incremental data ingestion from files. We will continue using our online school dataset, consisting of three tables: students, enrollments, and courses.

In this demonstration, we will use a new Python notebook titled "5.2 - Auto Loader." We begin by running the "School-Setup" helper notebook to prepare our environment:

```
%run ../Includes/School-Setup
```

In this scenario, we will leverage Auto Loader to incrementally ingest student enrollment data from JSON files into a target Delta table. Before setting up our Auto Loader stream, let's inspect our source directory:

```
files = dbutils.fs.ls(f"{dataset_school}/enrollments-json-raw")
display(files)
```

Figure 5-13 displays the contents of the source directory, showing that it currently hosts a single JSON file.

ᴬᴮᴄ path	ᴬᴮᴄ name	₁²₃ size	₁²₃ modificationTime
dbfs:/mnt/DE-Associate-Book/datasets/school/enrollments-json-raw/01.json	01.json	179874	1714529091000

Figure 5-13. The content of the source directory

Now, we'll set up Auto Loader to efficiently handle the ingestion of this file and any new files arriving in the directory.

Setting up Auto Loader

Remember, Auto Loader uses the readStream and writeStream methods from Spark's Structured Streaming API. Here's an example of how to set up Auto Loader for our use case:

```
(spark.readStream
        .format("cloudFiles")
        .option("cloudFiles.format", "json")
        .option("cloudFiles.inferColumnTypes","true")
        .option("cloudFiles.schemaLocation",
            "dbfs:/mnt/DEA-Book/checkpoints/enrollments")
        .load(f"{dataset_school}/enrollments-json-raw")
```

```
    .writeStream
        .option("checkpointLocation",
                "dbfs:/mnt/DEA-Book/checkpoints/enrollments")
        .table("enrollments_updates")
)
```

In this configuration, the cloudFiles format represents the Auto Loader stream, with three additional options:

cloudFiles.format

Specifies the format of the data files being ingested, in this case, JSON.

cloudFiles.inferColumnTypes

Enables Auto Loader to automatically determine the data types of the columns.

cloudFiles.schemaLocation

Sets the directory where Auto Loader can store the inferred schema information.

Subsequently, we use the load method to define the location of our data source files.

Following that, we immediately chain a writeStream method to write the ingested data into a target table called enrollments_updates. Furthermore, we provide a location for storing checkpoint information, enabling Auto Loader to track the ingestion process. It's worth noting that both schema and checkpoint information are stored within the same directory.

Upon executing the previous command, a streaming query is initiated, as illustrated in Figure 5-14. This query remains active, continuously processing new data as it arrives in the data source directory.

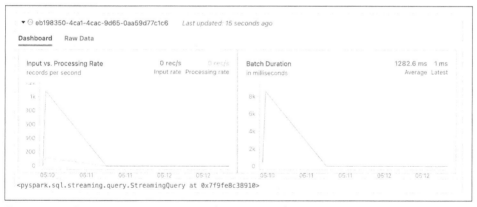

Figure 5-14. Streaming write operation by Auto Loader

To confirm the successful data ingestion, we can review the contents of the updated table by executing a standard SELECT statement:

```
%sql
SELECT * FROM enrollments_updates
```

Figure 5-15 displays the result of querying our target table after the initial ingestion. At this point, the table contains 1,000 records, confirming that our stream is correctly configured and that data is being successfully processed and stored in the target table.

^A_C courses	^A_C enroll_id	^A_C enroll_timestamp	^A_C quantity	^A_C stud
1 [{"course_id":"C08","discount_percent":75,"subtotal":10.25}]	000000000006341	1657520256	1	S00788
2 [{"course_id":"C08","discount_percent":75,"subtotal":10.25}]	000000000006342	1657520256	1	S00788
3 [{"course_id":"C02","discount_percent":65,"subtotal":9.8}]	000000000006343	1657531717	1	S00654
4 [{"course_id":"C02","discount_percent":70,"subtotal":8.4}]	000000000006344	1657531717	1	S00654

⬇ 1,000 rows | 2.04 seconds runtime

Figure 5-15. The result of querying the `enrollments_updates` *table*

Observing Auto Loader

As part of this demonstration, we can simulate an external system adding new data files to our source directory. This is achieved by the `load_new_data` helper function, which is provided with our online school dataset. Each execution of this function mimics the external system adding a single file of 1,000 records:

```
load_new_data()
```

After running the command, a new file is successfully copied to our source directory, as shown in Figure 5-16.

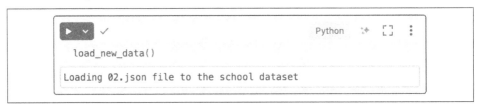

Figure 5-16. The output of executing the `load_new_data` *function*

To further increase the volume of data for our demonstration, let's run the previous command a second time for adding another file.

With two new files added, we can re-examine the contents of our source directory to confirm their presence:

```
files = dbutils.fs.ls(f"{dataset_school}/enrollments-json-raw")
display(files)
```

Figure 5-17 displays the updated contents of the source directory, confirming the addition of two new files. Remember, our Auto Loader stream is still active, continuously scanning the directory for new files and processing any that are detected. With this set up, the new files will be processed automatically.

ABc path	ABc name	1²₃ size	1²₃ modificationTime
dbfs:/mnt/DE-Associate-Book/datasets/school/enrollments-json-raw/01.json	01.json	179874	1714529091000
dbfs:/mnt/DE-Associate-Book/datasets/school/enrollments-json-raw/02.json	02.json	179833	1714619542000
dbfs:/mnt/DE-Associate-Book/datasets/school/enrollments-json-raw/03.json	03.json	179758	1714623297000

Figure 5-17. The content of the source directory after landing a new data file

Returning to our Auto Loader stream above, you can observe its current activity through the provided dashboard. It indeed indicates the reception of new batches of data, as illustrated in Figure 5-18.

Figure 5-18. Auto Loader stream processing after landing two new data files

To confirm that the new data has been successfully processed and ingested into our target table, we can check the number of records in the table:

```sql
%sql
SELECT count(*) FROM enrollments_updates
```

This command reveals that our `enrollments_updates` table now has a total of 3,000 records, confirming the insertion of data from the new files. This highlights Auto Loader's capability to detect and process new files as soon as they appear in the source directory, demonstrating its efficiency and reliability for near-real-time data ingestion. Of course, you can also execute Auto Loader in incremental batch mode by using the `availableNow` trigger option.

Exploring table history

After successfully updating our Delta Lake table using Auto Loader, it's valuable to review the history of changes made to the table during this process. To achieve this, let's run the DESCRIBE HISTORY command on the enrollments_updates table:

```
%sql
DESCRIBE HISTORY enrollments_updates
```

Figure 5-19 displays our table history, revealing three new table versions, each corresponding to an update triggered by the Auto Loader stream. It's evident that each of these entries aligns with the arrival of one of our data files at the source. Note in particular that writeSteam registers the operation as a streaming update rather than a normal write operation (see Chapter 2 for more on the Dela Lake transaction log).

Figure 5-19. The history log of the enrollments_updates table

Cleaning up

At the end of this demonstration, we can tidy up by performing two cleanup actions: dropping the table and removing the checkpoint directory. However, let's first revisit our Auto Loader query and stop the active streaming job.

With the streaming job interrupted, we can proceed to drop the enroll ments_updates table:

```
%sql
DROP TABLE enrollments_updates
```

Finally, we remove the checkpoint location associated with our Auto Loader stream by running the dbutils.fs.rm function:

```
dbutils.fs.rm("dbfs:/mnt/DEA-Book/checkpoints/enrollments", True)
```

In summary, Auto Loader has proven to be a powerful tool for automating the data ingestion process, allowing for efficient and scalable data loading. Its ability to handle high volumes of data makes it an essential component of many modern data pipelines. In the next section, we'll explore how to take Auto Loader to the next level by using it in a medallion architecture, enabling even more complex and scalable data processing workflows.

Medallion Architecture

A medallion architecture is a robust approach for efficiently processing data through multiple stages of transformation. In this section, we will delve into the fundamental concepts and benefits of this architecture. Following this, we will explore a step-by-step guide on implementing a medallion architecture on the Databricks platform.

Introducing Medallion Architecture

A medallion architecture, also referred to as multi-hop architecture, is a data design pattern that logically organizes data in a multi-layered approach. Its primary objective is to gradually enhance both the structure and the quality of data as it progresses through successive processing layers.

The layered approach

The medallion architecture is structured into three principal layers, each serving a distinct purpose in the data refinement process. These layers are symbolically termed bronze, silver, and gold, indicating their ascending order of quality and value, as illustrated in Figure 5-20.

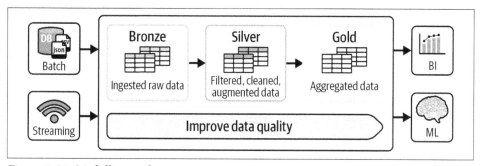

Figure 5-20. Medallion architecture

Let's dive deeper to gain a comprehensive understanding of each of these layers.

Bronze layer. The foundation of the medallion architecture starts at the bronze layer, which is the initial stage of data ingestion. At this layer, data is ingested from external systems and stored in its rawest form. This raw data is retained in tables known as bronze tables, which serve as repositories for unprocessed data. The data stored in these tables is exactly as it was received from the source systems, without any transformations or modifications. This approach ensures that the original data is preserved, preventing data loss and enabling easy auditing and traceability.

The data sources that feed into the bronze layer are diverse and varied. They can range from structured data files to operational databases. Moreover, the bronze tables are also common destinations for streaming data from platforms like Kafka, enabling real-time data ingestion and processing.

So, the bronze layer's primary function is to ensure that all data is captured and stored, regardless of its source or quality. This provides a comprehensive snapshot of information in its original form, serving as a single source of truth for your data projects.

Silver layer.   As data moves up to the silver layer, it goes through significant processing to improve its quality and utility for further analysis. This middle layer focuses on data cleansing, normalization, and validation. Incorrect or irrelevant data points are filtered out, and inconsistencies are resolved to ensure data reliability. Moreover, this stage often involves enriching the data by joining fields from various datasets, thereby providing a more integrated and coherent view. For instance, data from different departmental databases might be consolidated to provide a comprehensive view of organizational operations.

So, the enhancements made at the silver layer are designed to prepare the data for various analytical tasks that require a higher degree of data integrity and accuracy.

Gold layer.   The final layer is the gold tables, where data reaches its most business-ready form. This layer is characterized by its role in facilitating high-level business analytics and intelligence. Data at this stage is often aggregated and summarized to support specific business needs, such as performance metrics, financial summaries, and customer insights.

So, the transformations at the gold layer make the data ready for reporting, dashboarding, and advanced analytics in machine learning and AI.

Benefits of Medallion Architectures

The medallion architecture offers several advantages that can be summarized by the following key points:

Simplicity
> The architecture represents a simplified data model that is intuitive and easy to understand and implement. By organizing data into distinct layers, each serving a specific purpose, the complexity of data management and maintenance is significantly reduced.

Incremental ETL
> This architecture enables incrementally transforming and loading data as it arrives. This facilitates integrating new data and propagating it through each layer of the architecture.

Hybrid workloads

The architecture offers the flexibility to combine both streaming and batch processing within a unified pipeline. Each stage can be configured to operate either as a batch or a streaming job, depending on the nature of the data and the desired processing latency.

Table reconstruction

Another major benefit of this architecture is the ability to regenerate downstream tables from raw data at any time. This capability is particularly valuable in scenarios where data quality issues are detected during post-processing and must be solved at the source.

Building Medallion Architectures

In this section, we will walk through a step-by-step process to implement a complete medallion architecture in Databricks. As a practical example, we will demonstrate how to manage our school enrollments using this approach. So, we will continue using our dataset, consisting of three tables: students, enrollments, and courses.

In this exercise, we will use a new Python notebook titled "5.3 - Medallion Architecture." We begin by running the "School-Setup" helper notebook to prepare our environment:

```
%run ../Includes/School-Setup
```

Let's start by revisiting the contents of our source directory:

```
files = dbutils.fs.ls(f"{dataset_school}/enrollments-json-raw")
display(files)
```

At present, there are three JSON files within the directory, as illustrated in Figure 5-21.

$\mathrm{^A_C}$ path	$\mathrm{^A_C}$ name	$\mathrm{1^2_3}$ size	$\mathrm{1^2_3}$ modificationTime
dbfs:/mnt/DE-Associate-Book/datasets/school/enrollments-json-raw/01.json	01.json	179874	1714529091000
dbfs:/mnt/DE-Associate-Book/datasets/school/enrollments-json-raw/02.json	02.json	179833	1714619542000
dbfs:/mnt/DE-Associate-Book/datasets/school/enrollments-json-raw/03.json	03.json	179758	1714623297000

Figure 5-21. The content of the source directory enrollments-json-raw

These files represent the raw material of our data pipeline, awaiting ingestion into the bronze layer tables.

Establishing the bronze layer

Our journey of implementing a medallion architecture begins in the bronze layer, which is the foundational layer for data ingestion. It serves as the initial repository that captures all incoming data in its rawest form, before any transformation or cleansing occurs.

Configuring Auto Loader.   The first step in the bronze layer typically involves configuring Auto Loader against the source directory. Here, we configure our Auto Loader stream to process the input files and load the data into a Delta Lake table:

```
import pyspark.sql.functions as F

(spark.readStream
          .format("cloudFiles")
          .option("cloudFiles.format", "json")
          .option("cloudFiles.inferColumnTypes","true")
          .option("cloudFiles.schemaLocation",
                  f"{checkpoint_path}/enrollments_bronze")
          .load(f"{dataset_school}/enrollments-json-raw")
          .select("*",
                  F.current_timestamp().alias("arrival_time"),
                  F.input_file_name().alias("source_file"))
      .writeStream
          .format("delta")
          .option("checkpointLocation",
                  f"{checkpoint_path}/enrollments_bronze")
          .outputMode("append")
          .table("enrollments_bronze")
)
```

In this segment, we start by initiating a streaming read operation from our JSON source files. The reader is set to infer the columns' data types automatically, ensuring that they are correctly identified without explicit declaration. The data is then combined with two supplementary pieces of metadata available through Auto Loader:

`arrival_time`
: Timestamp of when the data is ingested, which is valuable for tracking and auditing purposes.

`source_file`
: The name of the file from which the data is sourced, aiding in data lineage and troubleshooting.

After the data is read and supplemented with this metadata, it is streamed directly into a Delta table named `enrollments_bronze`.

Upon activating this Auto Loader stream, we can observe that a new batch of data has been detected and processed, as illustrated in Figure 5-22.

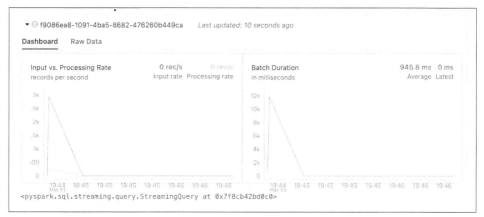

<pyspark.sql.streaming.query.StreamingQuery at 0x7f8cb42bd0c0>

Figure 5-22. Streaming write operation by Auto Loader

To inspect the raw data that has been captured, we can simply query the enroll
ments_bronze table:

```sql
%sql
SELECT * FROM enrollments_bronze
```

Figure 5-23 displays the result of this query, confirming the successful ingestion of
the data along with the added metadata fields: arrival_time and source_file.

🔗 courses	ᴬᴮ꜀ enroll_id	1²₃ enroll_tim...	1²₃ quantity	ᴬᴮ꜀ student_id	📅 arrival_time	ᴬᴮ꜀ source_file
1 > [{"course_id":"...	000000000006341	1657520256	1	S00788	2024-05-03T17:4...	dbfs:/mnt/DE-Associate:
2 > [{"course_id":"...	000000000006342	1657520256	1	S00788	2024-05-03T17:4...	dbfs:/mnt/DE-Associate:
3 > [{"course_id":"...	000000000006343	1657531717	1	S00654	2024-05-03T17:4...	dbfs:/mnt/DE-Associate:
4 > [{"course_id":"...	000000000006344	1657531717	1	S00654	2024-05-03T17:4	dbfs:/mnt/DE-Associate:

⤓ 3,000 rows | 0.91 seconds runtime

Figure 5-23. The result of querying the enrollments_bronze table

Next, we can verify the volume of data that has been written into the bronze layer:

```sql
%sql
SELECT count(1) FROM enrollments_bronze
```

This command reveals that 3,000 records have been persisted, which corresponds to
our three source files, each containing 1,000 records. This confirms that our ingestion
process is correctly configured and functioning as expected.

To demonstrate the stream processing capabilities of our data pipeline, let's simulate
the arrival of new data in the source directory using our load_new_data function:

```
load_new_data()
```

Output: Loading 04.json file to the school dataset

Returning to our previous active stream, we observe that the new data is immediately detected and processed by the streaming query, as illustrated in Figure 5-24.

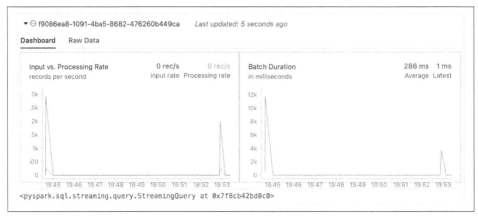

Figure 5-24. Auto Loader stream processing after landing the new data file

By re-querying the number of records in the bronze table, we can verify that the new data has been successfully ingested. As shown in Figure 5-25, the table now contains 4,000 records, reflecting an increase of 1,000 records since our last ingestion process.

```
%sql
SELECT count(1) FROM enrollments_bronze
```

Table ⌄ +

1^2_3 count(1)
1   4000

Figure 5-25. The number of records in the `enrollments_bronze` table after loading the new input file

Creating a static lookup table. In preparation for data processing within the subsequent layers, we may need to integrate additional data sources that can enrich our primary datasets. In our case, we require a static lookup table of student information. This table will be used in the silver layer to join with the enrollment data in order to add more depth and context to our analysis. To create our static lookup, we use the `spark.read` method to construct a static DataFrame from the students' JSON files:

```
students_lookup_df = (spark.read
                      .format("json")
                      .load(f"{dataset_school}/students-json"))
```

Before proceeding further, let's examine the structure and contents of the newly created lookup DataFrame:

```
display(students_lookup_df)
```

The results, visualized in Figure 5-26, illustrate that the `students` lookup DataFrame consists of several columns such as student ID, email, and profile information.

A^B_C email	1.2 gpa	A^B_C profile	A^B_C student_id	A^B_C upda
thomas.lane@gmail.com	1.06	> {"first_name":"Thomas","last_name":"Lan...	S00301	2021-12
ocolegatele@blogger.com	1.13	> {"first_name":"Odilia","last_name":"Coleg...	S00302	2021-12
acolledged2@nbcnews.com	3.62	> {"first_name":"Andros","last_name":"Colle...	S00303	2021-12
null	1.18	> {"first_name":"Iver","last_name":"Collet","...	S00304	2021-12
pcollier5r@cmu.edu	1.02	> {"first_name":"Page","last_name":"Collier"	S00305	2021-12

Figure 5-26. Displaying the `students_lookup_df` DataFrame

With our bronze layer established, we can now progress to the next phase of our data processing pipeline—the silver layer.

Transitioning to the silver layer

In the silver layer, our focus shifts to refining and enhancing the data acquired from the bronze layer. At this stage, we refine the raw data by adding contextual information, formatting values, and performing data quality checks. Our objective is to ensure that the data is clean, structured, and optimized for downstream processing and analysis.

In the following code snippet, we initiate a streaming read operation on the `enroll ments_bronze` table, and then we apply a series of transformations to enrich and refine the data:

```
enrollments_enriched_df = (spark.readStream
    .table("enrollments_bronze")
    .where("quantity > 0")
    .withColumn("formatted_timestamp",
            F.from_unixtime("enroll_timestamp",
                            "yyyy-MM-dd HH:mm:ss").cast("timestamp") )
    .join(students_lookup_df, "student_id")
    .select("enroll_id", "quantity", "student_id", "email",
            "formatted_timestamp", "courses")
)
```

The transformations applied in this step include the following:

Data cleansing
>   We exclude any enrollments with no items (quantity > 0), ensuring that only valid records are processed further.

Timestamp formatting
>   We parse the enrollment timestamp from the Unix time format into a human-readable format using the `from_unixtime` function to facilitate easier understanding and interpretation.

Data enrichment
>   We enrich the enrollment data by joining it with the student information from our static lookup DataFrame `students_lookup_df`. This adds the students' email addresses to the enrollment records.

Column selection
>   Finally, we select specific columns of interest for further analysis, including enrollment ID, quantity, student ID, email, formatted timestamp, and course information.

These transformations are executed using the PySpark API. However, it's worth noting that similar operations can also be achieved using Spark SQL. By registering a streaming temporary view against the bronze table, we can leverage SQL queries to perform the same transformations, just like we did earlier in this chapter.

Subsequently, we proceed to persist this processed streaming data into a dedicated silver table. We accomplish this by performing a stream write operation on the `enroll ments_enriched_df` DataFrame:

```
(enrollments_enriched_df.writeStream
                    .format("delta")
                    .option("checkpointLocation",
                            f"{checkpoint_path}/enrollments_silver")
                    .outputMode("append")
                    .table("enrollments_silver"))
```

This code snippet sets up a continuous streaming write into the `enrollments_silver` table. By specifying the output mode as `"append"`, new records will be added to the table as they are processed, ensuring that the table is incrementally populated with the latest data from the bronze layer.

Upon executing the previous command, our stream is activated, and data starts flowing into the silver table, as illustrated in Figure 5-27.

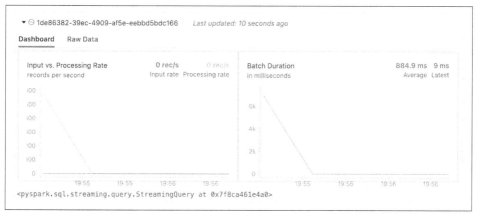

```
▾ ⊙ 1de86382-39ec-4909-af5e-eebbd5bdc166     Last updated: 10 seconds ago

Dashboard    Raw Data

Input vs. Processing Rate          0 rec/s      0 rec/s   Batch Duration                    884.9 ms  9 ms
records per second             Input rate  Processing rate   in milliseconds                   Average  Latest
```

```
<pyspark.sql.streaming.query.StreamingQuery at 0x7f8ca461e4a0>
```

Figure 5-27. Stream processing in the silver layer

To verify the written data, let's query the `enrollments_silver` table:

```
%sql
SELECT * FROM enrollments_silver
```

Figure 5-28 displays the result of querying our silver table. The presence of all 4,000 records confirms the successful data processing and writing.

ᴬᵇᴄ enroll_id	₁²₃ quantity	ᴬᵇᴄ studen...	ᴬᵇᴄ email	🕘 formatted_timestamp	♣ courses
1 000000000009397	1	S00494	sfairbardfh@reuters.com	2022-07-12T17:13:57.00...	> [{"course_id"
2 000000000009396	1	S00494	sfairbardfh@reuters.com	2022-07-12T17:13:57.00...	> [{"course_id"
3 000000000008397	1	S00494	sfairbardfh@reuters.com	2022-07-12T17:13:57.00...	> [{"course_id"
4 000000000008396	1	S00494	sfairbardfh@reuters.com	2022-07-12T17:13:57.00...	> [{"course_id"

⤓ 4,000 rows | 1.41 seconds runtime

Figure 5-28. The result of querying the `enrollments_silver` table

To further demonstrate the dynamic capabilities of our data pipeline, let's trigger the arrival of new data files in our source directory using the `load_new_data` function. We then monitor the propagation of this new data through the bronze layer and into the silver layer.

```
load_new_data()
```

Output: Loading 05.json file to the school dataset

The new data now seamlessly propagates through the pipeline, starting from the active Auto Loader steam and continuing through to the silver layer. We can track the progress of processing using the dashboard associated with each stream. Figure 5-29 showcases the latest updates in the silver layer, confirming the successful handling of the new data by our stream.

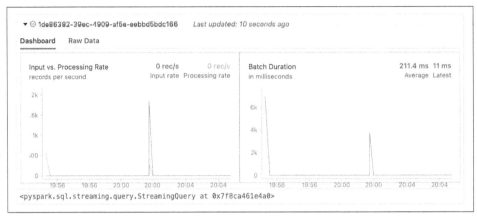

```
<pyspark.sql.streaming.query.StreamingQuery at 0x7f8ca461e4a0>
```

Figure 5-29. Stream processing in the silver layer after landing the new data file

With the addition of 1,000 records from the latest file, the total count in the `enroll`
`ments_silver` table now stands at 5,000 records, as shown in Figure 5-30.

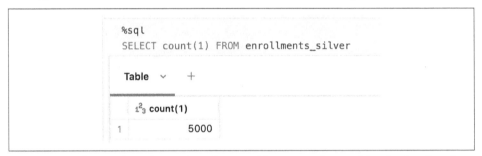

*Figure 5-30. The number of records in the `enrollments_silver` table after loading the
new input file*

From here, we can now advance to the final phase of our medallion architecture—the
gold layer.

Advancing to the gold layer

In the gold layer, we concentrate on providing high-level aggregations and summaries. This layer is important for supporting business intelligence and analytics applications by presenting the data in its most refined form.

Our task here involves creating an aggregate table that summarizes the daily number
of course enrollments per student. To accomplish this, we initiate a streaming read
operation on the `enrollments_silver` table, and then we perform the necessary
transformations to aggregate the data by student ID, email, and day:

```
enrollments_agg_df =(spark.readStream
            .table("enrollments_silver")
            .withColumn("day", F.date_trunc("DD", "formatted_timestamp"))
            .groupBy("student_id", "email", "day")
            .agg(F.sum("quantity").alias("courses_counts"))
            .select("student_id", "email", "day", "courses_counts")
)
```

In the previous code, the date_trunc function is used to truncate the timestamp to the day level, allowing us to group the data by day.

Once this aggregation logic is applied, we can proceed to persist the aggregated data into a dedicated gold table named daily_student_courses:

```
(enrollments_agg_df.writeStream
            .format("delta")
            .outputMode("complete")
            .option("checkpointLocation",
                    f"{checkpoint_path}/daily_student_courses")
            .trigger(availableNow=True)
            .table("daily_student_courses"))
```

In this configuration, we specify the output mode as "complete", indicating that the entire aggregation result should be rewritten each time the logic runs.

Structured Streaming assumes data is being appended only in the upstream tables. Once a table is updated or overwritten, it becomes invalid for streaming reads. Therefore, reading a stream from such a gold table is not supported. To alter this behavior, options like skipChangeCommits can be utilized, although they may come with other implications that need to be considered. See the Databricks documentation for more information (*https://oreil.ly/8ZrqL*).

By running this streaming query, our stream will process all available data in micro-batches and then stop automatically, thanks to the availableNow trigger option. This approach allows us to seamlessly integrate streaming and batch workloads within the same pipeline.

Now, we can inspect the aggregated data written into the daily_student_courses table:

```
%sql
SELECT * FROM daily_student_courses
```

Figure 5-31 displays the contents of our gold table, showcasing the daily enrollment statistics. You can observe that the students currently have course counts ranging between 5 and 10, reflecting the cumulative enrollment till now.

Aᴮc student_id	Aᴮc email	🗓 day	1²₃ courses_counts
S01165	holler19@google.co.uk	2022-07-14T00:00:00.000+00:00	5
S00657	lhampekl@ebay.co.uk	2022-07-24T00:00:00.000+00:00	10
S00849	zlackmann11@prnewswire.com	2022-07-20T00:00:00.000+00:00	5
S00864	flankester95@smugmug.com	2022-07-12T00:00:00.000+00:00	5
S00702	shollymanfk@xrea.com	2022-07-23T00:00:00.000+00:00	10
S00903	plequeux9p@delicious.com	2022-07-23T00:00:00.000+00:00	5

Figure 5-31. The result of querying the `daily_student_courses` table

Let's simulate the arrival of more new data by triggering the ingestion of another file into our source directory. This action initiates the propagation of data through our pipeline, from the bronze to the silver and gold layers:

```
load_new_data()
```

Output: Loading 06.json file to the school dataset

The new data will automatically propagate into both the bronze and silver layers as they maintain active continuous streams in place. Figure 5-32 illustrates the updated progress of the stream processing in the silver sayer after receiving the new data.

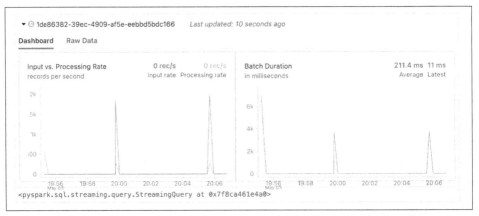

Figure 5-32. Stream processing in the silver layer after landing the new data file

However, for the gold layer, it's necessary to explicitly rerun its streaming query to update the table. Remember, this query was configured as an incremental batch job using the `availableNow` trigger option.

Upon re-executing the streaming write query of our gold table, the newly ingested data is processed to reflect the latest changes. To confirm the successful update, we can again query the `daily_student_courses` table. Figure 5-33 illustrates the updated content of this gold table, showcasing students with an increased number of course enrollments.

ᴬᴮc student_id	ᴬᴮc email	🕓 day	₁²₃ courses_counts
S00836	dkovnot1r@columbia.edu	2022-07-17T00:00:00.000+00:00	6
S00657	lhampekl@ebay.co.uk	2022-07-24T00:00:00.000+00:00	12
S00702	shollymanfk@xrea.com	2022-07-23T00:00:00.000+00:00	12
S01091	lmooganjy@4shared.com	2022-07-18T00:00:00.000+00:00	6
S01030	bmcilvoray9h@netvibes.com	2022-07-19T00:00:00.000+00:00	6
S01112	imoves1w@godaddy.com	2022-07-15T00:00:00.000+00:00	6

Figure 5-33. The result of querying the `daily_student_courses` table after processing the new data

Stopping active streams

Finally, at the end of this demonstration, it's important to ensure that all active streams in our notebook are properly terminated. This can be easily achieved by executing a loop that iterates through each active stream in the current Spark session and stops them:

```
for s in spark.streams.active:
    print("Stopping stream: " + s.id)
    s.stop()
    s.awaitTermination()

Stopping stream: 1de86382-39ec-4909-af5e-eebbd5bdc166
Stopping stream: f9086ea8-1091-4ba5-8682-476260b449ca
```

Conclusion

In conclusion, the medallion architecture provides a structured and incremental approach to data processing, which is highly beneficial for modern data engineering tasks. By organizing data into distinct layers based on its level of refinement, this architecture enables you to efficiently process and analyze data, while ensuring data quality and accuracy. This makes it the ideal choice for building data pipelines in the lakehouse that can support a wide range of data-driven applications and analytics.

Sample Exam Questions

Conceptual Question

1. A data engineering team is working on a large-scale data pipeline for a global e-commerce platform. The platform collects vast amounts of customer transaction data, which is continuously landed into a cloud storage system in file format. The team needs to process this incoming data in near real-time, ensuring that all new files are ingested efficiently, without missing any records. The team decides to use Auto Loader for this task.

Based on this scenario, which of the following statements best describes how Auto Loader can help the data engineering team in this situation?

A. Auto Loader requires no computing resources, allowing users to process unlimited amounts of data without affecting performance.

B. Auto Loader automatically detects and processes new data files as they arrive in cloud storage, without reprocessing previously processed files.

C. Auto Loader reprocesses the entire set of files in cloud storage each time new data is added, which ensures that no file is missed.

D. Auto Loader is based on the COPY INTO command to ensure new files are detected and processed in real-time.

E. Auto Loader supports only batch processing, making it unsuitable for streaming or continuously updating data pipelines.

Code-Based Question

2. A data engineer uses the following Structured Streaming query to process incoming orders and compute the total cost of each order, including tax. The processed data is then written to a table named new_orders:

```
( spark.table("orders")
        .withColumn("total_after_tax", col("total")+col("tax"))
        .writeStream
        .option("checkpointLocation", checkpointPath)
        .outputMode("append")
        ._____
        .table("new_orders"))
```

The engineer needs the query to execute multiple micro-batches to process all available data, and then stop automatically when there is no more data left to process.

Which of the following lines of code fills in the blank to achieve the desired outcome?

A. `trigger("micro-batches")`

B. `trigger(once=True)`

C. `trigger(processingTime="0 seconds")`

D. `trigger(micro-batches=True)`

E. `trigger(availableNow=True)`

The correct answers to these questions are listed in Appendix C.

Building Production Pipelines

As our data pipelines grow in complexity, we need to consider how to productionize them to ensure reliability, scalability, and maintainability. This is where building production pipelines comes in, and it's the focus of the following pages. In this chapter, we'll explore how to create robust and efficient production pipelines using Delta Live Tables and Databricks Jobs. We will delve into the nuances of controlling data quality, capturing data changes, and orchestrating workflows to automate our pipelines.

Exploring Delta Live Tables

Delta Live Tables (DLT) is a powerful tool that enables you to build production data pipelines with ease. By providing a simple and intuitive way to manage data pipelines, DLT empowers you to focus on extracting insights from your data. In this section, we will delve into the world of Delta Live Tables, exploring its key features, benefits, and use cases.

Introducing Delta Live Tables

Delta Live Tables is a declarative ETL framework powered by Apache Spark for building reliable and maintainable data pipelines. It's designed to simplify the process of creating large-scale data processing pipelines, while maintaining table dependencies and data quality.

Figure 6-1 illustrates a sample DLT pipeline, which will be built in the subsequent section of this chapter.

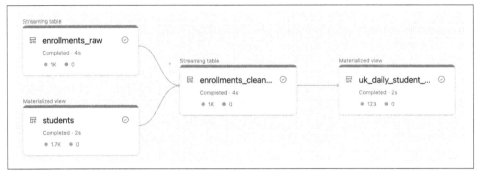

Figure 6-1. Example of a DLT pipeline

As shown, the DLT pipeline is well-visualized, allowing you to easily identify your tables and the dependencies between them.

Benefits of Delta Live Tables

DLT provides several advantages over Apache Spark and other traditional ETL frameworks, including the following:

Simplified pipeline construction
> DLT offers a declarative approach to pipeline construction, enabling you to write less code and thereby reduce complexity and development time.

Maintain table dependencies
> DLT uses directed acyclic graphs (DAGs) to efficiently manage table dependencies within data pipelines, enhancing their reliability and maintainability.

Support for data quality control
> DLT provides built-in support for data quality control, ensuring the production of high-quality data outputs.

Comparison of DLT and Spark Structured Streaming

The primary goal of DLT is to reduce the overhead associated with constructing and maintaining complex pipelines. To better understand the differences between DLT and Spark Structured Streaming, let's compare their key features, outlined in Table 6-1.

Table 6-1. Comparison of DLT and Spark Structured Streaming

	Spark Structured Streaming	DLT
Python syntax	```spark.readStream` ` .format("cloudFiles")` ` .option("cloudFiles.format",` ` "json")` ` .load('/some/path/')` `.writeStream` ` .option("checkpointLocation",` ` "/path")` ` .table("orders_raw")```	```import dlt`  `@dlt.table` `def orders_raw():` ` return (spark.readStream` ` .format("cloudFiles")` ` .option("cloudFiles.format",` ` "json")` ` .load("/some/path")` `)```
SQL support	Cannot create streaming tables in Spark SQL syntax only. It needs to pass by PySpark to register streaming tables.	Supports creating streaming tables in SQL via CREATE STREAMING TABLE syntax.
Data quality control	Supports basic data quality control using Delta Lake table constraints.	Provides advanced data quality control using DLT expectations.

Let's dive deeper to gain a comprehensive understanding of these differences.

Syntax. One of the most notable differences between DLT and Spark Structured Streaming lies in their Python syntax. Spark Structured Streaming employs the read Stream and writeStream methods to define incremental tables. In contrast, DLT simplifies this process through the use of the @dlt.table decorator, which defines incremental tables without the need for explicit stream writing. This decorator abstracts the complexities of streaming data management, including checkpointing, which is automatically managed by DLT.

SQL support. SQL support is another area where DLT and Spark Structured Streaming diverge significantly. As discussed in Chapter 5, Spark Structured Streaming does not inherently support the creation of streaming tables solely using SQL syntax. Instead, you must use PySpark to read and write streaming tables. On the other hand, DLT supports the creation of incremental tables using simple SQL syntax via the CREATE STREAMING TABLE statement. This feature allows users to leverage their SQL skills directly without needing to delve into PySpark or Scala.

Data quality control. Another significant difference between DLT and Spark is their support for data quality control. Apache Spark lacks native support for data quality control, leaving it up to developers to implement their own solutions. While Delta Lake table constraints (e.g., check constraints) do help in this area, DLT, by contrast, can natively enforce advanced data quality standards using DLT expectations. These expectations provide enhanced capabilities for validation conditions, actions, and tracking violations. This built-in support for advanced data quality control makes DLT a more robust and reliable choice for data processing.

In essence, while the DLT framework is built on top of Apache Spark, their differences mean that any code written for Spark cannot be directly deployed within the DLT framework. You must refactor your existing Spark code to conform to the DLT syntax and leverage its features, such as the DLT expectations.

DLT object types

Delta Live Tables provides various object types to handle different use cases and requirements. In DLT, you can create three primary types of objects: streaming tables, live tables, and live views. Each type has distinct characteristics and purposes.

Streaming tables. A streaming table in DLT is designed to process only the new data added since the last pipeline run. This type of table is particularly useful for scenarios where continuous data ingestion and near-real-time processing are crucial. To create a streaming table in DLT using SQL syntax, you can use the following statement:

```
CREATE OR REFRESH STREAMING TABLE my_table AS
SELECT * FROM <streaming source>
```

The input data source for this type of tables must be a streaming source, such as an autoloader stream or an append-only Delta table, which can be read using the STREAM function in SQL. For example, the following statement demonstrates how to create a new streaming table, table_2, that streams data from an existing append-only table, table_1:

```
CREATE OR REFRESH STREAMING TABLE table_2 AS
SELECT * FROM STREAM(table_1)
```

Each time the pipeline runs, the streaming table table_2 will process only the new data that has been added to table_1 since the previous pipeline run.

Materialized views. In addition to streaming tables, DLT also supports the creation of nonstreaming table objects, known as *materialized views*. Materialized views, previously known as live tables, reprocess the entire source dataset each time the pipeline runs. This type of object is suitable for scenarios where data sources don't adhere to the append-only pattern required by streaming sources. This means that materialized views can handle input data that contains updates, deletes, or overwrites. The SQL syntax for creating a materialized view in DLT is straightforward:

```
CREATE OR REPLACE MATERIALIZED VIEW my_mview AS
SELECT * FROM <batch source>
```

For instance, the following statement illustrates how to create a new materialized view, mview_1, from an existing table, table_3:

```
CREATE OR REPLACE MATERIALIZED VIEW mview_1 AS
SELECT * FROM table_3
```

Each time the pipeline runs, the materialized view, mview_1, is completely updated to reflect the latest data in table_3, replacing any existing data in mview_1 with the new results of the query.

Table 6-2 summarizes the main differences between streaming tables and materialized views in DLT.

Table 6-2. Comparison of streaming tables and materialized views in DLT

	Streaming tables	Materialized views (live tables)
Data processing	Processes only new data added since the last pipeline run	Reprocesses the entire source dataset with each pipeline run
SQL syntax	`CREATE STREAMING TABLE my_table AS <streaming query>`	`CREATE MATERIALIZED VIEW my_mview AS <batch query>`
Input data source	Input data source must be a streaming source, such as • Auto Loader • Append-only table read via STREAM function	Input data dataset is static, or contains data updated, deleted, or overwritten

Live views. Live views in DLT are temporary view objects that are scoped to the DLT pipeline they belong to. Unlike tables in DLT, live views are not persisted to the catalog, and they exist only for the duration of the current pipeline run. This makes them ideal for intermediate data transformations and quality checks, where the results do not need to be saved for long-term access. To create a live view in DLT, simply use the CREATE LIVE VIEW statement, followed by the logic to define the transformation or computation:

```
CREATE TEMPORARY LIVE VIEW my_temp_view AS <query>
```

Once created, the live view can be queried like a regular DLT table, allowing you to easily integrate it into your pipeline workflow.

With this foundation, we can now turn our attention to the next important aspect of working with DLT objects, which is defining constraints on them.

DLT Expectations

One of the advanced features of DLT is the ability to enforce data quality through constraints, which are specified using the `CONSTRAINT` keyword in SQL syntax. This capability allows defining conditions that data must meet to be considered valid, thereby enhancing the overall data integrity and reliability.

When creating a DLT table or view using SQL syntax, constraints are used to collect metrics on constraint violations. This is achieved through the following syntax:

```
CONSTRAINT <constraint_name> EXPECT (<condition>) ON VIOLATION <action>
```

The `CONSTRAINT` keyword allows for the definition of conditions that the data must satisfy. If the data fails to meet these conditions, it is considered a violation. The `ON VIOLATION` clause specifies the action that should be taken when such violations occur. This clause can significantly influence how data is handled during the pipeline processing.

The `ON VIOLATION` clause provides three main actions that can be taken when a constraint is violated:

DROP ROW

> This action removes records that do not meet the specified constraints. It ensures that only data conforming to the defined quality rules is retained in the dataset. This mode is useful for cleansing data by removing invalid entries automatically.

FAIL UPDATE

> In this mode, any violation of the constraints causes the entire pipeline to fail. This strict approach ensures that no invalid data passes through, thus maintaining the highest level of data integrity. This action is beneficial in scenarios where data correctness is critical, and any deviation from the expected quality must be addressed immediately.

No action (default)

> If the `ON VIOLATION` clause is omitted, records that violate the constraints are still included in the dataset, but the violations are reported in the metrics. This approach allows for tracking data quality issues without interrupting the pipeline's operation. It provides visibility into the data quality problems while allowing the workflow to proceed.

These actions are summarized in Table 6-3.

Table 6-3. List of actions for violations of DLT constraints

ON VIOLATION actions	Behavior
DROP ROW	Discards records that violate constraints
FAIL UPDATE	Causes the pipeline to fail when a constraint is violated
No action	Keeps records violating constraints, but reports them in metrics

The ability to choose from these different actions provides flexibility in handling data quality issues according to specific business requirements and priorities.

Now that we've learned the essential concepts behind Delta Live Tables, it's time to get hands-on and apply these concepts in practical settings.

Implementing DLT Pipelines

In this section, we will delve into the construction of a medallion architecture using Delta Live Tables. As in the previous chapter, our primary focus remains on the management of school enrollments. So, we will continue to employ our existing dataset, which includes three primary tables: students, enrollments, and courses, as illustrated in Figure 6-2.

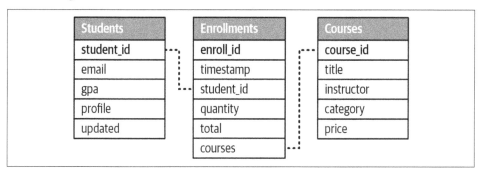

Figure 6-2. Entity-relationship diagram of the online school dataset

DLT pipelines are implemented using Databricks notebooks written in either Python or SQL. For this demonstration, we will work in a new SQL notebook titled "6.1 - Delta Live Tables." Within this notebook, we will declare all DLT tables that together implement a simple medallion architecture.

The first step in the process involves specifying the path to our dataset. We use the SET command to declare a variable that holds the location of our dataset:

```
SET school.dataset_path=dbfs:/mnt/DE-Associate-Book/datasets/school;
```

This command sets a variable named `school.dataset_path` with a default value referring to the directory containing our input data. We will explore later how to define this variable as a parameter when configuring our DLT pipelines. This approach will allow us to pass the dataset location dynamically to the pipeline, further enhancing the flexibility of our data architecture.

Bronze layer

Remember, in the medallion architecture, tables are organized into layers that represent different stages of data processing. The bronze layer is the initial layer that captures data in its most raw form. At this stage, we will create two DLT objects that represent our two data sources before any transformation or cleansing.

Creating a streaming table. We first declare a DLT table to handle incremental data ingestion from our source directory using Auto Loader. Since our source data is incremental, we must declare the DLT table as a streaming table to support this type of data feed. To do this, we simply add the `STREAMING` keyword to the table declaration:

```
CREATE OR REFRESH STREAMING TABLE enrollments_raw
COMMENT "The raw courses enrollments, ingested from enrollments-dlt-raw folder"
AS SELECT * FROM cloud_files("${school.dataset_path}/enrollments-dlt-raw",
                "json",
                map("cloudFiles.inferColumnTypes", "true"))
```

In the previous SQL statement, we create a streaming table named `enrollments_raw` to ingest JSON-formatted data incrementally using Auto Loader. The `cloud_files` method provides a direct way to use Auto Loader in SQL. This method accepts three parameters: the source location of the data files, the file format, and an optional map containing key-value pairs of reader settings. In this example, the map function specifies the `cloudFiles.inferColumnTypes` option as true, allowing Auto Loader to automatically infer column types based on the data.

Note that we also add the `COMMENT` clause to annotate the table with a description, providing additional context and metadata. This information is particularly useful for enhancing the discoverability and understandability of the data source for other users.

Upon running this query, you will notice that it only displays the schema of the table, as illustrated in Figure 6-3.

```
┌─────────────────────────────────────────────────────────────────────────┐
│                                                                           │
│  enrollments_raw  is defined as a Delta Live Tables dataset with schema:  │
│                                                                           │
│  Name                Type                                                  │
│  courses             array<struct<course_id:string,discount_percent:bigint,subtotal:double>>│
│  enroll_id           string                                                │
│  enroll_timestamp    bigint                                                │
│  quantity            bigint                                                │
│  student_id          string                                                │
│  total               double                                                │
│  _rescued_data       string                                                │
│                                                                           │
│  To populate your table you must either:                                  │
│                                                                           │
│   ◦ Run an existing pipeline using the Delta Live Tables menu             │
│   ◦ Create a new pipeline:  [ Create Pipeline ]                           │
│                                                                           │
└─────────────────────────────────────────────────────────────────────────┘
```

Figure 6-3. Output of creating the enrollments_raw *DLT table*

In Databricks notebooks, executing a DLT query only performs a syntax validation of the statement, without actually processing the data. To populate DLT tables with data, you need to create and run a DLT pipeline, which will be covered in the next section.

The displayed schema includes details about the columns, their data types, and any other relevant metadata inferred from the raw JSON data files. This immediate feedback is useful for verifying that the structure of the data aligns with expectations.

Creating a materialized view. The second object in the bronze layer is the students materialized view, which contains student data that is sourced from JSON input files. This object plays an essential role as a lookup table in the silver layer of this data pipeline.

```
CREATE OR REPLACE MATERIALIZED VIEW students
COMMENT "The students lookup table, ingested from students-json"
AS SELECT * FROM json.`${school.dataset_path}/students-json`
```

Since our student information may be updated or deleted in the source, we create this object as a materialized view. Remember, sources that update, delete, or overwrite data break the append-only requirement of streaming source, preventing us from creating DLT streaming tables. By employing materialized views, we ensure that the entire dataset from the source is reprocessed with each pipeline run, thus handling any new changes in the data.

Silver layer

The next step in our data pipeline is the implementation of the silver layer. At this stage, we apply essential data processing operations, including data cleansing and enrichment, to transform raw data into a more structured and meaningful format.

In this context, we declare a silver table, enrollments_cleaned, which enhances the enrollment data and integrates it with additional student information. Notably, when referencing other DLT tables within the same pipeline, it is essential to use the correct syntax. Specifically, we employ the LIVE prefix and the STREAM method to query these tables:

```
CREATE OR REFRESH STREAMING TABLE enrollments_cleaned (
  CONSTRAINT valid_order_number EXPECT (enroll_id IS NOT NULL) ON VIOLATION
        DROP ROW
)
COMMENT "The cleaned courses enrollments with valid enroll_id"
AS
  SELECT enroll_id, quantity, o.student_id,
        c.profile:first_name as f_name, c.profile:last_name as l_name,
        cast(from_unixtime(enroll_timestamp,
            'yyyy-MM-dd HH:mm:ss') AS timestamp) formatted_timestamp,
        o.courses, c.profile:address:country as country
  FROM STREAM(LIVE.enrollments_raw) o
  LEFT JOIN LIVE.students c
    ON o.student_id = c.student_id
```

The LIVE keyword serves as a namespace required to refer to any DLT object in the same pipeline. The STREAM method allows us to query a table as a streaming source, enabling incremental data processing. Note that reading from a streaming source using the STREAM method requires defining the target table as a streaming table to write the data incrementally.

Furthermore, in this example, we leverage DLT expectations to add a quality control measure using the CONSTRAINT keyword. We define a constraint, valid_order_ number, to ensure that the order_id column is not null. If a row violates this constraint, it will be automatically dropped, as defined by the ON VIOLATION clause. This prevents invalid records from being written to the table.

Gold layer

The gold layer represents the final and most refined stage of our data pipeline. At this layer, data is typically transformed into highly aggregated, analytically optimized formats designed to support business intelligence, and advanced analytics.

Here, we create a gold object that provides the daily number of courses per student in a specific region, namely the United Kingdom. This object is declared as a materialized view, enabling it to replace the aggregated values with each pipeline update:

```
CREATE OR REPLACE MATERIALIZED VIEW uk_daily_student_courses
COMMENT "Daily number of courses per student in United Kingdom"
AS
  SELECT student_id, f_name, l_name,
         date_trunc("DD", formatted_timestamp) order_date,
         sum(quantity) courses_counts
  FROM LIVE.enrollments_cleaned
  WHERE country = "United Kingdom"
  GROUP BY student_id, f_name, l_name, date_trunc("DD", formatted_timestamp)
```

Now that we have established our multi-hop layers, we can proceed to configure and run a DLT pipeline from this notebook.

Configuring DLT Pipelines

In this section, we will explore how to use our notebook to create a new DLT pipeline. To get started, navigate to the Workflows tab on the left sidebar in your Databricks workspace. On the top, select the Delta Live Tables tab. This will take you to the DLT page, where you can create and manage your DLT pipelines, as shown in Figure 6-4. Alternatively, you can directly access the DLT page by clicking the Delta Live Tables option under the Data Engineering section in the left sidebar.

Figure 6-4. Delta Live Tables page

Once you are on this DLT page, click the "Create pipeline" button to start configuring your new DLT pipeline.

The pipeline configuration process consists of five main steps: General configurations, Source code, Destination, Compute, and Advanced configurations, as displayed in Figure 6-5.

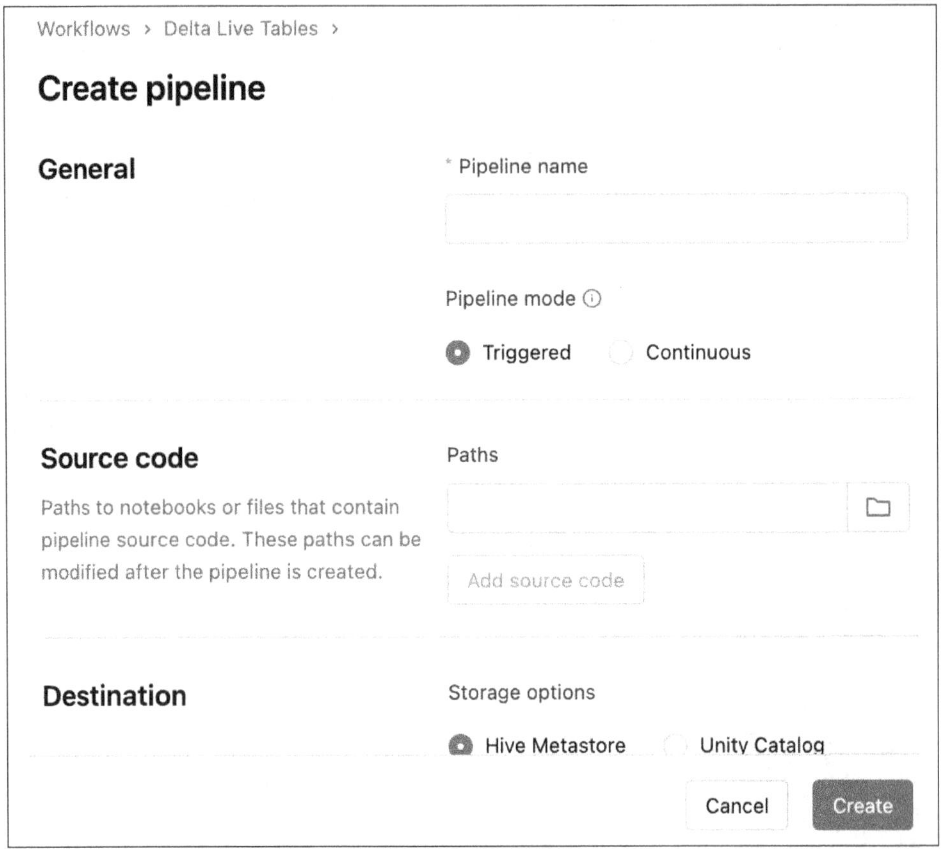

Figure 6-5. The "Create pipeline" interface

General configurations

In this step, we need first to fill in a pipeline name, for instance, "School Demo DLT." This will help identify our pipeline in the Delta Live Tables page.

Next, we need to choose our pipeline mode. The pipeline mode is the trigger method that specifies how often the pipeline should process incoming data. Similar to Spark Structured Streaming, there are two primary pipeline modes: continuous and triggered, as summarized in Table 6-4.

Table 6-4. Pipeline modes of Delta Live Tables

Mode	Behavior	Additional configurations
Continuous	The pipeline continuously runs to process incoming data at regular intervals (e.g., every 2 minutes).	`SET pipelines.trigger.interval=2 minutes`
Triggered	The pipeline runs once to process all available data, then shuts down until the next manual or scheduled execution.	No additional configurations required

Choosing between continuous and triggered modes depends on your specific use case and requirements. For this demonstration, we will be running our pipeline in the triggered mode.

Source code. In this step, you need to specify the source code for your DLT pipeline. Use the navigator to locate and select the notebook with your DLT tables definition. In our case, we will choose the notebook "6.1 - Delta Live Tables," which we developed in the previous section.

Destination. In the Destination section, we need to specify the storage options for our DLT pipeline. Let's choose the Hive metastore option and fill in a database name in the "Target schema" field. For example, let's use `school_dlt_db` as a schema name. This will define the schema where our DLT tables will be stored.

Next, in the "Storage location" field, let's enter a path where the pipeline logs and data files will be stored. In our case, we will use *dbfs:/mnt/DEA-Book/dlt*. This directory will contain all the files generated by our pipeline, including logs, data files, and other metadata. We will explore this directory in more detail in the upcoming section.

Figure 6-6 displays the completed Destination section of our DLT pipeline configuration.

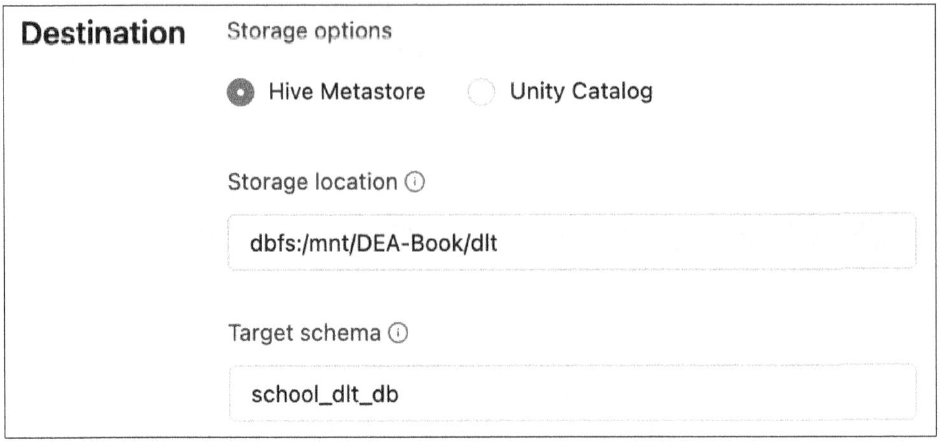

Destination   Storage options

　　　　　　　　● Hive Metastore　　○ Unity Catalog

　　　　　　　Storage location ⓘ

　　　　　　　　┌─────────────────────────────────────┐
　　　　　　　　│ dbfs:/mnt/DEA-Book/dlt   │
　　　　　　　　└─────────────────────────────────────┘

　　　　　　　Target schema ⓘ

　　　　　　　　┌─────────────────────────────────────┐
　　　　　　　　│ school_dlt_db   │
　　　　　　　　└─────────────────────────────────────┘

Figure 6-6. The completed Destination section of the DLT pipeline configuration

Compute.   In this step, we will configure the compute resources for our DLT pipeline, as a new cluster will be created for data processing. You can set the cluster mode to either Autoscaled or Fixed size. For our pipeline, let's choose Fixed size, as displayed in Figure 6-7. Then, set the number of workers to 0 to create a single-node cluster. This means your pipeline will run on a single machine, which is suitable for small-scale pipelines or development environments.

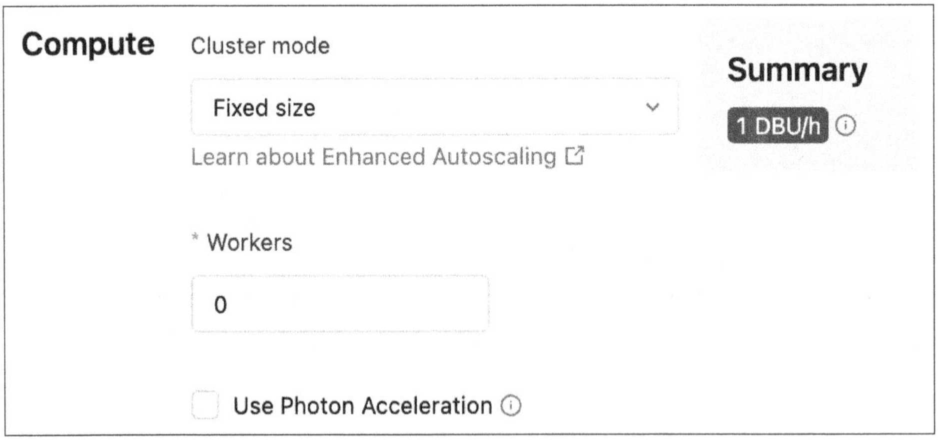

Compute   Cluster mode

　　　　　　　　　　　　　　　　　　　　　　　　　　Summary

　　　　　┌──────────────────────────────────┐
　　　　　│ Fixed size　　　　　　　　　　　 ∨ │　　 ▊1 DBU/h▊ ⓘ
　　　　　└──────────────────────────────────┘
　　　　　Learn about Enhanced Autoscaling ↗

　　　　　* Workers

　　　　　┌──────────────────────────────────┐
　　　　　│ 0   │
　　　　　└──────────────────────────────────┘

　　　　　☐ Use Photon Acceleration ⓘ

Figure 6-7. The completed Compute section of the DLT pipeline configuration

Notice the summary on the left side of the screen, which shows the DBU estimate. This estimate is similar to the one provided in the Databricks Compute UI when configuring all-purpose clusters.

Under Advanced configurations , you can further customize your pipeline's compute resources. You can choose the "Worker type" and "Driver type" to specify the machine types and size for your cluster, as shown in Figure 6-8.

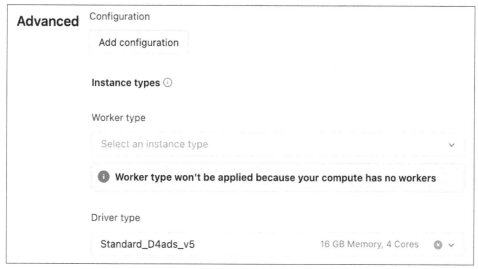

Figure 6-8. Instance types settings of the DLT pipeline's Advanced configuration

 If you are on a free tier on Microsoft Azure cloud, there is a compute limit of four cores. By default, DLT creates a cluster with eight cores, which leads to a quota exceeded error when running your DLT pipeline. To resolve this issue, you need to use a single-node cluster of a maximum of four cores. In the Advanced configuration section, make sure to choose a four-core cluster for the driver type. There's no need to set the Worker type since we configured a cluster of zero workers.

Advanced configurations

In the Advanced section, you can also customize your pipeline by adding configuration parameters. These parameters allow you to dynamically pass values to your pipeline, making it more flexible and easier to manage. To add a new configuration parameter, click the "Add configuration" button, and enter its key-value pair. In this example, we will define the path to our data source as follows:

- Key: Set the key to `school.dataset_path`. Remember, this parameter is used in our notebook to specify the path to our school dataset files.

- Value: Set the value to the location of our dataset, which is located at *dbfs:/mnt/ DE-Associate-Book/datasets/school*.

Figure 6-9 displays the completed Advanced section of our DLT pipeline configuration.

Figure 6-9. The completed Advanced section of the DLT pipeline configuration

Finally, let's click the Create button to complete the pipeline configuration process. As soon as we click Create, we will be redirected to our newly established pipeline interface, as illustrated in Figure 6-10.

Figure 6-10. DLT pipeline interface

Running DLT pipelines

With our pipeline now established, we are ready to run it and begin processing our data. However, before running DLT pipelines, you have the option to choose between two running modes: Development and Production, as illustrated in Figure 6-11.

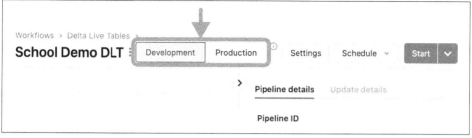

Figure 6-11. DLT pipeline running modes

Production mode. In Production mode, the DLT framework is optimized for reliability and scalability. When running a pipeline in this mode, the following occurs:

- A new job cluster is created for each pipeline run, and it is terminated when the pipeline is stopped.
- The cluster is restarted for recoverable errors, such as memory leaks or stale credentials.
- Execution is retried in case of specific errors, such as a failure to start a cluster.

This mode is suitable for production environments where data processing needs to be reliable, scalable, and fault-tolerant.

Development mode. In Development mode, the DLT framework is optimized for ease of development and testing. When running a pipeline in this mode, the following takes place:

- The job cluster is reused to avoid the overhead of restarts, making it faster to iterate and test changes. By default, the cluster runs for two hours, but this can be changed using the `pipelines.clusterShutdown.delay` setting in the pipeline configuration.
- Pipeline retries are disabled, allowing you to immediately detect and fix errors.

This mode is suitable for interactive development environments where rapid iteration and testing are essential.

For now, let us work in the Development mode and proceed by clicking the Start button to run the pipeline. The initial run may take several minutes while the job cluster is provisioned, as shown in Figure 6-12.

Figure 6-12. DLT pipeline execution

Once the pipeline has completed its run, you can monitor its execution and view its results in the interface, as illustrated in Figure 6-13.

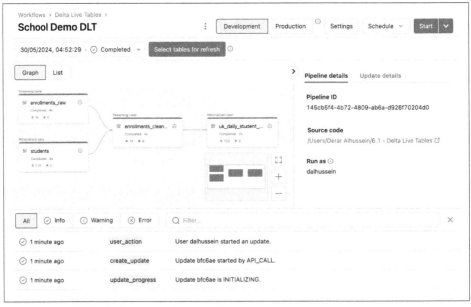

Figure 6-13. DLT pipeline execution result

The pipeline execution interface is divided into three main sections:

Directed acyclic graph (DAG)
> In the middle of the interface, you will find the DAG visualization that represents the entities involved in the pipeline and their relationships. The DAG provides a clear and concise overview of the pipeline's execution flow.

Pipeline details
> On the right-hand side, you can view detailed information about the pipeline, including its configuration, cluster details, and execution statistics.

Event log
> Located at the bottom of the interface, the event log displays all the events related to the running pipeline, including information, warnings, and errors.

By clicking any entity in the DAG, you can explore its details, as displayed in Figure 6-14. This includes its run status and other metadata information, such as the comment we set during the table definition. Additionally, under the Schema tab here, we can view the list of the table's columns and their data types.

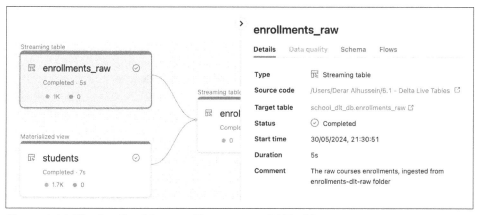

Figure 6-14. The details of the `enrollments_raw` *DLT table*

Data quality metrics. If you select the `enrollments_cleaned` table, you can view its data quality metrics in the right-hand side, as shown in Figure 6-15. Since this table has data expectations declared, the metrics are collected and displayed here.

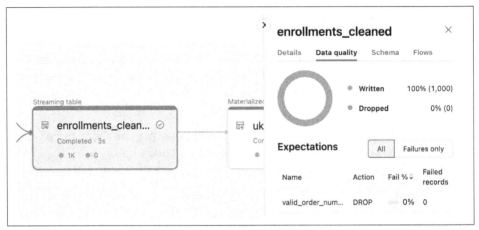

Figure 6-15. Data quality metrics of the `enrollments_cleaned` DLT table

In this case, the results show that there are no records violating the constraint, indicating that the data meets our expected quality standards.

Modifying DLT pipelines

Let's now return to our notebook and add another table to see how this change is reflected in the pipeline. To do this, we'll open the notebook associated with our pipeline by clicking the link in the "Pipeline details" section, as displayed in Figure 6-16.

Figure 6-16. Accessing the source code notebook for the DLT pipeline

At the end of the notebook, let's add a new DLT table definition similar to the previous gold table declaration. This time, we'll modify the filter to focus on France instead of the United Kingdom. Additionally, we'll experiment by intentionally omitting a keyword, specifically the LIVE prefix, to observe how this change affects the pipeline's behavior:

```
CREATE OR REPLACE MATERIALIZED VIEW fr_daily_student_courses
COMMENT "Daily number of courses per student in France"
AS
  SELECT student_id, f_name, l_name,
         date_trunc("DD", formatted_timestamp) order_date,
         sum(quantity) courses_counts
  --FROM LIVE.enrollments_cleaned
  FROM enrollments_cleaned
  WHERE country = "France"
  GROUP BY student_id, f_name, l_name, date_trunc("DD", formatted_timestamp)
```

Executing this query in the notebook only validates its syntax, and no runtime errors are thrown at this point. To observe the full impact of these changes, we need to rerun the pipeline. For this, let's return to our pipeline interface and click the Start button again.

As illustrated in Figure 6-17, the previous pipeline run resulted in an error.

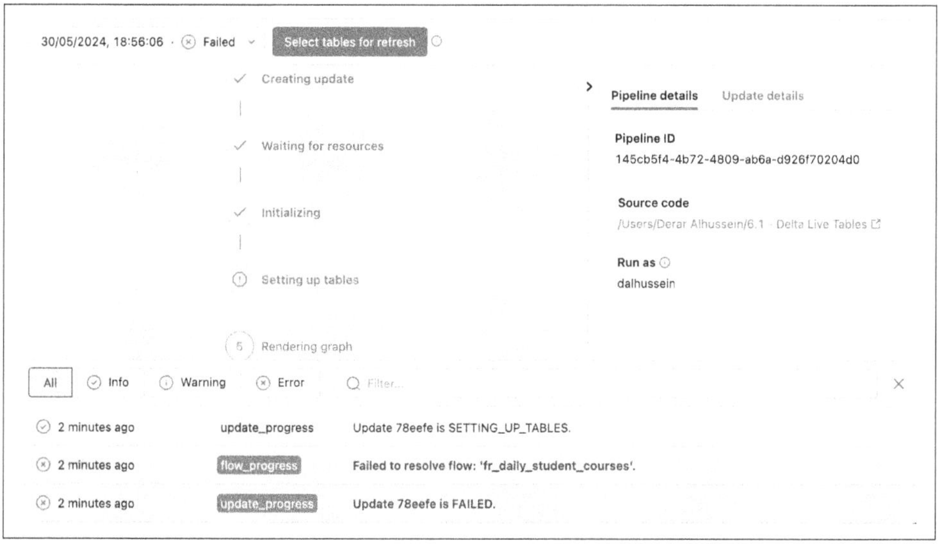

Figure 6-17. Failure of the DLT pipeline

By clicking the error in the event log, we can view the detailed error message. The error message indicates that a table or view is not found, which is due to the missing namespace keyword LIVE in the table definition. This confirms that the absence of the keyword caused the pipeline to fail, as it could not locate the enrollments_cleaned table in the DLT pipeline context.

To resolve this issue, we need to correct the table definition by adding the LIVE keyword before the table name, specifically LIVE.enrollments_cleaned.

Here is the corrected SQL query:

```
CREATE OR REPLACE MATERIALIZED VIEW fr_daily_student_courses
COMMENT "Daily number of courses per student in France"
AS
 SELECT student_id, f_name, l_name,
        date_trunc("DD", formatted_timestamp) order_date,
        sum(quantity) courses_counts
 FROM LIVE.enrollments_cleaned
 WHERE country = "France"
 GROUP BY student_id, f_name, l_name, date_trunc("DD", formatted_timestamp)
```

With this correction in place, we can proceed and restart our pipeline.

Figure 6-18 shows that our pipeline successfully completes after this modification, with the new gold table now integrated in the data flow.

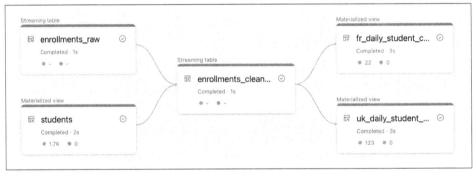

Figure 6-18. The updated DLT pipeline after the modification

Full refresh. In Delta Live Tables, there may be situations where you need to reprocess all available data from scratch, clearing all existing data and reloading it from streaming sources. This is where the "Full refresh" feature comes in, providing a convenient and efficient way to accomplish this task.

To initiate a "Full refresh" in DLT, follow these simple steps:

1. Click the drop-down arrow next to the Start button.

2. Select the "Full refresh all" option from the drop-down menu, as illustrated in Figure 6-19.

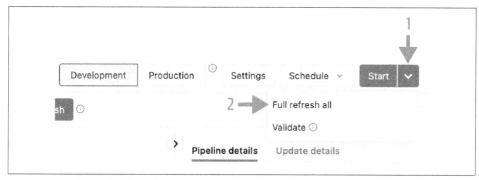

Figure 6-19. Full refresh of the DLT pipeline

When you trigger a "Full refresh," DLT clears all data from each table, effectively resetting the entire dataset. Then, it loads all data from the streaming sources, ensuring that your tables are refreshed with the latest information. This process is useful when you need to correct erroneous data or reload updated data after making changes to your streaming sources.

Examining DLT pipelines

Now, let's delve deeper into the underlying mechanisms of Delta Live Tables to better understand how it operates. Remember, the events and information displayed in the DLT pipeline interface are stored in the configured underlying storage. This storage configuration was provided during the initial setup and configuration of our DLT pipeline, as shown in Figure 6-20.

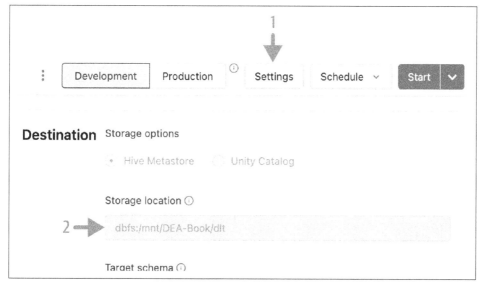

Figure 6-20. Configuration settings for the DLT pipeline

To gain insights into our pipeline storage location, we'll create a new SQL notebook named "6.2 - Output Exploration" and start our demo all-purpose cluster to run the commands.

Let us begin by exploring the content of the pipeline storage location:

```
%fs ls "dbfs:/mnt/DEA-Book/dlt"
```

Figure 6-21 illustrates the structure of our pipeline storage, revealing four main directories: *autoloader, checkpoints, system,* and *tables.*

A^Bc path	A^Bc name	1^2_3 size	1^2_3 modificationTime
dbfs:/mnt/DEA-Book/dlt/autoloader/	autoloader/	0	1717037550000
dbfs:/mnt/DEA-Book/dlt/checkpoint...	checkpoints/	0	1717037184000
dbfs:/mnt/DEA-Book/dlt/system/	system/	0	1717037138000
dbfs:/mnt/DEA-Book/dlt/tables/	tables/	0	1717037172000

Figure 6-21. The content of the pipeline storage location

The system directory captures all the activities associated with the DLT pipeline, including the event logs. To explore the events stored in the system directory, let's examine the events subfolder:

```
%fs ls "dbfs:/mnt/DEA-Book/dlt/system/events"
```

Figure 6-22 reveals that the pipeline events are stored as a Delta Lake table within this directory.

A^Bc name	1^2_3 size	1^2_3 modification...
_delta_log/	0	1717037138000
part-00000-0088a0db-f972-4033-87d7-052edb874eee-c000.snappy.parquet	12557	1717092027000
part-00000-0476f247-e525-452f-97db-6ac5d0a67bb8-c000.snappy.parquet	12385	1717042893000
part-00000-05b6d10d-8a2f-4dd9-97d6-7f9ad78852f1-c000.snappy.parquet	12559	1717090827000

Figure 6-22. The content of the pipeline events directory

To explore the event logs, let us query this Delta Lake table:

```
SELECT * FROM delta.`dbfs:/mnt/DEA-Book/dlt/system/events`
```

Figure 6-23 displays the result of querying the pipeline events table. It demonstrates that all events displayed in the DLT user interface are stored in this Delta table, including log messages, event levels (such as INFO, ERROR, or METRICS), and additional details.

message	level	maturity_level	error	details
Update 78eefe started by API_CALL.	INFO	STABLE	null	> {"create_up
Update 78eefe is WAITING_FOR_RESOURCES.	INFO	STABLE	null	{"update_prog
Failed to resolve flow: 'fr_daily_student_courses'.	ERROR	STABLE	> {"fatal":tru...	{"flow_progre:
Update 78eefe is FAILED.	ERROR	STABLE	> {"fatal":tru...	{"update_prog
Reported cluster resources metrics.	METRICS	STABLE	null	> {"cluster_re
Reported flow time metrics for flowName: 'pipe...	METRICS	STABLE	null	{"flow_progre:

Figure 6-23. The result of querying the pipeline events table

Analyzing such event logs provides valuable insights into pipeline execution, performance, and potential issues or errors encountered during processing.

Continuing our exploration of the DLT pipeline storage, let's focus now on the tables directory, which contains the DLT tables generated by the pipeline:

```
%fs ls "dbfs:/mnt/DEA-Book/dlt/tables"
```

Figure 6-24 illustrates the contents of the tables directory, showcasing our five DLT tables stored within it.

path	name	size	modificationTime
dbfs:/mnt/DEA-Book/dlt/tables/cn_daily_student_courses/	cn_daily_student_courses/	0	1717037180000
dbfs:/mnt/DEA-Book/dlt/tables/enrollments_cleaned/	enrollments_cleaned/	0	1717037178000
dbfs:/mnt/DEA-Book/dlt/tables/enrollments_raw/	enrollments_raw/	0	1717037172000
dbfs:/mnt/DEA-Book/dlt/tables/fr_daily_student_courses/	fr_daily_student_courses/	0	1717037181000
dbfs:/mnt/DEA-Book/dlt/tables/students/	students/	0	1717037176000

Figure 6-24. The content of the pipeline tables directory

Instead of querying these tables directly, we can access them through the catalog. To do this, we will first return to our DLT pipeline interface, where we can get their database and catalog name. Selecting any table in the DAG visualization, we can view the database information associated with that table, as illustrated in Figure 6-25.

Figure 6-25. The database information of the uk_daily_student_courses DLT table

Clicking the target table link opens the table details in the Catalog Explorer. As shown in Figure 6-26, our pipeline database and its associated tables are listed in the Hive metastore.

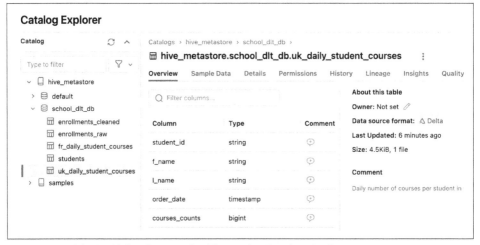

Figure 6-26. The DLT database and tables in the Catalog Explorer

Returning to the "6.2 - Output Exploration" notebook, we can now read our DLT tables. For instance, let's query the uk_daily_student_courses gold table:

```
SELECT * FROM hive_metastore.school_dlt_db.uk_daily_student_courses
```

Figure 6-27 illustrates the content of our gold table, indicating that it contains 123 records.

	A^B_C student_id	A^B_C f_name	A^B_C l_name	⏱ order_date	1^2_3 courses_counts
1	S01139	Jasmin	Northleigh	2022-07-16T00:0...	1
2	S00742	Maxine	Isack	2022-07-28T00:0...	2
3	S00817	Arturo	Kleinmann	2022-07-15T00:0...	1
4	S00825	Gail	Klulicek	2022-07-27T00:0	1

↓ 123 rows | 1.11 seconds runtime

Figure 6-27. The result of querying the uk_daily_student_courses DLT table

Finally, at the end of our pipeline development, it's essential to terminate the pipeline cluster to avoid unnecessary costs. To do this, navigate to the Cluster section in the pipeline details panel and click "View details," as shown in Figure 6-28.

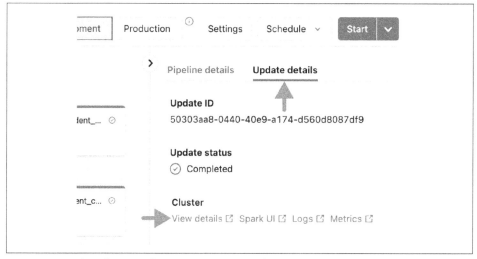

Figure 6-28. The Cluster information section in the pipeline details panel

This action will redirect you to the cluster configuration page, where you can simply click the Terminate button.

In summary, DLT is an innovative solution for building ETL pipelines that offers several advantages over Spark Structured Streaming. DLT provides simplified syntax, automatic checkpointing, and built-in support for data quality control. With this solid understanding of DLT, we can now delve into more advanced topics, specifically the mechanism for capturing data changes and its implementation within DLT.

Capturing Data Changes

Capturing and replicating data changes is a crucial aspect of building robust ETL pipelines, as it ensures that the data reflects the latest source modifications. This process, known as change data capture (CDC), is the primary focus of this section. Here, we'll explore the fundamental concepts of CDC and provide guidance on implementing this process using Delta Live Tables.

Definition

Change data capture (CDC) is a process that identifies and captures changes made to data in a data source and delivers a record of those changes to a target. This technique is essential for keeping data systems synchronized and ensuring that any updates in the source are accurately reflected in the target.

CDC captures three types of row-level changes, as illustrated in Figure 6-29:

Insertions
New records that are added to the source and need to be inserted into the target.

Updates
Existing records in the source that have been modified and need to be updated in the target.

Deletions
Records that have been removed from the source and need to be deleted from the target.

Figure 6-29. Change data capture (CDC)

By capturing and processing row-level changes, CDC ensures that a target database reflects the current state of the source database.

CDC Feed

Changes are logged at the source as events, each containing the data of the affected records along with relevant metadata information. This metadata includes the following:

Operation type

Indicates whether the record was inserted, updated, or deleted.

Timestamp/version number

Indicates the order in which changes occurred, ensuring that changes can be applied in the correct sequence.

Figure 6-30 presents an example of CDC events for state temperatures, illustrating the modifications that need to be applied to a target table.

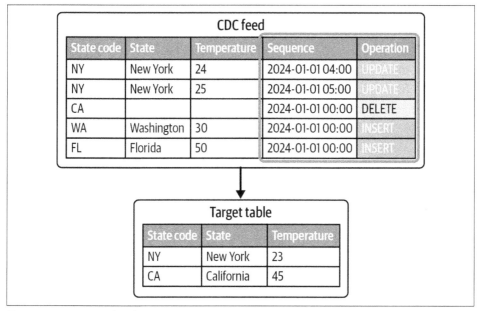

Figure 6-30. Example of CDC events

This CDC feed contains the following events:

New York

This state has two update events targeting the existing record for New York. In this case, only the most recent change must be applied, meaning only the latest version of the record will be reflected in the target table.

California

This record is marked for deletion. In such a case, the full record data is not required; only the record identifier and the metadata information indicating the deletion are needed.

Washington and Florida

These are new records that need to be inserted into the target table.

So, this CDC feed provides the data of the records, the metadata that indicates the type of change (insert, update, or delete), and the order of changes.

Figure 6-31 shows the latest version of the target table after applying the previous CDC feed.

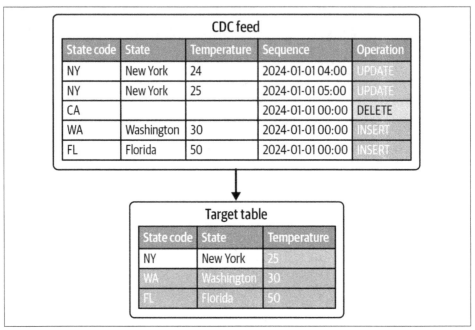

Figure 6-31. Applying a CDC feed into a target table

The following changes are reflected:

New York
> The target table shows the most recent record for New York, as the existing record was overwritten by the latest update.

California
> This record is absent in the target table because it was marked for deletion in the CDC feed.

Washington and Florida
> Both of these records are present in the target table as new entries.

This confirms that the target table has been successfully synchronized with the latest updates from the source, ensuring data integrity and consistency are maintained.

CDC Sources

CDC data typically originates from two main sources: databases with built-in CDC features, and third-party software known as CDC agents.

Databases with built-in CDC features

Many modern databases come equipped with built-in change data capture features. These databases maintain change logs that record every change made to the data within the database. These logs capture detailed information about inserts, updates, and deletes performed on the tables within the database.

For example, Microsoft SQL Server change data capture is a feature that tracks changes to SQL Server tables. This logs the details of these changes, including the type of operation and the affected rows, enabling efficient and accurate data synchronization. Delta Lake also has a built-in change data feed (CDF) feature for this purpose.

CDC agents

CDC agents are third-party software processes that continuously monitor a database for any changes. When a change is detected, these agents capture the details of the change, including the type of operation (insert, update, delete), the affected rows, and the data before and after the change. These agents can work with various database systems and provide a flexible solution for CDC.

For instance, Debezium (*https://debezium.io*) is an open source CDC platform that supports several popular databases, including MySQL, PostgreSQL, SQL Server, and MongoDB. It captures and streams changes in real time, providing a powerful tool for keeping data in sync across different systems.

CDC Feed Delivery

CDC feeds can be delivered from the source in various formats. Two common methods are as follows:

Data stream
> The CDC events are continuously streamed from the source to the target system, allowing for near-real-time data synchronization.

JSON files
> The CDC events can be periodically captured and stored in JSON files, which are then processed to apply the changes to the target system.

Both methods ensure that the target system remains synchronized with the source, reflecting all changes accurately and promptly.

CDC in DLT

Delta Live Tables provides robust support for processing CDC feeds using the APPLY CHANGES INTO command. This command is designed to simplify the application of CDC events into a target table, ensuring that the target table accurately reflects the changes captured from the source. This DLT implementation for CDC eliminates many common errors associated with applying change records, making the process more accurate and reliable.

APPLY CHANGES INTO command

The APPLY CHANGES INTO command allows you to apply changes from a CDC feed table into a DLT table, which serves as the target table. Here's an example of the command:

```
APPLY CHANGES INTO LIVE.target_table
FROM STREAM(LIVE.cdc_feed_table)
KEYS (key_field)
APPLY AS DELETE WHEN operation_field = "DELETE"
SEQUENCE BY sequence_field
COLUMNS *
```

This command is composed of several key elements, including the following:

Target table specification

LIVE.target_table is the DLT table into which the changes will be applied. This table must be created before executing the APPLY CHANGES INTO command.

Source table

STREAM(LIVE.cdc_feed_table) specifies the CDC feed table as a streaming source. This table contains the change events that need to be processed.

Primary keys

KEYS identifies the primary key fields used to determine if a record already exists in the target table. If the key exists, the record will be updated; if not, a new record will be inserted. As a reminder, keys must be unique.

Delete condition

APPLY AS DELETE WHEN specifies that records representing deletion operation should be removed from the target table.

Sequencing key

SEQUENCE BY indicates the field used to order the operations. This ensures that changes are applied in the correct sequence.

Columns

COLUMNS * specifies that all fields from the CDC feed should be included in the target table. You can also specify a subset of columns if needed.

By using this command, you can efficiently synchronize changes from a source into a target table, ensuring that it remains up-to-date and accurately reflects the latest state of the data.

Advantages of APPLY CHANGES INTO

The APPLY CHANGES INTO command offers several advantages for processing CDC feeds in the DLT framework:

Reduced code complexity
> Traditionally, handling CDC involved extensive custom logic, potentially spanning hundreds of lines of code. Implementing this logic manually requires steps to handle inserts, updates, and deletes, along with mechanisms for ordering, deduplication, and merging. With APPLY CHANGES INTO, much of this complexity is abstracted away, reducing the code required to a few lines and making it more manageable and maintainable.

Automatic ordering of late-arriving records
> The command leverages the user-provided sequencing key to automatically order records, ensuring that downstream results are accurately recomputed if records arrive out of order.

Performing upsert operations
> The default behavior for insert and update operations is to upsert the CDC events into the target table. This means that the command updates existing rows that match the specified key or inserts new records if no matching record exists.

Flexible delete handling
> Optional handling for delete events can be specified with the APPLY AS DELETE WHEN condition.

Multiple key fields
> You can specify one or many fields as the primary key for a table.

Excluding columns
> You can use the EXCEPT keyword to specify columns to ignore, enabling precise control over column selection during CDC processing.

Built-in support for slowly changing dimensions
> The command supports storing records as slowly changing dimensions (*https:// oreil.ly/NbWkE*) (SCD), type 1 or type 2. By default, it creates a type 1 SCD table, meaning that each unique key has at most one record, and updates overwrite the original information.

Disadvantages of APPLY CHANGES INTO

Despite its numerous benefits, the APPLY CHANGES INTO command has a notable disadvantage:

Breaking append-only requirement for streaming sources
> Since the command involves updating and deleting data in the target table, it breaks the append-only requirement for streaming table sources. Consequently, the updated table can no longer be used as a streaming source in subsequent layers.

Now that we've covered the essential concepts of CDC feed processing, we're ready to take the next step and apply them in a practical, hands-on exercise. Let's move on to the next section to put our knowledge into action!

Processing Change Data Capture

In this section, we will delve into the process of handling CDC feeds in Delta Live Tables. The objective here is to modify our school DLT pipeline to add CDC processing capabilities. Through this process, we will gain a deeper understanding of CDC feeds and unlock the full potential of data processing in the DLT framework.

Before we dive into the DLT pipeline implementation, let's first examine the CDC data that we will process in this demonstration. The data is delivered as JSON files, which contain a series of change events captured from our source system. To begin, we will create a simple SQL notebook titled "6.3 - Land New Data" to land these new files in our source directory and explore the data.

In this notebook, we start by running the "School-Setup" helper notebook to prepare our environment:

```
%run ../Includes/School-Setup
```

Next, we load a new file of the CDC feed using the following helper function:

```
load_new_json_data()
```

Upon execution, the function loads the file *02.json* into our school dataset directory, as indicated by the output:

```
Output: Loading 02.json courses file to the school dataset
```

With this new file now available, let's take a closer look at its content. We use the following SQL command to directly query the JSON file:

```
%sql
SELECT * from json.`${dataset.school}/courses-cdc/02.json`
```

This command retrieves all the records from the specified JSON file, displaying CDC records for our courses table, as shown in Figure 6-32.

$^{A}_{C}$ course_id	$^{A}_{C}$ title	$^{A}_{C}$ instructor	$^{A}_{C}$ price	$^{A}_{C}$ row_status	$^{A}_{C}$ row_time	$\equiv\uparrow$
B03	Neural Network	Adam R.	30	UPDATE	2022-11-05T18:11:33.507+01:00	
B04	Robot Dynamics and Control	Mark G.	20	INSERT	2022-11-05T18:12:05.419+01:00	
B05	Python Programming	Luciano C.	47	INSERT	2022-11-05T18:12:05.419+01:00	
B06	Deep Learning	François R.	22	INSERT	2022-11-05T18:12:05.419+01:00	
B01	null	null	null	DELETE	2022-11-05T18:17:50.236+01:00	
B02	JavaScript Design Patterns	Ali M.	40	UPDATE	2022-11-05T18:17:50.236+01:00	

Figure 6-32. The result of querying the `courses` *CDC data*

As shown, in addition to the course's information data, the results also include two operational columns: `row_status` and `row_time`:

`row_status`

This column indicates the type of operation performed on each record. It can have one of the following values:

Insert

Indicates a new record has been added

Update

Indicates an existing record has been modified

Delete

Indicates a record has been removed

It's important to recognize that insert and update operations always involve complete and valid records, whereas delete operations have null values for all fields except the key columns, which in this case is `course_id`.

`row_time`

This column records the timestamp of the operation, which will serve as a sequence key in our CDC data processing. This key is crucial for maintaining the order of changes and ensuring data consistency during the processing stage.

Extending DLT Pipelines with New Notebooks

Building on the simple DLT pipeline we implemented earlier in this chapter, we will now expand it by adding a new notebook. This new notebook will define additional DLT tables for processing the `courses` CDC data.

Figure 6-33 illustrates the target result of our updated DLT pipeline. It shows the integration of the new notebook with our existing DLT pipeline. This approach demonstrates the flexibility of DLT, allowing us to seamlessly incorporate new data processing tasks into existing pipelines. Later in this section, we will cover how to modify an existing pipeline to incorporate additional notebooks.

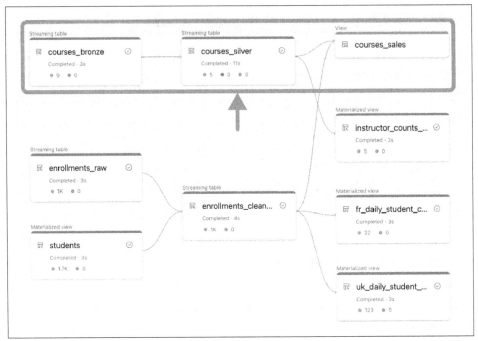

Figure 6-33. The updated DLT pipeline after integrating the CDC processing

To achieve this result, let's begin by creating a new SQL notebook named "6.4 - CDC Pipeline" where we'll define our new DLT tables. In this notebook, we start by specifying the path to our source dataset:

```
SET school.dataset_path=dbfs:/mnt/DE-Associate-Book/datasets/school;
```

The next step involves creating a bronze table to ingest the `courses` CDC feed. For this purpose, we use Auto Loader to incrementally load the input JSON files from our source directory:

```
CREATE OR REFRESH STREAMING TABLE courses_bronze
COMMENT "The raw courses data, ingested from CDC feed"
AS SELECT * FROM cloud_files("${school.dataset_path}/courses-cdc", "json")
```

With the bronze table established and ingesting the raw CDC feed, we now proceed to create the silver table. The silver table is our target table, where we will apply the changes from the CDC feed to maintain up-to-date course data.

The process of creating the silver table begins with its declaration. Remember, we need to declare the table separately before applying the changes, since the APPLY CHANGES INTO command requires a pre-existing target table:

```
CREATE OR REFRESH STREAMING TABLE courses_silver;
```

This command initializes the silver table if it doesn't already exist, ensuring it's ready to receive and apply changes from the CDC feed.

Once the silver table is declared, we can use the APPLY CHANGES INTO command to specify how changes from the bronze table should be applied to the silver table. The following command accomplishes this:

```
APPLY CHANGES INTO LIVE.courses_silver
  FROM STREAM(LIVE.courses_bronze)
  KEYS (course_id)
  APPLY AS DELETE WHEN row_status = "DELETE"
  SEQUENCE BY row_time
  COLUMNS * EXCEPT (row_status, row_time)
```

Let's break down the components of this command:

APPLY CHANGES INTO LIVE.courses_silver

This specifies the target table, courses_silver, where the changes from the CDC feed will be applied.

FROM STREAM(LIVE.courses_bronze)

This specifies the courses_bronze table as the streaming source of our CDC feed.

KEYS (course_id)

This identifies course_id as the primary key for matching records. If a record with the same course_id exists in the target table, it will be updated; otherwise, a new record will be inserted.

APPLY AS DELETE WHEN row_status = "DELETE"

This condition specifies that records with a row_status of "DELETE" should be removed from the target table.

SEQUENCE BY row_time

This clause orders the operations by the row_time field. This ensures that changes are applied in the correct sequence, preserving the chronological order of events.

COLUMNS * EXCEPT (row_status, row_time)

This clause indicates that all columns from the CDC feed should be included in the target table, except for the operational columns row_status and row_time. These columns are used for processing changes but are not needed in the final table.

By running this command, we can maintain an up-to-date and accurate view of the courses_silver data, which can then be leveraged in the subsequent layers.

At this point, we've reached the last stage of our data pipeline: the gold layer. Here, we'll define a simple aggregate query to create a materialized view that provides a higher-level summary of our course data:

```
CREATE OR REPLACE MATERIALIZED VIEW instructor_counts_stats
  COMMENT "Number of courses per instructor"
AS SELECT instructor, count(*) as courses_count,
        current_timestamp() updated_time
  FROM LIVE.courses_silver
  GROUP BY instructor
```

It is crucial to note that this gold table is not defined as a streaming table. This is because the `courses_silver` table, which is the source of our data here, is being updated and deleted. As a result, it's no longer valid to use it as a streaming source for this new table. Remember that, in a streaming context, data sources are expected to be append-only, meaning new records are continuously added without updates or deletions.

In the final step of our data pipeline, we'll also demonstrate how to define a DLT view that joins and references tables across notebooks. This capability is a powerful feature of Delta Live Tables, allowing you to create complex data pipelines that span multiple notebooks.

In the following command, we create a DLT view that joins two tables from different notebooks:

```
CREATE TEMPORARY LIVE VIEW courses_sales
  AS SELECT b.title, o.quantity
    FROM (
      SELECT *, explode(courses) AS course
      FROM LIVE.enrollments_cleaned) o
    INNER JOIN LIVE.courses_silver b
    ON o.course.course_id = b.course_id;
```

In this example, we are joining our `courses_silver` table to the `enrollments_cleaned` table, which was created in a previous notebook ("6.1 - Delta Live Tables"). This capability is enabled by DLT's support for combining multiple notebooks into a unified pipeline. Consequently, any notebook within the pipeline can reference tables and views defined in other notebooks using the `LIVE` keyword. This means that the `LIVE` namespace allows you to access objects at the DLT pipeline level, instead of being limited to individual notebooks.

Now that we have completed our new notebook ("6.4 - CDC Pipeline"), let's integrate it into the "School Demo" DLT pipeline that we built earlier. To achieve this, follow the steps outlined here and illustrated in Figure 6-34:

1. Go to the pipeline interface and click the Settings button.

2. Under the Source code configuration section, click "Add source code."

3. Navigate to select the "6.4 - CDC Pipeline" notebook.

4. Once added, click Save to confirm the changes.

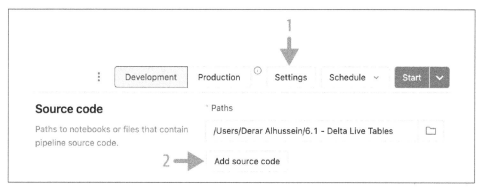

Figure 6-34. Adding the new notebook to the "School Demo" DLT pipeline

Upon saving, you'll notice that the Pipeline details panel now references two notebooks instead of one, as displayed in Figure 6-35.

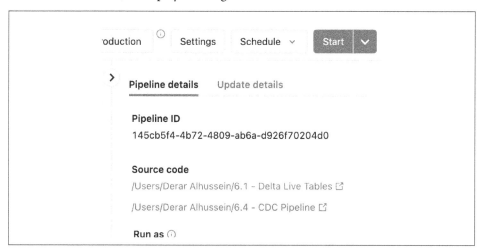

Figure 6-35. The pipeline details after adding the new notebook

With the updated configuration in place, let's run the pipeline by clicking the Start button.

Upon executing the pipeline, the updated DAG is generated, as displayed in Figure 6-36. As expected, the updated pipeline includes the additional tables created by the new notebook, as well as the `courses_sales` view that combines data from both notebooks' tables.

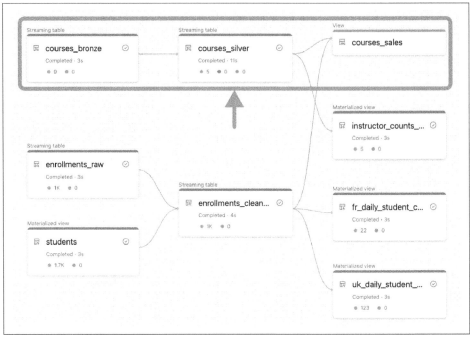

Figure 6-36. The updated DLT pipeline after integrating the CDC processing

By incorporating the new notebook into our "School" DLT pipeline, we've successfully expanded our data processing capabilities and created a more comprehensive data pipeline.

In conclusion, the DLT framework provides a powerful mechanism for processing CDC feeds, offering a range of features that enhance data integrity and freshness. By keeping your data up-to-date and responsive to changes, you can ensure that your analytics are always accurate and reflect the most recent information.

Orchestrating Workflows

Databricks offers an advanced job orchestration capability to build and automate data workflows. In this section, we will dive into the details of Databricks Jobs, exploring how to create, configure, run, and debug jobs to optimize your workflow orchestration.

Introducing Databricks Jobs

Databricks Jobs is an integrated workflow orchestration tool within the Databricks platform. It is designed to facilitate the creation, scheduling, and monitoring of complex data workflows in the lakehouse environment. This feature can be leveraged to automate the processing of data pipelines, train and deploy machine learning models, and execute various data analysis activities.

With Databricks Jobs, you can easily automate your workflows by defining a series of tasks that need to be executed in a specific order, as illustrated in Figure 6-37. Each task within the job serves a specific purpose, contributing to the overall objective of the workflow.

Figure 6-37. Example of a Databricks job

A key feature of Databricks Jobs is its flexibility in terms of task execution. A task can be anything from executing a notebook or saved SQL query to running an entire DLT pipeline, Python script, or JAR file. Additionally, tasks can evaluate conditional logic, such as if-else statements, and even trigger the execution of another job. This range of options allows you to create customized workflows that meet your specific needs, making it an essential tool for your data projects.

To illustrate the capabilities of Databricks Jobs, we will now create a multi-task job and explore its features in a hands-on demonstration.

Creating Databricks Jobs

In this practical section, I will guide you through a step-by-step process for creating a multi-task job in Databricks. The job will automate the data management of our online school scenario. This involves retrieving data into a source directory, transforming and processing the data, and lastly analyzing and validating the results.

Our demonstration will focus on creating a multi-task job that consists of three interconnected tasks, as illustrated in Figure 6-38. The first task involves executing a notebook that imports a new batch of data into our source directory. The second task triggers our "School Demo" DLT pipeline, which processes the new data through a series of tables. Finally, the third task executes the output exploration notebook to verify the results of the pipeline. By combining these tasks into a single multi-task job, we can automate our data ingestion, processing, and analysis.

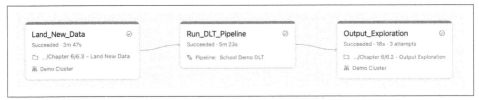

Figure 6-38. Demo multi-task job

To create such a job in Databricks, you can follow these steps:

1. Navigate to the Workflows tab from the left sidebar.
2. Under the Jobs tab, click the "Create job" button, as displayed in Figure 6-39.

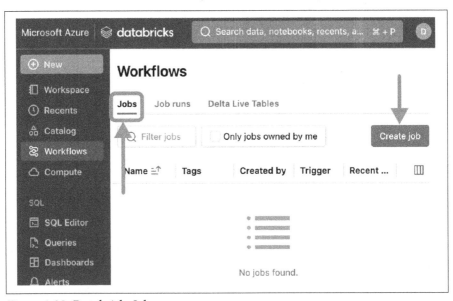

Figure 6-39. Databricks Jobs page

After clicking the "Create job" button, you will be presented with the job configuration interface, as shown in Figure 6-40. This interface allows you to define the details of your job, including its name, tasks, and schedule.

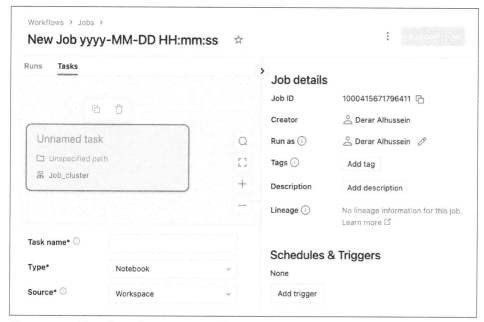

Figure 6-40. The job configuration interface

At the top of the job configuration interface, you will see a default name assigned to the job (*New Job yyyy-MM-DD HH:mm:ss*). Click this name to rename it to something more descriptive, such as "School Demo Job." This will help you identify the job and its purpose in your Databricks workspace.

With the job name updated, you can now start configuring each of the tasks that will be executed as part of the job.

Task 1: Landing data

As shown in Figure 6-40, the interface defaults to configure the first task in the job. So, let's fill in the details for our first task dedicated to landing new data in our source directory:

Task name

Enter a name for the task, such as Land_New_Data. This name clearly indicates the purpose of the task, which is to land a new batch of data in the source directory.

Task type

From the drop-down menu, select Notebook. This indicates that the task will run a Databricks notebook.

Source

Specify the location of the notebook. It can be in your Databricks workspace or in a remote Git repository. For this example, the notebook is located within the workspace.

Path

Browse to select the notebook named "6.3 - Land New Data." This notebook contains a simple call to our `land_new_data` function.

Cluster configuration

From the cluster drop-down, under Existing All-Purpose Clusters, select your "Demo Cluster." We're choosing this here as a matter of convenience for the example. It's important to note that for production jobs, ephemeral job clusters are preferred due to their lower cost. Remember, job clusters are temporary and automatically terminated after the job is completed, reducing unnecessary resource usage.

After filling out these details, click the "Create task" button. This action will create a job consisting of a single task, as shown in Figure 6-41.

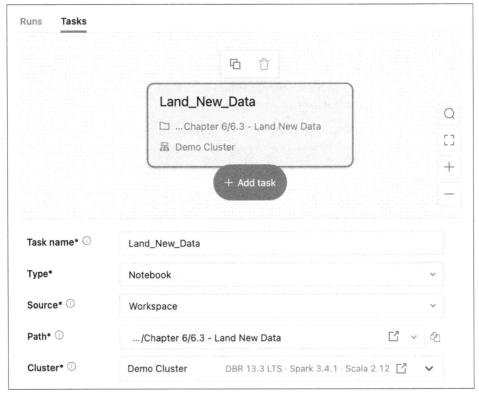

Figure 6-41. A single-task job

This is just the beginning—we can add more tasks to our job to create a multi-task workflow.

Task 2: DLT pipeline

The next step involves adding a Delta Live Tables pipeline task. This task should be executed following the successful completion of the first task to process the newly received data. This will ensure a seamless and logical progression in our workflow.

To add another task, click the "+ Add task" blue button shown at the bottom of the task flow chart. Select its type as "Delta Live Tables pipeline," and configure it as follows:

Task name
> Enter Run_DLT_Pipeline as the name for the new task.

Task type
> Keep the "Delta Live Tables pipeline" type selected. This indicates that the task will run a DLT pipeline.

Pipeline selection
> Select our "School Demo DLT" pipeline that we created during the previous section.

Dependency configuration
> The "Depends on" field will default to your previously defined task, Land_New_Data, so no changes are needed here. This ensures that the DLT pipeline task will run only after the successful completion of the data landing task. Note that tasks can have multiple dependencies, if desired.

Now, click the "Create task" button to finalize the addition of the new task.

At this point, your workflow will include two tasks: the initial Land_New_Data task and the subsequent Run_DLT_Pipeline task just created, as shown in Figure 6-42. The dependency defined between these tasks ensures that the DLT pipeline processes the newly landed data, maintaining the integrity and sequence of operations.

Figure 6-42. Job with two tasks

Task 3: Output exploration

The final step involves adding a task for output exploration and verification. This task will run an additional notebook designed to explore and display the results of the DLT pipeline, ensuring that the data processed through the previous tasks is accessible and correctly formatted for further analysis.

Before adding the new task, make sure to click the Run_DLT_Pipeline task in the flow chart. This ensures that the new task will be correctly linked to follow the DLT pipeline execution. Now, click the "+ Add task" blue button, choose Notebook as the task type from the menu, and enter the following details for the new task:

Task name
    Enter a name for the new task, such as Output_Exploration.

Task type
    Leave the Notebook type selected. This specifies that the task will execute a Databricks notebook.

Source
    Select Workspace since our notebook is located within the Databricks workspace.

Path

Browse to select the "6.2 - Output Exploration" notebook from the previous session, which is specifically designed to show the pipeline results. Remember, this notebook contains code to display the content of the pipeline's storage location and query the gold table where the processed data is stored.

Cluster selection

From the cluster drop-down, select the Demo Cluster. As with previous tasks, the Demo Cluster is used here for demonstration purposes, but job clusters should be used in production to optimize costs and resource management.

Dependency configuration

The "Depends on" field will automatically default to the previously selected task, which is the Run_DLT_Pipeline task in this case. This ensures that the Out put_Exploration task will run only after the DLT pipeline task has successfully completed. If the "Depends on" field is not correctly set, manually adjust it to ensure proper task sequencing.

Now, click the "Create task" button to complete the task creation process.

With the addition of the output exploration task, your workflow now includes three interconnected tasks, as illustrated in Figure 6-43. This setup ensures a complete and systematic data processing and validation cycle.

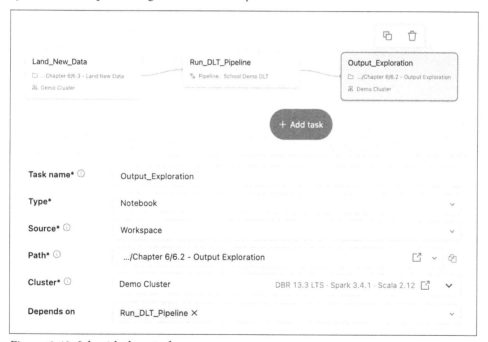

Figure 6-43. Job with three tasks

Now, our attention turns to configuring the job settings to ensure seamless execution and management.

Configuring Job Settings

With the job structure in place, the next step involves managing its settings through the right-hand side panel, as illustrated in Figure 6-44. This allows you to control various aspects of your job, including scheduling, notifications, and permissions.

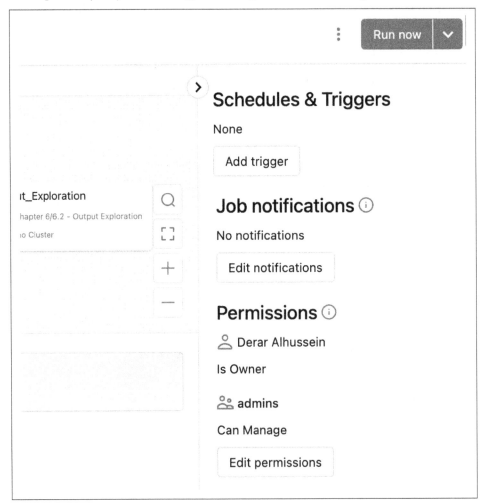

Figure 6-44. Job settings panel

Scheduling the job

The Schedules section is where you can set up and manage job execution timing. Simply click the "Add trigger" button to explore scheduling options.

The Scheduled trigger type allows you to specify when and how often the job should run, as shown in Figure 6-45.

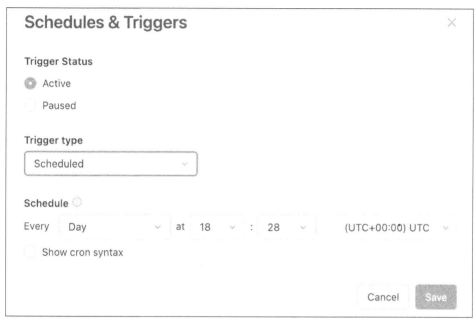

Figure 6-45. Job scheduling settings

Additionally, you can define the schedule using Quartz Cron syntax (*https://oreil.ly/ sGxSa*), which provides more precise advanced control over job execution timing, as illustrated in Figure 6-46. For example, you might set the job to run at specific times on certain days of the week.

For the purposes of this demonstration, no schedule needs to be set, so you can cancel out of the scheduling window. In a production environment, setting a schedule can be crucial for automating workflows.

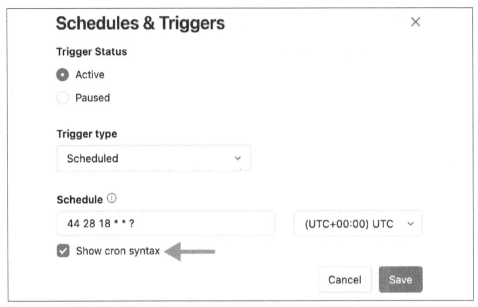

Figure 6-46. Job scheduling using cron syntax

Setting job notifications

Job notifications keep you informed about the status of your job, allowing you to respond quickly to any issues that may arise. You can receive notifications at multiple email addresses or through pre-defined system destinations such as Slack, Microsoft Teams, or any webhook-based service.

To configure job notifications, click the "Edit notifications" button in the job settings panel. From there, you can add notifications to alert you at various stages of the job's lifecycle, such as when the job starts, succeeds, or fails. These notifications can be sent via email or through system destinations, as shown in Figure 6-47.

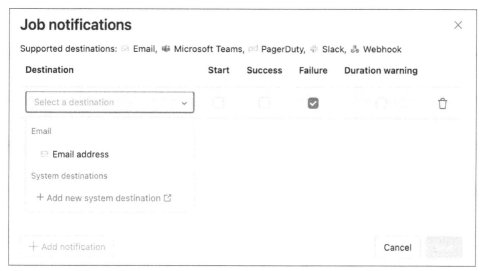

Figure 6-47. Job notifications settings

With notifications in place, you can rest assured that you'll be promptly alerted to any changes in your job's status, enabling efficient job monitoring.

Managing permissions

The permissions section allows you to control access and management rights for the job. This includes defining who can run, manage, or review the job, as shown in Figure 6-48. You can assign these permissions to individual users or user groups defined in the workspace. Additionally, you can also transfer ownership of the job to another user or group, which is particularly useful in collaborative environments or when team roles change.

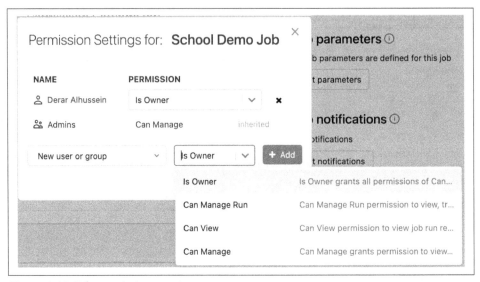

Figure 6-48. Job permissions settings

Properly managing permissions ensures that only authorized personnel can modify or execute the job or access potentially sensitive information, enhancing security and control over your workflows.

Running the Job

With all tasks and configurations in place, the final step is to execute the job and review its output. This ensures that each task runs as expected and produces the desired results.

To start the job, simply click the "Run now" button at the top right of the job interface since we didn't define a pre-set schedule. This initiates the execution of all configured tasks in the specified order.

To view the job's execution, navigate to the Runs tab, where you can see the list of all runs associated with the job, as illustrated in Figure 6-49.

Figure 6-49. Job permissions settings

To delve deeper into the job execution, click the highlighted "Start time" link of the current run to open its detailed view. This allows you to track the real-time status of each task's run in the job, as displayed in Figure 6-50. The task's flow chart updates in real time, indicating which tasks are currently running, completed, or have encountered issues. This enables you to identify any potential problems and take corrective action promptly.

Figure 6-50. The current run of the "School Demo Job" job

Reviewing task results

Upon the job's run completion, it's essential to review the results of each task to ensure that they have executed correctly and produced the expected outcomes.

Task 1: Landing data

Clicking the first task, in the job's run interface, reveals its results within an executed copy of the notebook, as shown in Figure 6-51. This shows that two new input files have been successfully landed in the source directory, confirming that the data landing process executed correctly.

Figure 6-51. The result of executing the Land_New_Data task

With the data landing confirmed, let's move forward to Task 2 and examine the DLT Pipeline.

Task 2: DLT pipeline

When reviewing the output of the DLT task, you'll notice that it doesn't display results directly in the run interface. Instead, a link is provided that directs you to the DLT pipeline UI, as shown in Figure 6-52.

Figure 6-52. The output of the Run_DLT_Pipeline task

By clicking this link, you'll be redirected to the DLT interface, where you can view the status of the pipeline run with the new data. This allows you to explore the pipeline's execution and verify that it has processed the data correctly.

Task 3: Output exploration

Clicking the third task reveals the output of its associated notebook, showcasing the final processed data. This displays the output of all cells in the notebook, including the content of the pipeline storage location and the results from the gold table. The updated table results provide a clear confirmation that the data workflow has been successfully executed through each processing stage of the task sequence.

Debugging Jobs

In our previous scenario, we demonstrated the successful execution of a data work-flow, where every task was carefully designed to produce a correct output. However, in the real world, things don't always go as planned. In this section, we'll explore what happens when our data workflow encounters an unexpected error, leading to a job failure.

Let's consider a simple example in the "6.2 - Output Exploration" notebook, which is the source notebook for the third task in our job. Let's try to query a table that doesn't exist in our database, such as a table for the daily students' courses in the USA:

```
SELECT * FROM hive_metastore.school_dlt_db.usa_daily_student_courses
```

When we run the job, the system attempts to access the specified table. However, due to the table's nonexistence, the job fails as expected, as illustrated in Figure 6-53.

Figure 6-53. The failed run of the "School Demo Job" job

To diagnose the issue, we click the failed task, where detailed error messages can be accessed. In this case, the error message indicates a "table or view not found" `AnalysisException`, as shown in Figure 6-54.

Figure 6-54. The result of executing the "Output Exploration" task

Repairing runs

Let's explore how to correct the error and successfully rerun the job. This involves fixing the erroneous query and utilizing the "Repair run" feature in Databricks Jobs.

To resolve the issue caused by querying a nonexistent table, we need to correct the table name in our notebook. As an alternative, let's query the daily students' courses in an existing region, such as France, instead of the USA:

```
SELECT * FROM hive_metastore.school_dlt_db.fr_daily_student_courses
```

With this correction in place, we can revisit our failed run and explore our options for recovery.

Upon reviewing the details page for the failed run, we're presented with a valuable feature—the "Repair run" button, as displayed in Figure 6-55. This button offers a convenient way to handle such scenarios, allowing you to rerun only the failed tasks, rather than re-executing the entire job from scratch.

Figure 6-55. The" Repair run" feature

By clicking the "Repair run" button, we can choose which tasks to rerun, as illustrated in Figure 6-56. In our case, only the Output_Exploration task is selected by default to be re-executed.

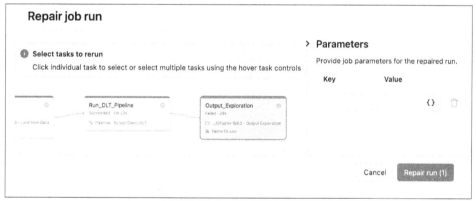

Figure 6-56. Task selection for run repair

After confirming the tasks to be rerun, we click "Repair run (1)" to initiate the process. Databricks intelligently manages the workflow, executing only the corrected task while preserving the results of previously successful tasks.

Upon completion of the run repair, the job status should reflect success, confirming that the job has been successfully repaired. You can verify that the output now includes the data from the gold table of France, indicating that the corrected query has been executed without issues.

This seamless recovery process showcases the robustness and flexibility of Databricks Jobs, empowering you to rapidly recover from errors and restore your workflows to optimal performance.

Conclusion

In conclusion, we've reached the end of our journey through the world of production pipeline development and orchestration. We've explored how to create and execute a complete data workflow, how to handle its errors and exceptions, and how to repair it and recover from failures. With these skills in hand, you can now confidently tackle complex data workflows, ensuring efficient and reliable data processing.

Sample Exam Questions

Conceptual Question

1. An ETL solution uses a declarative approach to establish reliable and maintainable data processing pipelines, while preserving table dependencies and ensuring data quality.

Which of the following technologies corresponds to this definition?

A. Delta Live tables

B. Delta Lake

C. Spark Structured Streaming

D. Databricks jobs

E. Databricks workflows

Code-Based Question

2. A data engineer is developing a Delta Live Tables pipeline to handle data ingestion from a source system that generates events reflecting dataset changes. Each change event includes metadata indicating whether a record was inserted, updated, or deleted, along with a timestamp for ordering the events.

Which command would best enable the data engineer to solve this problem?

A. `UPSERT`

B. `COPY INTO`

C. `INSERT INTO`

D. `MERGE INTO`

E. `APPLY CHANGES INTO`

The correct answers to these questions are listed in Appendix C.

Exploring Databricks SQL

Databricks SQL is an essential component within the Databricks ecosystem, simplifying the process of querying, visualizing, and alerting on data. It empowers data analysts and business intelligence professionals to easily uncover insights and extract value from their data. This chapter explores Databricks SQL, covering its various components, such as SQL endpoints, dashboards, and alerts.

What Is Databricks SQL?

Databricks SQL (DBSQL) is a data warehousing solution specifically designed for scalable business intelligence applications. It offers features for executing and managing SQL queries, creating interactive dashboards, and setting up alerts, all while maintaining unified governance. With Databricks SQL, teams can easily analyze and visualize large datasets, share insights, and make data-driven decisions.

In the Databricks workspace, you can find Databricks SQL tools in the left sidebar, under the SQL section, as illustrated in Figure 7-1.

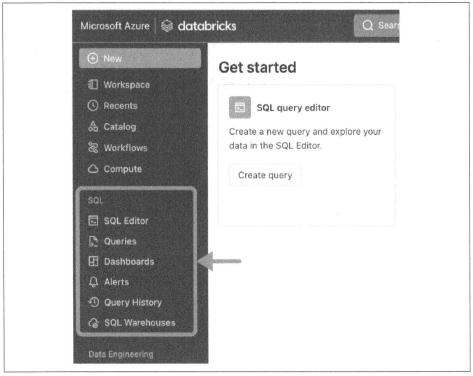

Figure 7-1. Databricks SQL menu

As shown, Databricks SQL offers a range of new options, including the following:

SQL editor
An intuitive interface for writing and executing SQL queries

Queries
A repository for storing and managing frequently used queries

Dashboards
A visualization tool for creating interactive dashboards

Alerts
A feature for setting up custom alerts and notifications based on data changes

Query history
A log of executed queries, facilitating tracking and auditing

SQL warehouses
Scalable compute resources optimized for executing SQL workloads

Each of these components plays a crucial role in leveraging the full potential of Databricks SQL. Let's take a closer look at each of them, starting with SQL warehouses.

Creating SQL Warehouses

SQL warehouses are the backbone of Databricks SQL, providing the computational power necessary to run SQL queries at scale. They are essentially compute clusters based on Apache Spark and the Photon engine. These clusters are highly optimized for SQL workloads and provide some additional benefits that enhance performance and increase concurrency compared to traditional clusters. This enables you to efficiently manage and execute your queries and dashboards.

To get started with SQL warehouses, let's navigate to the SQL Warehouses tab in the left sidebar of the Databricks workspace. This page is the control center for creating and managing your SQL computational resources, as shown in Figure 7-2.

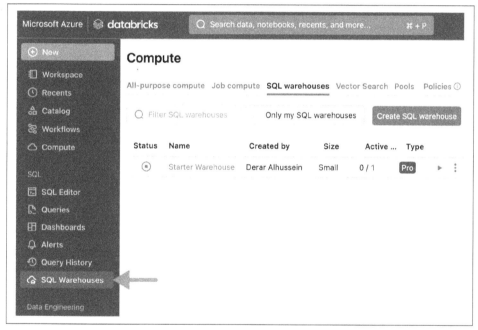

Figure 7-2. SQL warehouses page

Configuring a SQL Warehouse

To set up a new SQL warehouse, click the "Create SQL warehouse" blue button, which will prompt a configuration window, as illustrated in Figure 7-3. Here, we can specify the details of our new warehouse.

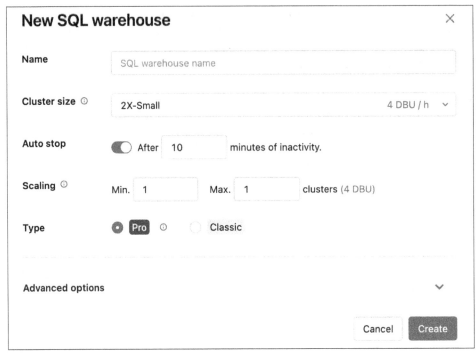

Figure 7-3. SQL warehouse configuration window

Let's create a SQL warehouse instance, which we'll call "Demo Warehouse." For this demonstration, we'll set the cluster size to 2X-Small to allocate minimal resources suitable for light workloads. We will leave all other options at their default settings and proceed to click Create.

SQL warehouses typically take a few minutes to start. However, you may also have the option to choose a Serverless compute type, as illustrated in Figure 7-4. This offers a fully managed service by Databricks that does not require managing infrastructure in your cloud account. It starts instantly, without the need to wait for provisioning any resources.

Figure 7-4. SQL warehouse configuration window with Serverless compute type

Once the creation process is complete, our SQL warehouse is running and ready to be used, as shown in Figure 7-5.

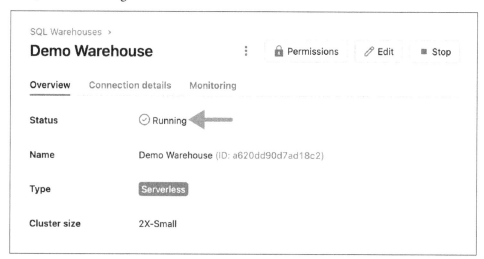

Figure 7-5. Fully operational SQL warehouse

SQL Endpoints

A key feature of SQL Warehouses is the provisioning of SQL endpoints, which allow external business intelligence (BI) or other SQL-based tools to connect and access data in the lakehouse. To connect to your SQL warehouse, you can refer to the connection information provided under the "Connection details" tab, as shown in Figure 7-6.

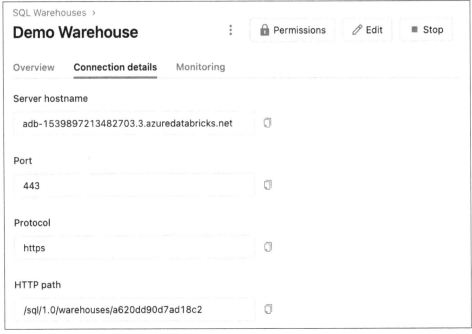

Figure 7-6. Connection details of the SQL warehouse

With our SQL warehouse up and running, we can now leverage its capabilities for an array of SQL workloads. In the next sections, we will explore how to use the SQL warehouse to create dashboards, run queries, and more.

Designing Dashboards

Dashboards in Databricks SQL offer a dynamic way to visualize data and insights derived from SQL queries. They enable you to create interactive and shareable visualizations of your data, making it easier to understand and communicate complex information.

To begin working with dashboards, navigate to the Dashboards tab in the left sidebar of your Databricks workspace. Here, you can manage your existing dashboards or create new ones, as shown in Figure 7-7. You can also explore sample dashboards by clicking the "View samples gallery" button.

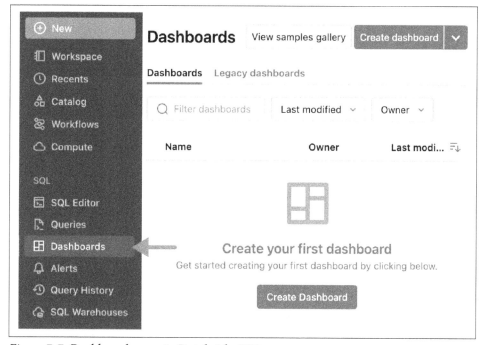

Figure 7-7. Dashboards page in Databricks SQL

Creating a New Dashboard

To create a new dashboard, click the "Create dashboard" button in the upper-right corner of the page. This opens the dashboard editor interface, which consists of two panes: the Canvas pane and the Data pane, as illustrated in Figure 7-8:

Canvas pane
This is where you design your dashboard. You can drag and drop different visual elements, such as charts, graphs, and tables, to create a visually appealing and informative layout.

Data pane
In this pane, you define the source datasets for your dashboard. There, you can specify the data sources that will feed data to your visualizations.

Figure 7-8. Dashboard editor interface

At the top of the dashboard editor interface interface, you will see a default name assigned to the dashboard (*New Dashboard yyyy-MM-dd HH:mm:ss*). Click this name to rename it to something more descriptive, such as "School Demo Dashboard." This gives our dashboard a clear and descriptive title.

Before you can start building your dashboard, make sure you have a SQL warehouse connected, as displayed in Figure 7-9.

Figure 7-9. Connecting a running SQL warehouse to the dashboard

The dashboard's functionality depends on the SQL warehouse, as it is responsible for retrieving data and displaying the visualizations.

Creating data sources

The Data pane in the dashboard editor interface allows you to define the source data-sets for your dashboard, as displayed in Figure 7-10. This is a crucial step in building a functional dashboard, as these datasets provide the input data for your visualizations.

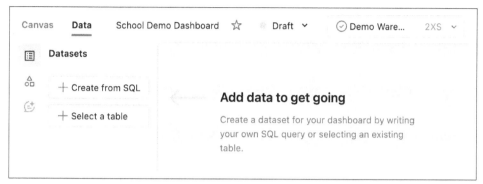

Figure 7-10. Dashboard Data pane

Each dataset is defined as either a SQL query or a table, which provides flexibility and power in shaping your data insights. Let's add a new dataset by clicking the "+ Create from SQL" button in the left panel. This opens a SQL editor to write our custom query, as shown in Figure 7-11.

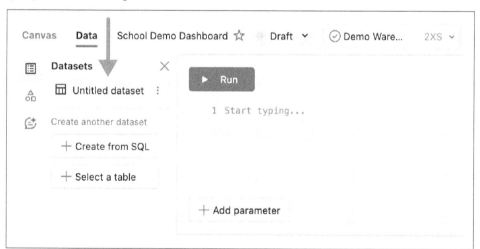

Figure 7-11. Dashboard Data pane

For this demonstration, we will write a SQL query that combines the two gold tables created previously by the "School" DLT pipeline. But before we dive into the query, let's rename the dataset to a meaningful name that can be easily identified in the

Canvas pane. To do this, simply double-click the default dataset name (*Untitled dataset*) in the left panel and enter a new name, such as "Daily Student Courses."

Now, let's write our SQL query that consolidates the school statistics data from two regions: the United Kingdom and France.

```sql
SELECT "United Kingdom" region, student_id, f_name, l_name,
       order_date, courses_counts
FROM hive_metastore.school_dlt_db.uk_daily_student_courses


UNION


SELECT "France" region, student_id, f_name, l_name,
       order_date, courses_counts
FROM hive_metastore.school_dlt_db.fr_daily_student_courses
```

After writing the query, click the Run button to view and verify the query output. This ensures that your dataset is correctly defined and ready for use in your dashboard.

Remember, you can add additional datasets depending on your requirements, allowing you to incorporate multiple data sources and insights into your dashboard. These datasets can also be queries that leverage functions during execution or provide advanced filtering logic, which can be very useful for gaining deeper insights into your data.

With our dataset created, we can now switch to the Canvas pane to start building our dashboard. This is where we will design and lay out our visualizations, leveraging the data from our newly created dataset.

Designing visualizations

The Canvas pane enables you to design your dashboard by adding visualizations and filters. From the toolbar at the bottom, you can pick a widget to add, including a visualization, text box, or filter, as illustrated in Figure 7-12.

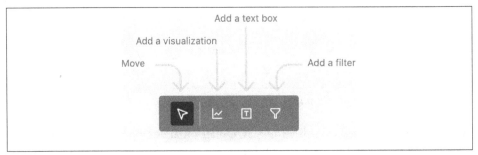

Figure 7-12. Toolbar in the Canvas pane

To create a visualization, simply pick the visualization widget and place it on the Canvas pane. Databricks SQL supports a wide range of visualization types, including area, bar, combo, counter, heatmap, histogram, line, pie, pivot, scatter, and table charts. This flexibility allows you to choose the most appropriate and effective visualization type to communicate your data insights.

Once you've added a visualization widget to the Canvas pane, a configuration panel for this visualization will appear on the right side, as illustrated in Figure 7-13. Here, you can specify the details of your visualization, including the dataset, visualization type, aggregation, and formatting options.

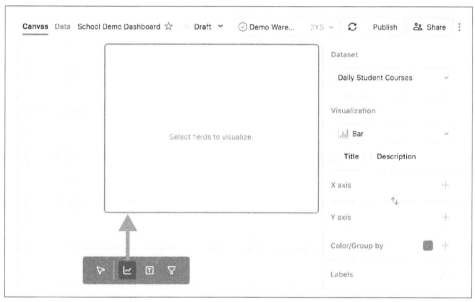

Figure 7-13. The configuration panel of a visualization widget

Let's configure this visualization widget to display a pie graph that shows the total course counts per region. To achieve this, complete the following steps:

1. Selecting the dataset: First, select the dataset "Daily Student Courses" that we created in the Data pane. This dataset contains the data we want to visualize.

2. Choosing the visualization type: Next, select the visualization type. In this case, we want to create a pie graph, so we choose the "Pie" option from the list of supported visualizations.

3. Customize the visualization settings: For a pie graph, we need to set the angle field and group by field. To do this, we do the following:

a. Set the angle field to SUM(courses_counts) by clicking the plus (+) button and selecting the courses_counts field. This will default to the sum aggregation function, which calculates the total number of courses. If needed, choose an alternative aggregation function to match your application.

b. Choose the "region" field as the color/group by field to display multiple categories in the graph.

After configuring these settings, you should see a pie graph that displays the total course counts per region, as illustrated in Figure 7-14.

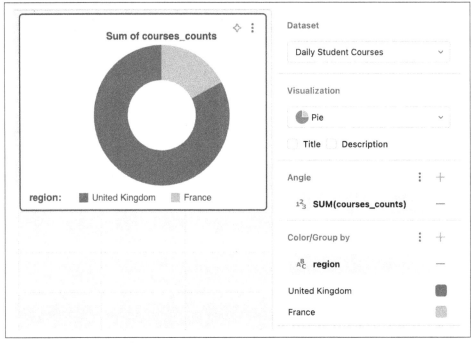

Figure 7-14. Pie graph for the total course counts per region

You can further customize this visualization by giving it a descriptive title, modifying its color scheme, and adjusting its size and position. This helps make the visualization more visually appealing and easier to understand for viewers.

In the same way, you can add other visualizations of different types depending on your business needs. By combining various visualizations, you can create a rich and informative dashboard that provides a comprehensive view of your data.

Defining filters

In addition to visualizations, Databricks SQL allows you to add dynamic filters to your dashboard. These filters enable viewers to refine the data presented in visualizations by filtering on specific fields. To add a filter to your dashboard, simply pick the filter widget from the toolbar at the bottom and place it on the Canvas pane, as shown in Figure 7-15.

Figure 7-15. Adding a filter to the dashboard

Next, we need to configure the widget to filter based on a specific field—in this case, the "region" field. To achieve this, follow these simple steps:

1. Navigate to the right-hand panel of the selected filter widget.
2. Locate the Fields section and click the plus (+) button.
3. Select the "region" field.

Figure 7-16 displays the updated canvas after configuring the region filter.

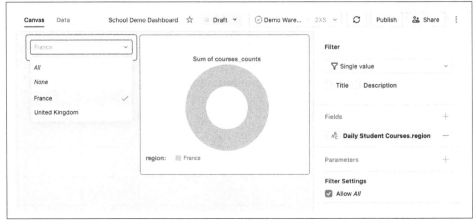

Figure 7-16. Dashboard view after applying the region filter

With this filter in place, our visualizations will update dynamically depending on the selected region. This means that when a user selects a specific region from the filter, the visualizations will automatically refresh to display only the data relevant to that region. This interactive filtering capability enables users to quickly and easily explore the data from different perspectives.

Sharing a Dashboard

When you create a new dashboard, it is initially saved as a draft, indicated by the Draft label in the top bar, as shown in Figure 7-17. This draft status allows you to refine and finalize your dashboard before sharing it with others.

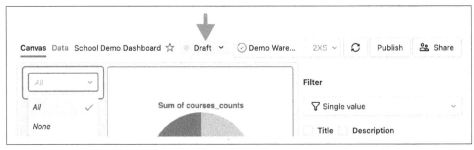

Figure 7-17. Draft version of the dashboard

You can share the draft with other users in your workspace to facilitate collaborative development and feedback. To share a dashboard, simply click the Share button at the top right of the dashboard editor. This opens a window where you can add users and set their permissions, allowing you to control who can manage, edit, run, or view the dashboard draft (Figure 7-18).

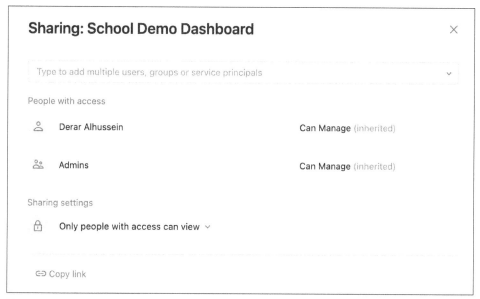

Figure 7-18. Setting permissions for sharing the dashboard draft

By assigning appropriate permissions, you can control the level of access each user has to your dashboard, ensuring a secure and controlled environment for collaboration. It's worth mentioning that when you share a dashboard draft, all users interact with the data and visualizations using their own credentials. This means that their individual permissions and access levels are applied, preventing unauthorized access to the underlying data.

Publishing a Dashboard

Once you're satisfied with your dashboard draft, you can publish it to create a clean copy that can be shared with any user in your organization. Publishing a dashboard allows others to view and interact with the visualizations and make data-driven decisions.

To publish your dashboard, click the Publish button at the top right, as displayed in Figure 7-19.

Figure 7-19. Publishing the dashboard

This will open a window that prompts you to choose how the published dashboard will access live data and run queries. You can select to use either your own embedded credentials or those of the viewing user, as shown in Figure 7-20.

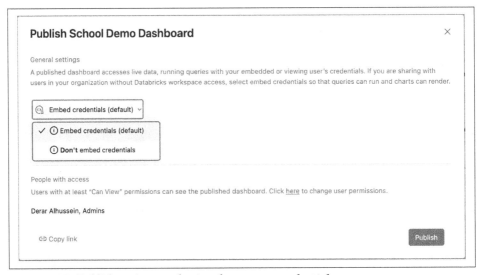

Figure 7-20. Publish options—selecting data access credentials

If you are publishing the dashboard for users in your organization without access to your Databricks workspace, select the option to embed credentials. This ensures that the dashboard's queries can run and visualizations can render properly for these users.

After publishing, you can view the live dashboard by clicking the Draft label at the top bar and selecting the published version, as displayed in Figure 7-21. This indicates that the dashboard is now live and accessible to others via its published link.

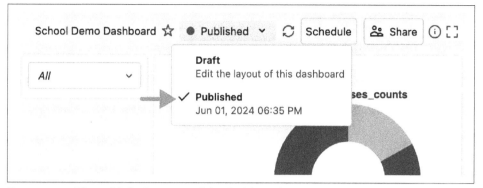

Figure 7-21. The published version of the dashboard

Republishing a New Version

The published version of your dashboard remains unchanged until you publish again. Meanwhile, you can continue making modifications and improvements in the draft version without affecting the publicly shared copy. This allows you to easily design and test a newer version of your dashboard before resharing it with your audience.

To switch from the published to the draft version, simply click the label at the top bar and select Draft, as illustrated in Figure 7-22.

Figure 7-22. Switching between published and draft versions of the dashboard

By effectively managing draft and published versions, you can continuously improve your dashboards while providing a consistent experience for end users.

Managing SQL Queries

Databricks SQL provides a comprehensive solution for managing SQL queries, enabling you to create ad hoc queries, save them in a workspace directory, and schedule automatic refreshes or alerts based on their results. This flexibility enables efficient data exploration and reporting.

To start creating SQL queries, let's navigate to the SQL Editor tab from the left sidebar of the workspace. This interface provides an integrated environment for writing, executing, and scheduling SQL queries, as illustrated in Figure 7-23.

Figure 7-23. SQL editor in Databricks SQL

Before writing any queries, ensure you are connected to a running SQL warehouse, as illustrated in Figure 7-24. This connection provides you with the computational power necessary for executing your SQL queries. If you attach it to a warehouse that has shut down, it will start automatically.

Figure 7-24. Connecting a running SQL warehouse to the SQL editor

On the left panel of the SQL editor, you'll find the schema browser where you can navigate your databases and tables. Expand the hive_metastore catalog to view the school_dlt_db database, which contains all the tables created by your DLT pipeline.

To view the columns of a table, simply expand the table in the schema browser, as shown in Figure 7-25. This provides a detailed list of columns as well as some indicators for column types, enabling you to understand the structure of your data and write more informed and accurate queries.

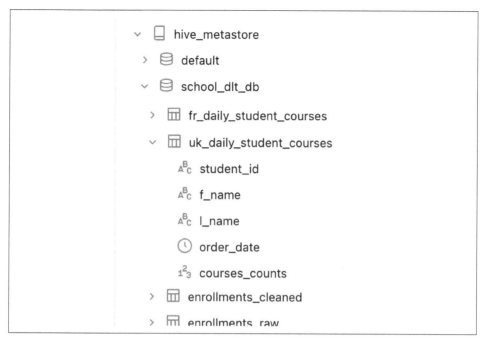

Figure 7-25. Exploring table columns in the schema browser

Writing a SQL Query

The SQL editor simplifies the process of writing queries by allowing you to interactively insert tables and columns into the query text. This feature allows you to quickly add the necessary objects to your query without having to type them out manually.

To insert a table or column into your query text, you can simply hover over the object name and click the double arrows button next to it, as illustrated in Figure 7-26.

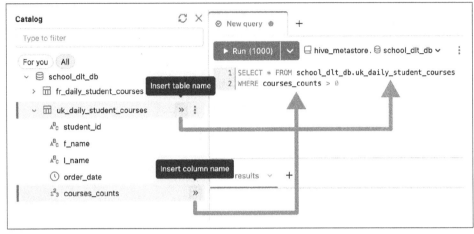

Figure 7-26. Inserting tables and columns into the query text

This convenient feature significantly speeds up query composition, ensuring accuracy and reducing manual input errors.

To illustrate the simplicity of writing queries in Databricks SQL, let's construct a basic query. Here is an example:

```
SELECT * FROM hive_metastore.school_dlt_db.uk_daily_student_courses
WHERE courses_counts > 0
```

Once the query is written, you can execute it by clicking the Run button in the SQL editor. The results will be displayed in the results pane below the editor. Figure 7-27 showcases the results of our query, which returns 123 records that meet the specified criteria.

	A^B_C st	Create custom table	e	📈 Visualization	ourses_counts
1	S011		1	▽ Filter	1
2	S007	Download CSV		{} Parameter	2
3	S008	Download TSV	1		1
4	S008	Download Excel		2022-07-27T00:00:00.000	1
5	S005	Copy results to clipboard		2022-07-16T00:00:00.000	2
6	S010..			2022-07-21T00:00:00.000	1
7	S00502	Elke	Feedome	2022-07-26T00:00:00.000	2

Raw results ⌄   +   ✕

🕐 502 ms | 123 rows returned   Refreshed **just now**

Figure 7-27. Query results in the SQL editor

From this pane, you can download the result set or create standalone visualizations, which can easily be added to new or existing dashboards.

Saving a Query

Once we have written and executed our query, we may want to save it for future use. Databricks SQL provides a convenient way to save our queries, making it easy to reuse them or share them with others.

To save our query, we simply click the Save button located at the top bar of the query editor. This will prompt us to give our query a name, as displayed in Figure 7-28. In our case, let's name our query `school_stats`. Note that you can also name your query directly in the query tab, just like other objects in the workspace.

Figure 7-28. Saving a query in the SQL editor

Later in this chapter, we'll discuss how to effectively manage our saved SQL queries and leverage them to set up customizable alerts.

Scheduling a Query

Scheduling queries in Databricks SQL allows you to automate the refresh of query results, ensuring that data is up-to-date without manual intervention. This feature is particularly useful when working with dynamic data that changes frequently, as it allows you to stay informed about the latest insights and trends.

To add a schedule to our query, we click the Schedule button located at the top bar of the query editor and then click "Add schedule," as shown in Figure 7-29.

Figure 7-29. Adding a schedule to a query in the SQL editor

This opens a window with scheduling options, allowing us to specify when and how often the query should run, as illustrated in Figure 7-30.

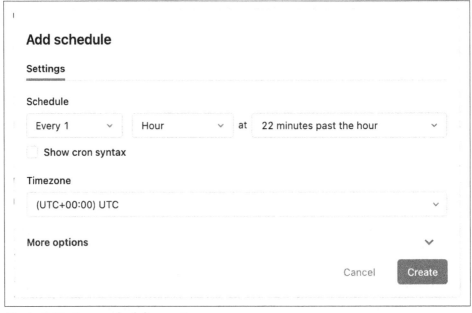

Figure 7-30. Query scheduling options

By scheduling queries to run at regular intervals, you significantly reduce the manual workload involved in maintaining up-to-date datasets. This is particularly useful for reports and other scenarios where fresh insights are critical or where queries may have long running times.

Browsing Saved Queries

Once we have saved our queries, we need a convenient way to access and manage them. Databricks SQL provides a dedicated interface for browsing saved queries, making it easy to find, organize, and reuse our queries.

To explore our saved queries, we navigate to the Queries tab on the left sidebar of the workspace, as shown in Figure 7-31. This tab provides a centralized location for all our saved queries, allowing us to quickly find and access the queries we need.

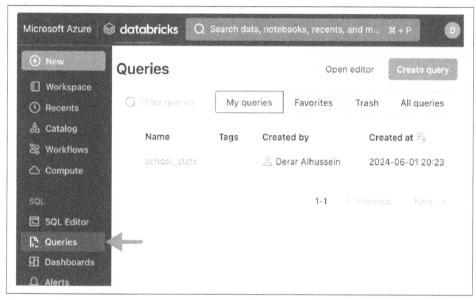

Figure 7-31. Queries interface in Databricks SQL

As shown, this tab displays a list of all our saved queries, along with relevant information such as the query name, creator name, and creation time. We can sort and filter the list to narrow down our search, making it easy to find specific queries or groups of queries.

At the top of the interface, there are also tabs for favorite queries we might reference frequently and trashed queries we want to review from time to time. Overall, the Queries page provides an organized and efficient way to manage our queries, allowing us to reuse our work and accelerate our data analysis tasks.

Setting Up Alerts

In Databricks SQL, we can take our data analysis to the next level by setting up alerts. Alerts are a powerful feature that enables us to monitor our data and receive notifications when reported values deviate from expected thresholds. By leveraging our saved queries, we can create alerts that periodically run queries, evaluate defined conditions, and send notifications when a condition is met.

In this demonstration, we will create an alert that notifies us when there is high demand for courses. This alert will be triggered when the number of course enrollments exceeds a threshold of 1,000, indicating high demand.

Creating an Alert

To create an alert, we navigate to the Alerts page from the left sidebar, as displayed in Figure 7-32. This interface displays all previously created alerts and their most recent statuses, serving as a reference for managing alerts. From here, we click "Create alert" in the top-right corner to start configuring the new alert.

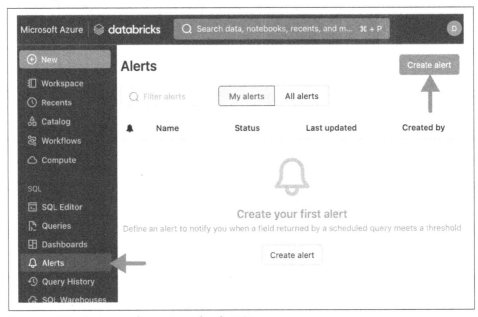

Figure 7-32. Alerts interface in Databricks SQL

First, let's configure the basis details of the alert, as shown in Figure 7-33.

Figure 7-33. Basic configurations of the new alert

Provide a descriptive name for the alert that reflects its purpose or the specific metric and source it monitors. For instance, let's name our alert `courses_high_demand`. Then, choose the saved query that will be executed to evaluate the alert condition. This query should return the data you want to monitor. In our case, let's choose our saved query titled `school_stats`.

Next, let's proceed by defining the condition that will trigger the alert, as illustrated in Figure 7-34.

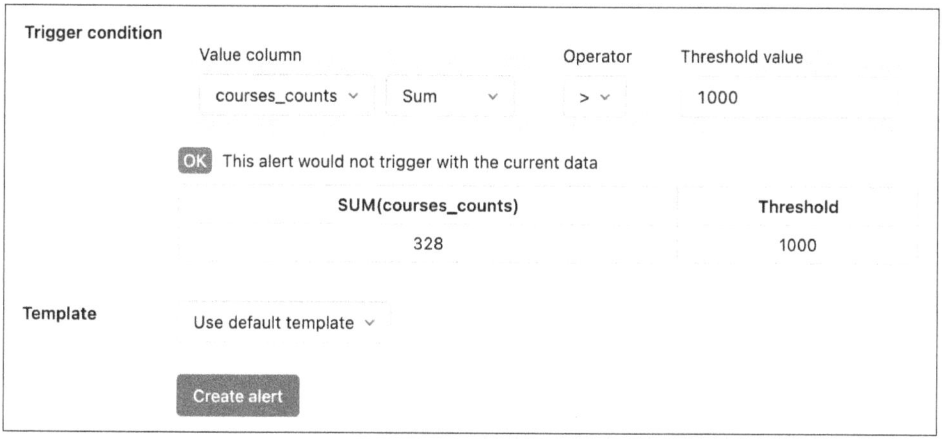

Figure 7-34. Condition configurations of the new alert

In this example, we set the value column to `courses_counts` with a threshold of a sum greater than 1,000. This means the alert will trigger if the total count of courses exceeds 1,000. Currently, the value in the table is 328, which is below the defined threshold.

Leave all other options at their default settings (*https://oreil.ly/GMEjA*), and click "Create alert" to finalize the creation process. Figure 7-35 displays the newly created alert, showcasing the configured settings.

Figure 7-35. *The* courses_high_demand *alert*

Now that we've successfully created our alert, the next essential step is to set its schedule.

Scheduling the Alert

To ensure timely notifications, it is important to schedule how frequently you want to check for alerts. When you schedule an alert, it periodically runs its underlying query and evaluates the alert criteria according to this schedule. If the criteria are met, notifications are sent to defined destinations. Notably, this scheduling is separate from any other schedule that may be associated with the underlying query.

To add a schedule to our alert, we click the "Add schedule" link in the schedules section, as illustrated in Figure 7-36.

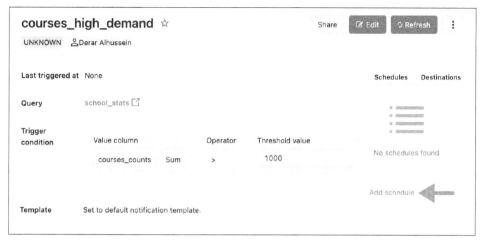

Figure 7-36. Adding a schedule to the courses_high_demand alert

This opens a window with scheduling options, allowing you to specify when and how often the alert should be evaluated, as shown in Figure 7-37.

Add schedule ✕

Settings   Destinations

Schedule

| Every 1 ⌄ | Hour ⌄ | at | 54 minutes past the hour ⌄ |

☐ Show cron syntax

Timezone

(UTC+00:00) UTC ⌄

More options ⌄

Cancel   Create

Figure 7-37. Alert scheduling options

After defining the schedule settings, you need to configure the notification destinations by clicking the Destinations tab, as illustrated in Figure 7-38. You can set up notifications to be sent to multiple email addresses or to system destinations (*https://oreil.ly/YG1MH*) such as Slack, Microsoft Teams, or any webhook-based service.

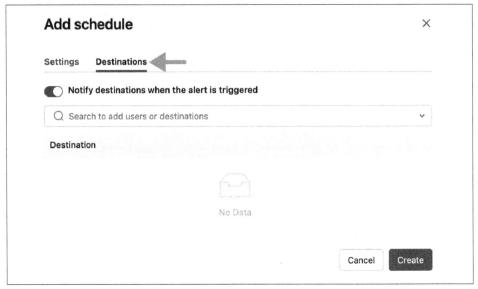

Figure 7-38. Alert destinations configuration

To add a destination, we use the drop-down menu to select an available notification destination or start typing a username from the workspace to add their email address. This allows us to customize the notification recipients and ensure that the right users are informed when the alert is triggered.

Finally, let's click Create to save our changes and activate the alert.

Now, on the next scheduled execution, if the total value of `courses_counts` changes and exceeds the defined threshold of 1,000, the alert will be triggered, and we will receive a notification at the configured destinations.

By setting up and scheduling alerts in Databricks SQL, you can ensure that critical business metrics are continuously monitored, and you receive timely notifications whenever important conditions are met. This allows for prompt actions and informed decision-making.

Conclusion

In conclusion, Databricks SQL provides a robust data warehousing solution, offering a comprehensive suite of tools for efficiently managing and analyzing data. Through its intuitive interface and robust features, you can easily create scalable SQL warehouses, design informative dashboards, and manage complex queries. By mastering these skills, you can unlock the full potential of your data and drive business insights at scale.

Sample Exam Questions

Conceptual Questions

1. Which of the following compute resources is required to render a dashboard in Databricks SQL?

A. A job cluster.

B. An all-purpose cluster.

C. A SQL warehouse.

D. A BI engine.

E. None of the above! Databricks dashboards don't require compute resources to render visualizations.

2. A data engineer is setting up an alert in Databricks SQL to ensure timely action is taken when an anomaly is detected in a data flow. They want to notify the data operations team when this alert is triggered.

Which of the following notification destinations is supported in Databricks and can be configured by the data engineer in response to a triggered alert?

A. Webhook-based service.

B. WhatsApp.

C. SMS.

D. All of the above options are valid notification destinations in Databricks.

E. None of the above notification destinations is supported in Databricks.

The correct answers to these questions are listed in Appendix C.

Implementing Data Governance

Databricks offers a robust data governance model designed to ensure the security, quality, and compliance of data throughout its lifecycle. This chapter delves into the key components of the Databricks data governance model, with a focus on data security. We will specifically examine data access management within the traditional Hive metastore and compare it with Databricks' governance solution, Unity Catalog.

What Is Data Governance?

Data governance is a strategic approach to managing data within an organization, ensuring that data is accurate, secure, and used responsibly. It involves the development and enforcement of policies and procedures to control data across various stages of its lifecycle—from ingestion and storage to processing and sharing. Data governance incorporates several key components, which are illustrated in Figure 8-1.

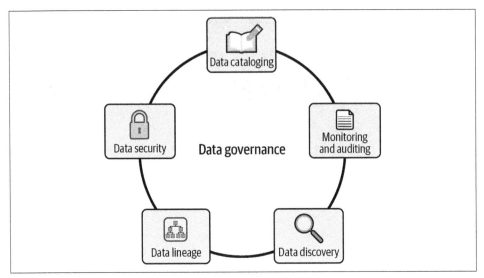

Figure 8-1. Components of data governance

Data cataloging
> Effective data governance requires a comprehensive understanding of an organization's data assets. A data catalog plays a crucial role in this process by serving as a centralized repository for metadata, which facilitates efficient data discovery and access.

Data security
> Robust data governance involves defining data access permissions to ensure that only authorized individuals or groups can access specific data. This practice is essential for maintaining data confidentiality and ensuring compliance with regulations such as the European General Data Protection Regulation (GDPR) (*https://gdpr-info.eu*).

Monitoring and auditing
> Comprehensive auditing of data access and usage is a fundamental aspect of strong data governance. It involves monitoring who is accessing the data, as well as when and how it is being used. This practice helps organizations ensure compliance with data protection regulations and reduce the risk of unauthorized access.

Data lineage
> Data lineage refers to the tracking and visualization of the flow of data assets from their origin to their final destination. This is vital for data governance as it ensures transparency, data reliability, and compliance. By mapping dependencies between different resources, data lineage facilitates troubleshooting and identifying potential impacts of changes.

Data discovery

A key element of data governance is ensuring that data is easily discoverable, allowing data teams to efficiently locate data assets across the organization. This helps prevent data duplication and promotes better data utilization.

Databricks addresses these components with its new governance solution, Unity Catalog. Unity Catalog offers advanced governance capabilities, including fine-grained access control, data auditing, lineage tracking, and enhanced data discovery. Previously, Databricks relied on the Hive metastore, which was primarily focused on managing metadata for tables and schemas and had limited governance features.

In the following sections, we will explore how data governance is implemented within Databricks by examining two key aspects: managing data security in the existing Hive metastore and exploring advanced data governance with Unity Catalog. By understanding the transition from the Hive metastore to Unity Catalog, you will gain insights into how Databricks has evolved its data governance strategy to meet the demands of modern data management.

Managing Data Security in the Hive Metastore

In Databricks, the Hive metastore is the traditional, legacy solution for managing metadata and ensuring data governance. It serves as a local repository for metadata about tables, columns, partitions, and databases in each workspace, facilitating efficient querying and data management. Effective data security in the Hive metastore is essential to ensure that sensitive data is protected and accessed only by authorized users.

The data governance model of the Hive metastore focuses on controlling access to data objects within the `hive_metastore` catalog. This model enables administrators to perform key operations programmatically through Spark SQL, including granting, denying, and revoking access permissions. These capabilities are used to manage who can view or manipulate data, thus supporting robust data governance.

Granting Permissions

The primary command used for managing data access is the GRANT statement. This command is used to provide a specific privilege on a data object to a user or group. The general syntax for this command is as follows:

```
GRANT <privilege> ON <object-type> <object-name> TO <user or group>
```

For example, to grant read access on a table named `product_info` to a user with the email *user_1@example.com*, the following command is used:

```
GRANT SELECT ON TABLE product_info TO user_1@example.com
```

In this example, user_1 is given permission to perform SELECT operations on the product_info table, allowing them to read data from this object. Such precise control helps ensure that users have access only to the data they need, thus maintaining data security and integrity.

Besides tables, permissions can also be granted on various other objects. Let's explore these different types of securable objects available in the Hive metastore.

Data object types

In the Hive metastore, permission management extends across various types of data objects. The hierarchy of these objects is structured into three primary levels, as illustrated in Figure 8-2.

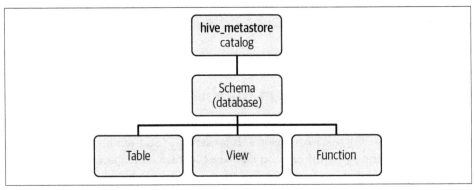

Figure 8-2. Data object hierarchy in the Hive metastore

The hive_metastore *catalog*
> At the top of this hierarchy is the hive_metastore catalog. This catalog acts as a container for all data objects managed by the metastore. In Databricks, the Hive metastore is limited to this single default catalog, meaning that you cannot create additional catalogs within the Hive metastore.

Schemas (databases)
> Within the hive_metastore catalog, there are schemas (also known as databases). A schema is a logical grouping of tables, views, and functions. Schemas facilitate granular access control, enabling administrators to manage permissions at a more detailed level than the catalog.

Tables, views, and functions
> These objects are fundamental data objects within a schema This level is ideal for situations where access needs to be restricted to particular entities within a database.

Databricks provides granular control over access to any of these data objects using the GRANT statement:

```
GRANT <privilege> ON <object-type> <object-name> TO <user or group>
```

In this context, `<object-type>` indicates the type of securable object, as outlined in Table 8-1.

Table 8-1. Types of securable objects in the Hive metastore

Object	Scope
CATALOG	Controls access to the entire data catalog
SCHEMA	Controls access to a specific database
TABLE	Controls access to a managed or external table
VIEW	Controls access to a SQL view
FUNCTION	Controls access to a specific named function
ANY FILE	Controls access to the underlying file system

By specifying the appropriate object types, administrators can precisely manage permissions and ensure secure and efficient access control.

Having identified these types of data objects on which privileges can be configured, let's now examine the specific privileges that can be granted.

Object privileges

Object privileges are permissions that can be granted to users or groups to perform various actions on data objects within the metastore. These privileges are granted using the GRANT statement:

```
GRANT <privilege> ON <object-type> <object-name> TO <user or group>
```

In this context, `<privilege>` represents the specific action being allowed. Table 8-2 outlines the various privileges available in the Hive metastore and the capabilities they grant.

Table 8-2. Object privileges in the Hive metastore

Privilege	Ability
SELECT	Read access to an object.
MODIFY	Add, delete, and modify data within an object.
CREATE	Create new objects.
READ_METADATA	View an object and its metadata.
USAGE	Required to perform any action on a database object, but has no direct effect on its own.
ALL PRIVILEGES	Grants all the above privileges simultaneously.

Let's dive deeper to gain a comprehensive understanding of these privileges.

SELECT privilege. This privilege grants read access to an object. Users with the SELECT privilege can query and retrieve data from the database object, such as a table, but cannot modify it:

```
GRANT SELECT ON TABLE product_info TO user_1@example.com;
```

MODIFY privilege. The MODIFY privilege allows users to add new data, delete existing data, and make modifications to the data within the object. This is translated by the ability to perform INSERT, UPDATE, and DELETE operations on a table:

```
GRANT MODIFY ON TABLE product_info TO user_1@example.com;
```

CREATE privilege. With the CREATE privilege, a user can create new objects. This is typically used for creating tables, views, or other schema objects within the database:

```
GRANT CREATE ON SCHEMA sales_db TO user_1@example.com;
```

READ_METADATA privilege. This privilege permits users to view an object along with its metadata. Metadata includes information about the structure of the object and its properties.

```
GRANT READ_METADATA ON TABLE product_info TO user_1@example.com;
```

USAGE privilege. The USAGE privilege, while not providing any direct access or ability on its own, is a prerequisite for performing any other actions on a database object. It is often combined with other privileges to enable their functionalities:

```
GRANT USAGE ON SCHEMA sales_db TO user_1@example.com;
```

ALL PRIVILEGES. This is a comprehensive privilege that grants all the individual privileges mentioned previously to a user or group. It simplifies the process of assigning multiple permissions by bundling them together.

To illustrate the application of these privileges, consider a scenario where we want to provide a user with full control over the sales_db schema. To achieve this, we would use the following command:

```
GRANT ALL PRIVILEGES ON SCHEMA sales_db TO user_1@example.com;
```

This command ensures that user1 can read data, modify data, create new objects, and view metadata, and has the necessary USAGE privilege on the sales_db schema.

Granting privileges by role

In the Hive metastore, managing access to data objects is restricted to certain roles. To grant privileges on an object, one must be either a Databricks administrator or the owner of that particular object. Table 8-3 illustrates the different roles in the Hive metastore and the privileges that can be granted by each of them.

Table 8-3. Roles in the Hive metastore

Role	Can grant access privileges for
Databricks administrator	All objects in the catalog and the underlying file system
Catalog owner	All objects in the catalog
Database owner	All objects in the database
Database object owner	Only the specific object within the database (table, view, ...)

Let's explore the details of each role and its abilities:

Databricks administrator
> This role has the highest level of access, capable of granting privileges for all objects within the hive_metastore catalog as well as the underlying file system. This broad scope of authority enables comprehensive management and oversight of the data infrastructure.

Catalog owner
> A catalog owner has the ability to grant access privileges for all objects contained within the hive_metastore catalog. This includes databases, tables, views, and functions, allowing for centralized control at the catalog level.

Database owner
> Database owners are empowered to grant privileges for all objects within a single database. This includes tables, views, and functions within that particular database, ensuring that database-specific access control is managed efficiently.

Database object owner
> Database object owners can grant privileges solely for the object they own within the database, such as a table, view, or function.

Understanding these roles and their associated privileges is crucial for maintaining a well-organized and secure data environment. Properly assigning and managing these roles ensures that access control is enforced at the appropriate levels, reducing the risk of unauthorized access while facilitating efficient data management.

Advanced Privilege Management

In the Hive metastore, managing object privileges extends beyond merely granting access. You can also explicitly deny access and revoke previously granted permissions, providing a comprehensive set of tools to ensure precise control over data access.

REVOKE operation

The REVOKE operation removes permissions that were previously granted to a user or group. This operation is essential for dynamically managing access as organizational roles and requirements change.

The syntax is as follows:

```
REVOKE <privilege> ON <object-type> <object-name> FROM <user or group>
```

Here is an example of the operation:

```
REVOKE  SELECT  ON  TABLE  product_info  FROM  user_1@example.com
```

In this example, the command removes the previously granted SELECT permission on the product_info table from user1.

DENY operation

The DENY operation is used to explicitly prevent a user or group from accessing specific resources or performing certain actions. This operation takes precedence over any other permissions that might otherwise allow access, ensuring that certain users or groups are definitively blocked from specific actions.

The syntax is as follows:

```
DENY <privilege> ON <object-type> <object-name> TO <user or group>
```

Here is an example:

```
DENY  SELECT  ON  TABLE  product_info  TO  user_1@example.com
```

This command will prevent user1 from performing the SELECT action on the prod uct_info table, regardless of other granted permissions.

SHOW GRANTS operation

The SHOW GRANTS operation allows administrators to view the current permissions assigned to a specific object. This command is useful for auditing and verifying access controls, ensuring that only authorized users have the necessary permissions.

The syntax is as follows:

```
SHOW GRANTS ON <object-type> <object-name>
```

Here is an example of the operation:

```
SHOW GRANTS ON TABLE product_info
```

This command will list all the permissions granted to each user or group for the prod uct_info table, providing a clear overview of who has access and what actions they can perform.

With this clear understanding of object privileges, let's now turn our attention to the Databricks platform to see how these concepts can be applied in Databricks SQL.

Managing Permissions with Databricks SQL

In this section, we'll explore the practical steps for managing permissions for databases, tables, and views in the Hive metastore within the context of an HR example. We'll first cover the process of adding users and groups specific to HR personnel within the Databricks workspace. Then, we'll discuss assigning the appropriate permissions through Databricks SQL to ensure secure access to sensitive HR data.

Adding users

To begin managing permissions in Databricks SQL, we need to first add the designated users within our Databricks workspace. For this demonstration, we will add three fictional users: Alice, Bob, and Eve. Here's a step-by-step guide to adding them:

1. Navigate to user settings: In the upper-right corner of any Databricks page, click your username and select Settings from the drop-down menu.

2. Access identity management: From the left sidebar, select "Identity and access," and then click Manage next to Users, as displayed in Figure 8-3.

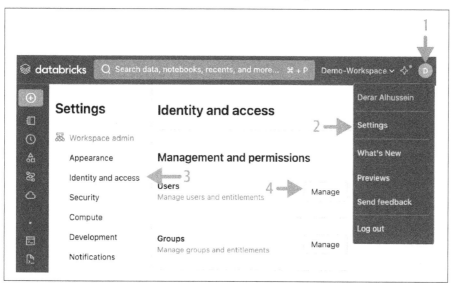

Figure 8-3. Identity and access settings in Databricks workspace

3. Add users: On the Users management page, click "Add user," and enter the email of each new user:

alice@example.com

bob@example.com

eve@example.com

Figure 8-4 illustrates the final outcome of the user additions.

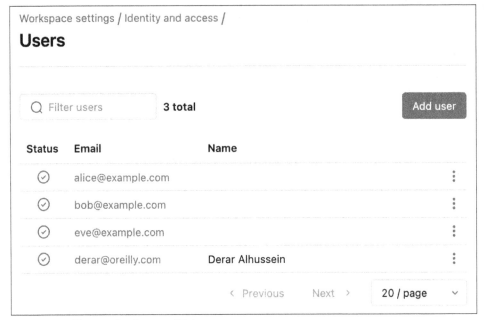

Figure 8-4. The result of user additions

With these users added to the workspace, we can now proceed to add a new group and assign permissions.

Adding groups

To streamline permission management and apply access controls across multiple users, groups can be utilized in Databricks. Here, we demonstrate how to add a group named hr_team and assign users to this group:

1. Access user settings: Navigate again to the Settings menu.

2. Access identity management: From the left sidebar, select "Identity and access," and then click Manage next to Groups, as shown in Figure 8-5.

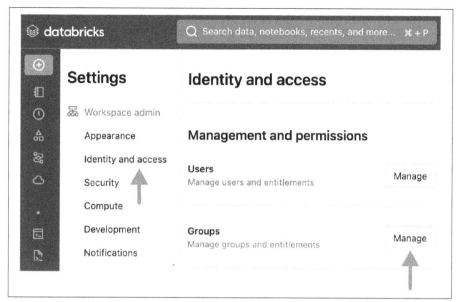

Figure 8-5. Identity and access management

3. Add group: On the Groups management page, click "Add group," enter the group name as hr_team, and confirm the addition. Figure 8-6 illustrates the result of the group addition.

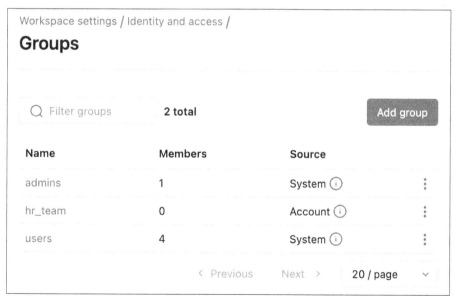

Figure 8-6. The Groups management page after adding the hr_team group

4. Add members to the group: Click the group name hr_team from the groups list to open the group settings. Under the Members tab, click "Add member," and add the users Alice (*alice@example.com*) and Bob (*bob@example.com*) to this group.

Figure 8-7 displays the final outcome of adding the hr_team group with its members.

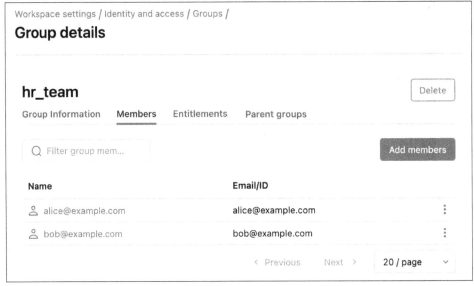

Figure 8-7. The result of adding the hr_team group with its members

By grouping users, permissions can be managed more efficiently. Permissions granted to the group will automatically apply to all its members, simplifying access control administration.

Creating data objects

For this demonstration, we will create some data objects in the Hive metastore, specifically focusing on creating a database and defining a table and a stored view within this database.

To follow along with this section, you will need to use Databricks SQL. Begin by navigating to the SQL editor located in the left sidebar of the Databricks workspace. Before executing any commands, ensure that a SQL warehouse you can use is running.

Our first step is to create a new database called hr_db within the hive_metastore catalog. The command for creating this database is as follows:

```
CREATE DATABASE IF NOT EXISTS hive_metastore.hr_db
LOCATION 'dbfs:/mnt/demo/hr_db.db';
```

After creating the database, the next step is to define a table and populate it with sample data. We will create a table named employees with columns for ID, name, salary, and city. To do this, execute the following SQL commands:

```
CREATE TABLE hive_metastore.hr_db.employees
(id INT, name STRING, salary DOUBLE, city STRING);


INSERT INTO hive_metastore.hr_db.employees
VALUES (1, "Felipe", 3000, "London"),
       (2, "Sachin", 3400, "New York"),
       (3, "Anna", 3600, "London"),
       (4, "Hong-Thai", 3200, "London"),
       (5, "Charlotte", 3500, "New York"),
       (6, "Amine", 3400, "New York"),
       (7, "Emily", 3200, "London");
```

In addition, create a view named london_employees_vw to display employees located in London:

```
CREATE VIEW hive_metastore.hr_db.london_employees_vw
AS SELECT * FROM hive_metastore.hr_db.employees WHERE city = 'London';
```

After executing these commands, you can explore the created objects in the Catalog Explorer. Figure 8-8 displays the structure and contents of the hr_db database within the hive_metastore catalog.

Now that we have created our database and its objects, the next step is configuring their permissions to control access. Properly setting permissions ensures that only authorized users and groups can access and manipulate data objects, thereby maintaining data security and integrity.

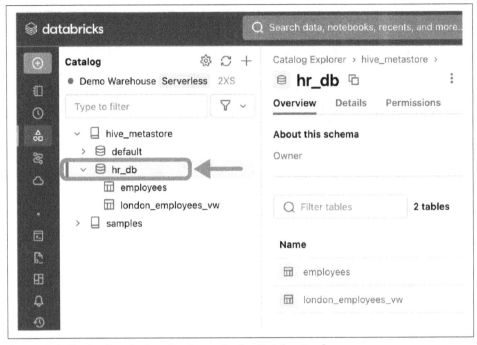

Figure 8-8. Reviewing the hr_db schema in the Catalog Explorer

Configuring object permissions

In this step, we will grant permissions to the necessary users and groups, allowing them to interact with our database and its objects effectively.

Granting privileges to a group. We begin by granting several privileges on the entire HR database (hr_db) to the hr_team group. This will enable all members of this group to read and modify the data, access metadata information, and create new objects such as tables and views within this database. The SQL command to achieve this is as follows:

```
GRANT SELECT, MODIFY, READ_METADATA, CREATE
ON SCHEMA hive_metastore.hr_db TO hr_team;
```

With this command, the HR team members will have the permissions to perform a range of actions on the hr_db schema, enhancing their ability to manage and utilize the HR data effectively.

In addition to the previously granted privileges, users must have the USAGE privilege to perform any action on database objects. Without this privilege, the objects within the database cannot be accessed or utilized by the group. The following command grants the USAGE privilege to the hr_team group:

```
GRANT USAGE ON SCHEMA hive_metastore.hr_db TO hr_team;
```

By executing this command, the hr_team group members will have the ability to use the database objects, ensuring they can interact with both data and metadata as needed.

Granting privileges to an individual user.   In addition to configuring permissions for groups, it is often necessary to assign specific privileges to individual users for more customized access control. To illustrate this, we will grant read access on the london_employees_vw view to the user Eve (*eve@example.com*), who is not a member of the hr_team.

The SQL command to grant the specified permission to Eve is as follows:

```
GRANT SELECT
ON VIEW hive_metastore.hr_db.london_employees_vw TO `eve@example.com`;
```

This selective permission allows Eve to access the information she needs without requiring her to be added to the hr_team group with broader permissions.

 While it is possible to assign privileges to individual users, it is generally recommended to grant permissions to groups. This practice simplifies permission management, especially in dynamic organizational environments where team structures frequently change.

Reviewing assigned permissions.   After configuring the necessary permissions for groups and individual users, it is important to verify that these permissions have been applied correctly. The SHOW GRANTS command is used to display the assigned privileges, ensuring transparency and accuracy in permission management.

To review the permissions assigned on the hr_db schema, we use the following SQL command:

```
SHOW GRANTS ON SCHEMA hive_metastore.hr_db;
```

Executing this command produces the list of granted privileges on our database, as displayed in Figure 8-9. This confirms that the HR team has all the required permissions.

ᴬᵇc Principal	ᴬᵇc ActionType	ᴬᵇc ObjectType	ᴬᵇc ObjectKey
hr_team	CREATE	DATABASE	hr_db
hr_team	READ_METADATA	DATABASE	hr_db
hr_team	SELECT	DATABASE	hr_db
hr_team	MODIFY	DATABASE	hr_db
hr_team	USAGE	DATABASE	hr_db
derar@oreilly.com	OWN	DATABASE	hr_db

Figure 8-9. *The output of the SHOW GRANTS command on the hr_db schema*

Additionally, this figure shows that the user who created the database (in this case, me) is the owner of the database.

To review the permissions assigned to the london_employees_vw view, we use the following SQL command:

```
SHOW GRANTS ON VIEW hive_metastore.hr_db.london_employees_vw;
```

This command produces the list of granted privileges on our view, confirming that Eve has the SELECT privilege, as illustrated in Figure 8-10.

ᴬᵇc Principal	ᴬᵇc ActionType	ᴬᵇc ObjectType	ᴬᵇc ObjectKey
eve@example.com	SELECT	TABLE	`hr_db`.`london_employees_vw`
derar@oreilly.com	OWN	TABLE	`hr_db`.`london_employees_vw`
hr_team	CREATE	DATABASE	hr_db
hr_team	READ_METADATA	DATABASE	hr_db
hr_team	SELECT	DATABASE	hr_db
hr_team	MODIFY	DATABASE	hr_db
hr_team	USAGE	DATABASE	hr_db

Figure 8-10. *The output of the SHOW GRANTS command on the london_employees_vw view*

Moreover, this figure shows that the HR team has inherited the relevant privileges on this view from the database level.

Managing permissions in Catalog Explorer

Beyond the SQL editor, we can also manage permissions through the Catalog Explorer. This simplifies the process of configuring access controls, making it easier for administrators who prefer a visual interface over writing SQL commands. To access the Catalog Explorer, click the Catalog tab in the left sidebar of your Databricks workspace.

In the Catalog Explorer, locate the database you previously created (hr_db). Clicking the database name will display a list of contained tables and views on the left-hand side. On the right-hand side, you will see detailed information about the database, such as owner information, as displayed in Figure 8-11.

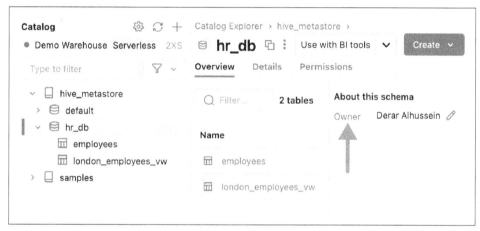

Figure 8-11. Reviewing the hr_db schema in the Catalog Explorer

From this interface, you can change the owner of the database by clicking the pencil icon next to the owner's name. It's worth noting that the owner of a database can be set as either an individual user or a group of users. This is necessary to ensure that the correct person or team has administrative control and access to the database, which is especially important when there are changes in personnel or when database management responsibilities need to be reassigned.

Reviewing and modifying permissions. Under the Permissions tab, you can review the current permissions for the database. This tab lists the granted privileges, such as those for the hr_team group, as illustrated in Figure 8-12.

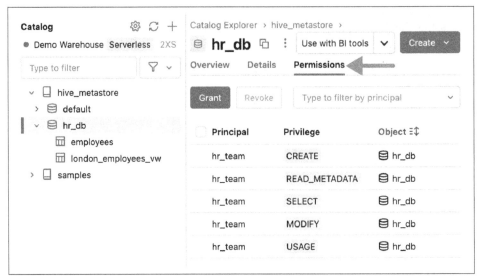

Figure 8-12. Reviewing the permissions of the hr_db schema in the Catalog Explorer

In the interface, you have the capability to manage access permissions, including granting and revoking privileges from users or groups. Next, we'll go through a step-by-step guide for each of these operations.

Granting new permissions. To grant new permissions, such as allowing all workspace users to review metadata about the database, use the following steps:

1. Click the Grant button: Begin by clicking the Grant blue button, which will open the grant permissions dialog, as shown in Figure 8-13.

2. Select the group: In the dialog, search for and select the "All workspace users" group from the list of available groups.

3. Choose privileges: Next, select the specific privileges you want to grant. In this case, you will choose both READ_METADATA and USAGE privileges.

4. Confirm granting of permissions: Finally, click the Grant button to apply the permissions.

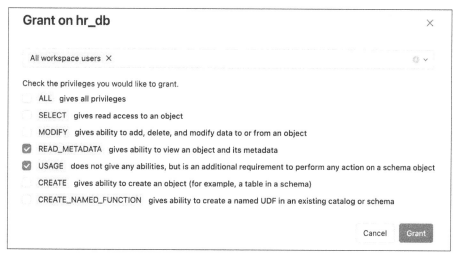

Figure 8-13. *The grant permissions dialog in the Catalog Explorer*

Figure 8-14 illustrates the interface where the two newly granted privileges to all the workspace users are displayed.

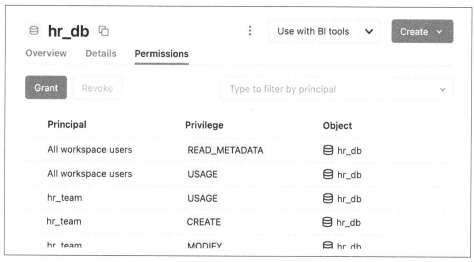

Figure 8-14. *The permissions interface of the hr_db schema showing the newly granted privileges*

This interface simplifies the process of granting permissions, eliminating the need to write complex SQL commands. Users can easily manage permissions through intuitive steps, making it accessible even for those with limited technical knowledge.

Revoking permissions. To remove existing privileges from a user or group, follow these steps:

1. Select the privilege(s) you want to revoke.
2. Click the Revoke button.

This action will remove the selected privilege from the designated user or group. For instance, consider the example shown in Figure 8-15. Here, the action of revoking the CREATE privilege from the hr_team is illustrated.

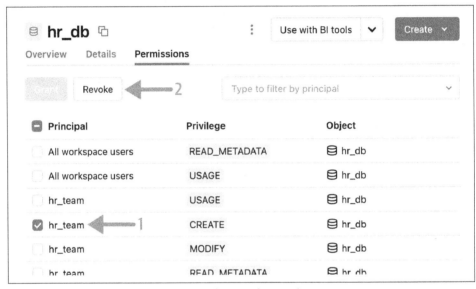

Figure 8-15. Revoking permissions via the Catalog Explorer

By revoking the CREATE privilege, the hr_team will no longer be able to create new objects within the hr_db schema.

Managing permissions for database objects. The Catalog Explorer not only allows you to manage database-level permissions but also extends this capability to individual data objects, such as tables and views. To manage permissions for these objects, click the desired table or view name from the left-side navigator, and open its Permissions tab, as displayed in Figure 8-16.

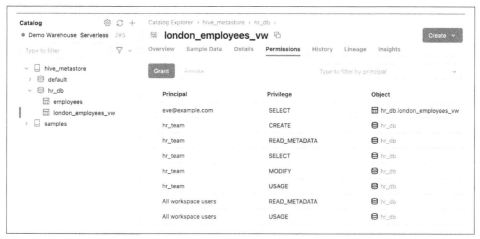

Figure 8-16. Reviewing the permissions of the `london_employees_vw` *view in the Catalog Explorer*

This figure illustrates the permissions interface for the `london_employees_vw` view, showing its current privileges and providing options to revoke and grant new permissions.

Limitations of the Catalog Explorer. While the Catalog Explorer is a versatile and powerful tool for managing data objects and permissions, there are some limitations. Specifically, the `ANY FILE` object cannot be managed through the Catalog Explorer and must be handled using the SQL editor.

Query History. One of the notable features of Databricks SQL is the query history functionality. This feature provides the ability to view all SQL queries executed in Databricks SQL, including those run behind the scenes by the Catalog Explorer.

To view these queries, simply select the Query History tab from the left sidebar of your Databricks workspace. This opens the query history interface, listing all executed queries along with details such as the query text, the execution time, and the executing user, as shown in Figure 8-17.

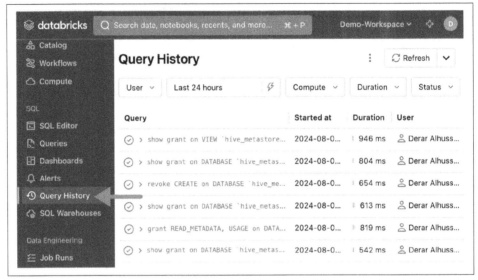

Figure 8-17. Query history in Databricks SQL

This transparency allows users to understand the exact commands being run and provides an opportunity to learn and replicate these commands manually if needed.

In conclusion, while the Hive metastore serves as a foundational component for metadata management, it offers only basic governance capabilities. It is clear that it lacks some advanced security and governance features required for modern data environments. This is where Unity Catalog comes into play, which will be the focus of our next section.

Governing Data with Unity Catalog

In the previous sections, we discussed the data governance model of Databricks with a default Hive metastore, highlighting its key features and limitations. Now, we turn our attention to Unity Catalog, the innovative governance solution introduced by Databricks. Unity Catalog represents a significant advancement in data management, offering a more robust and scalable architecture. This overview will delve into the key aspects of Unity Catalog, detailing its architecture, the hierarchical organization of its data objects, and its enhanced security model designed to meet the evolving needs of modern data governance.

What Is Unity Catalog?

Unity Catalog (UC) (*https://www.unitycatalog.io*) is an open source, centralized governance solution that spans across all your workspaces on any cloud. It unifies governance for all data and AI assets in your lakehouse, including files, tables, machine learning models, and dashboards. This centralization ensures consistent access controls, and simplified data management, which enhances overall data governance and security.

Unity Catalog Architecture

Before the introduction of Unity Catalog, metastore management, user and group definitions, as well as access control, were handled within individual workspaces. This approach required separate configurations for each workspace, which could lead to inconsistencies and inefficiencies.

With Unity Catalog, governance and access control have been centralized, significantly improving manageability and consistency across multiple workspaces, as illustrated in Figure 8-18. Unity Catalog operates independently of individual workspaces and is managed via the account console, a user interface designed for administrative tasks.

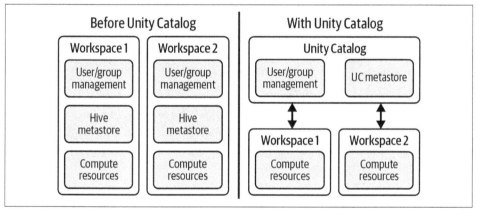

Figure 8-18. Databricks workspaces management before and after Unity Catalog

This figure illustrates how Unity Catalog decouples user, group, and metastore management from individual workspaces, offering a centralized approach to data governance.

Key Architectural Changes

There are three main components to the changes implemented by Unity Catalog:

Centralized user and group management
>   Unity Catalog utilizes the account console for managing users and groups, which can then be assigned to multiple workspaces. This approach means that user and group definitions are consistent across all workspaces assigned to Unity Catalog.

Separation of metastore management
> Unlike the workspace-specific metastore used previously, Unity Catalog's metastores are managed centrally per cloud region through the account console. A single Unity Catalog metastore can serve multiple workspaces, allowing them to share the same underlying storage. This consolidation simplifies data management, improves data accessibility, and reduces data duplication, as multiple workspaces can access the same data without needing to replicate it across different environments.

Centralized access control
> Access controls within Unity Catalog are controlled centrally and apply across all workspaces. This ensures that defined policies and permissions are enforced consistently across the organization, thereby enhancing overall security.

UC Three-Level Namespace

In the traditional Hive metastore, where there is only a single catalog, a two-level namespace (`schema.table`) was sufficient to address tables within schemas. While this structure is simple and effective for many use cases, it can become limiting as data volume and complexity increase, particularly in large-scale environments where a more granular level of organization is beneficial.

To address these limitations, Unity Catalog introduces a three-level namespace that enhances data organization and management. This new structure incorporates an additional layer called *catalogs*, which sits above schemas in the hierarchy. The updated format for accessing tables becomes `catalog.schema.table`, as illustrated in Figure 8-19.

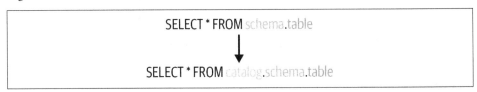

Figure 8-19. Transition to Unity Catalog's three-level namespace

To better understand the structure of Unity Catalog and its organization, let us explore the hierarchical model of its data objects in detail.

Data Object Hierarchy

The hierarchy of data objects in Unity Catalog begins with the metastore, which serves as the top-level logical container, as illustrated in Figure 8-20. The metastore holds metadata, including information about the objects it manages and the access control lists (ACLs) that govern access to these objects.

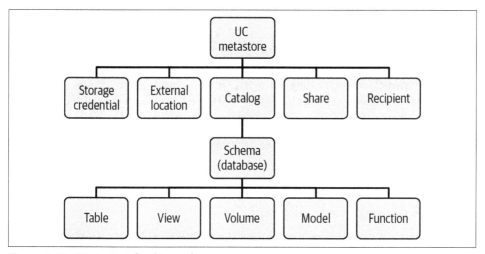

Figure 8-20. Unity Catalog hierarchy

Detailed Hierarchical Structure

Unity Catalog's hierarchical structure is based on relationships among a number of objects:

Metastore
> The metastore is the top-level entity in Unity Catalog, containing catalogs and managing metadata and access control. It operates independently from workspaces, providing enhanced security and a unified governance model.

Catalogs
> Within each metastore, catalogs act as high-level containers for organizing data objects. They represent the first part of the three-level namespace. A metastore can contain multiple catalogs, allowing for flexible and scalable data organization.

Schemas (databases)
> Schemas reside within catalogs and represent the second part of the three-level namespace. They are commonly referred to as databases. Schemas group related data and AI assets, facilitating organized data management.

Data and AI assets
> These are the third part of the three-level namespace. They reside within schemas and represent the actual data structures and AI artifacts managed by Unity Catalog, such as tables, views, storage volume, registered machine learning models, and functions.

Storage access objects

Unity Catalog allows you to set custom locations in cloud storage for storing managed and external tables. This introduces new securable objects to govern data access to these locations: storage credentials and external locations. A storage credential abstracts long-term access keys from cloud storage providers, while an external location links a given storage location with a storage credential.

Delta sharing entities

Unity Catalog also supports Delta Sharing, an open protocol designed for the efficient exchange of large datasets. Within Unity Catalog, shares represent collections of assets that can be shared with designated consumers (Recipients). Please note that Delta Sharing is not included as a topic in the Databricks Data Engineer Associate certification exam.

By understanding the relationships among these objects, you can effectively manage your data infrastructure and leverage Unity Catalog's capabilities.

Identity Management

Unity Catalog categorizes identities into three types: users, service principals, and groups. These identities are referred to as principals and play a vital role in managing access and permissions.

Users

Users are individuals who interact with the Databricks environment. Each user is uniquely identified by their email address, which serves as a unique identifier. Users can be assigned various roles, including administrative roles, allowing them to perform advanced tasks such as managing metastores, assigning metastores to workspaces, and managing other users.

Service principals

Service principals are designed to represent automated tools or applications. They are identified by an application ID, which ensures that automated processes have a distinct identity separate from human users. Service principals can be assigned administrative roles similar to users, allowing them to perform essential tasks programmatically. This capability is particularly useful for facilitating automation and integration with other systems.

Groups

Groups are collections of users and service principals, treated as a single entity. Groups simplify the management of permissions by allowing administrators to assign roles and privileges to a group rather than to individual users. Groups can be nested within other groups. For example, a parent group named "Employees" could contain subgroups such as "HR" and "Finance." This nesting capability mirrors organizational units or functional departments and allows for efficient delegation of access rights at different levels. Additionally, principals can belong to multiple non-nested groups.

By leveraging these identity types, administrators can streamline access control and ensure that both human and automated entities operate within their designated scopes.

Identity federation

In Databricks, identities are managed at two distinct levels: the account level and the workspace level. Unity Catalog introduces a feature called *identity federation*, which simplifies identity management by allowing identities to be created once at the account level and then assigned to multiple workspaces as needed. Figure 8-21 visually demonstrates how identities created at the account level can be federated across multiple workspaces.

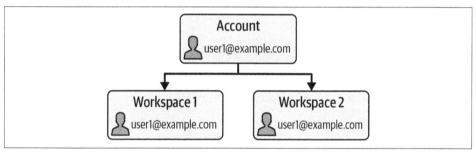

Figure 8-21. Identity federation in Unity Catalog

This approach is recommended for effective identity management across multiple workspaces. It significantly reduces the overhead associated with maintaining multiple copies of identities at workspace levels. As a result, it streamlines administrative tasks and enhances security and consistency across the Databricks environment.

UC Security Model

Unity Catalog offers a robust security model for permissions management based on standard ANSI SQL. It enhances data protection by offering granular access controls tailored to different types of operations and resources. This flexible and reliable model ensures efficient management and control over data access in the lakehouse.

Unity Catalog continues to use the GRANT statement for assigning privileges on securable objects to principals:

```
GRANT <privilege> ON <object-type> <object-name> TO <principal>
```

The UC security model provides a comprehensive set of privileges designed to efficiently manage access to various data and AI objects and underlying storage. Notably, two specific privileges now replace the legacy `ANY FILE` privilege from the Hive metastore, enhancing storage-related permissions. Here's a breakdown of the key categories:

Core privileges

CREATE

> Allows users to create new objects, such as a catalog (`CREATE CATALOG`), a schema (`CREATE SCHEMA`), a table or view (`CREATE TABLE`), or a function (`CREATE FUNCTION`).

USE

> Grants the ability to use a specified catalog (`USE CATALOG`) or schema (`USE SCHEMA`). Without this privilege, users cannot interact with the objects within the catalog or schema.

SELECT

> Permits users to read data from tables or views.

MODIFY

> Enables users to modify data within tables, including inserting, updating, and deleting records.

Storage-related privileges

READ FILES

> Allows users to read files directly from the underlying storage linked to volumes and external locations.

WRITE FILES

> Allows users to write files to the underlying storage.

Execution privilege

EXECUTE

> Grants permission to invoke user-defined functions or load a machine learning model for inference.

Figure 8-22 demonstrates the complete security model of Unity Catalog, highlighting its distinct approach compared to the Hive metastore's security model.

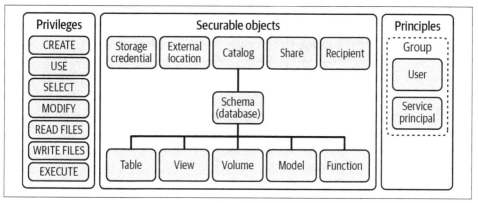

Figure 8-22. Security model of Unity Catalog

This comprehensive security model in Unity Catalog provides a clear and detailed framework for managing data access, supporting the needs of modern, data-driven organizations.

Accessing the Hive Metastore

Unity Catalog introduces advanced data governance and security features, but it is designed to be additive. This means that existing systems and data structures, such as the legacy Hive metastore, remain accessible and functional even after Unity Catalog is enabled.

When Unity Catalog is enabled in a Databricks workspace, the legacy Hive metastore remains available through its hive_metastore catalog, as illustrated in Figure 8-23. This catalog provides seamless access to the Hive metastore that is local to the workspace, ensuring that users can continue to interact with their existing data without interruption.

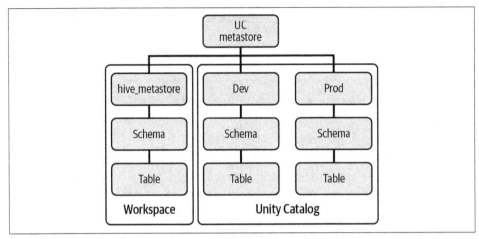

Figure 8-23. Coexistence of Unity Catalog and the legacy Hive metastore

This additive nature of Unity Catalog ensures a smooth transition to advanced data governance, and full compatibility with existing workflows and data assets.

Unity Catalog Features

In addition to its centralized and secure governance model, Unity Catalog offers the following features designed to enhance data management, accessibility, and traceability:

Automated lineage
> This feature tracks and visualizes the origin and usage of data assets across notebooks, workflows, queries, and dashboards, providing transparency and traceability.

Data search and discovery
> Unity Catalog offers capabilities for tagging and documenting data assets along with a powerful search interface, making it easier for users to find data.

System tables
> Unity Catalog provides access to your account's operational data through system tables, including audit logs, billable usage, and lineage information. This facilitates better monitoring and management of your data lakehouse.

Together, these features empower organizations to manage their data assets more efficiently, ensuring compliance and facilitating deeper insights.

Unity Catalog in Action

To leverage Unity Catalog, Databricks workspaces need to be properly configured and enabled. This process involves attaching the workspaces to a Unity Catalog metastore, which serves as a top-level container for all Unity Catalog metadata per cloud region.

Enabling workspaces for Unity Catalog

Databricks now automatically enables new workspaces for Unity Catalog. These workspaces are linked to a Unity Catalog metastore that is automatically provisioned in the same region. This simplifies the process for users and ensures that new workspaces are ready to take advantage of Unity Catalog's features right from the start.

Verifying Unity Catalog enablement.   To verify whether your Databricks workspace is enabled for Unity Catalog, simply review the list of catalogs available in the Catalog Explorer. A UC-enabled workspace will display at least two additional catalogs besides the legacy hive_metastore and samples catalogs, as displayed in Figure 8-24.

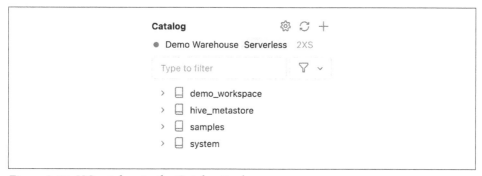

Figure 8-24. UC catalogs in the Catalog Explorer

These new catalogs include the following:

Main or workspace-named catalog
> This is a local workspace catalog. Depending on whether Unity Catalog was enabled manually or automatically, this catalog might be named main or reflect the name of your workspace.

System catalog
> This catalog hosts system tables that provide historical observability across your account, facilitating, among other things, operational insights and audit logging.

If you can see these catalogs, your workspace is all set up to utilize Unity Catalog's features. If not, you will need to manually enable your workspace for Unity Catalog.

Manual enabling of Unity Catalog. If your Databricks workspace was not automatically enabled for Unity Catalog, you can enable it by manually attaching it to a Unity Catalog metastore within the same region. If a Unity Catalog metastore is not already available in that region, you must create one through the Databricks account console.

Accessing account console. To manage your metastores and perform other administrative tasks in Unity Catalog, you need to access the Databricks account console as an account administrator. Depending on your cloud provider, you'll access the console via different URLs:

- AWS: *https://accounts.cloud.databricks.com*
- Azure: *https://accounts.azuredatabricks.net*
- GCP: *https://accounts.gcp.databricks.com*

Upon logging in, you will be directed to the account console homepage, as displayed in Figure 8-25.

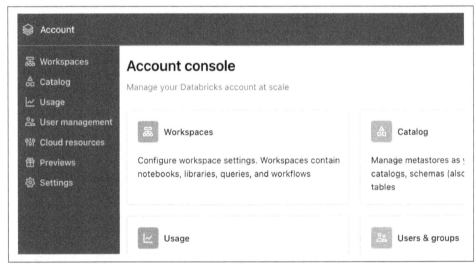

Figure 8-25. The Databricks account console

This interface provides tools for performing various administrative tasks at the account level, including managing workspaces, metastores, and identities, as well as monitoring account usage logs.

Creating a new metastore. In Databricks, each cloud region requires its own Unity Catalog metastore. This metastore can be linked to multiple workspaces within the same region, providing a unified view of the data across these workspaces. Data from other metastores can be accessed using Delta Sharing if needed to enable cross-regional federation.

To create a new metastore within a Databricks region, follow these steps:

1. Navigate to the account console and click Catalog from the left sidebar.
2. Click "Create metastore" to begin the setup process for your new metastore, as illustrated in Figure 8-26.

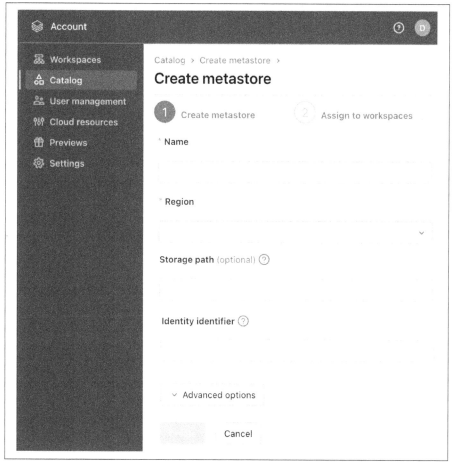

Figure 8-26. The configuration panel for creating a new metastore in Unity Catalog

3. Enter metastore details.

   a. Name: Provide a unique name for the new metastore.

   b. Region: Select the region where the metastore will be deployed. Ensure this is the same region as the workspaces that will access the data. Remember, only one metastore can be created per region.

   c. Root storage path (optional): Specify the path to the storage container or bucket that will serve as the default location for storing managed tables. If this is not provided, a storage path must be specified at the catalog level each time a new catalog is created in the metastore.

   d. Identity identifier: If a storage location is specified, provide the identifier of an identity that has the appropriate access permissions for that location. This information varies depending on your cloud provider:

      — AWS: Use an identity and access management (IAM) role.
      — Azure: Use an access connector for Azure Databricks resource.
      — GCP: A service account is automatically created for you. However, you must manually grant it access permissions to the specified storage location later.

   A full discussion of all this information is beyond the scope of the certification exam. For detailed instructions, refer to the respective Databricks documentation for your cloud provider.

4. Click Create to finalize the creation of the metastore.

In the next step, select the workspaces you want to link to the new metastore, as displayed in Figure 8-27. Remember, you can only select workspaces in the same region as the metastore.

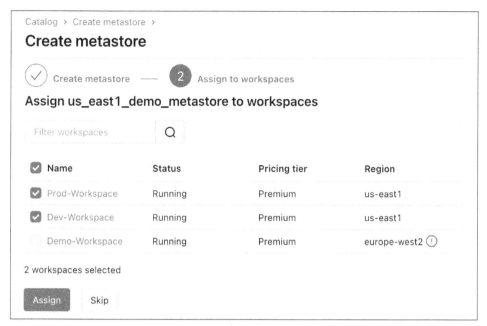

Figure 8-27. Metastore assignment to workspaces

Lastly, click Assign to activate Unity Catalog for the selected workspaces, or click Skip to proceed without linking any workspaces at this time. If you choose to skip, you can link workspaces to this metastore later.

Assigning existing metastore. Once a metastore has been created in Unity Catalog, you can assign it to workspaces at any time. Follow these steps to complete the assignment:

1. Navigate to the Databricks account console.
2. Click Catalog from the left sidebar.
3. Select the metastore you want to assign to workspaces.
4. Click the Workspaces tab within the metastore view, as illustrated in Figure 8-28.

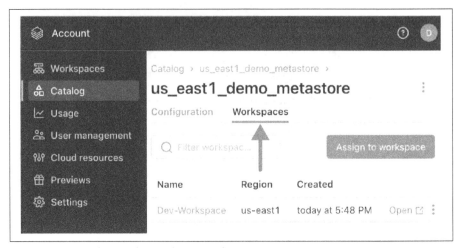

Figure 8-28. Exploring the workspaces of an existing metastore

5. Click "Assign to workspace."

6. Choose one or more workspaces in the same region in which the metastore is provisioned, as shown in Figure 8-29.

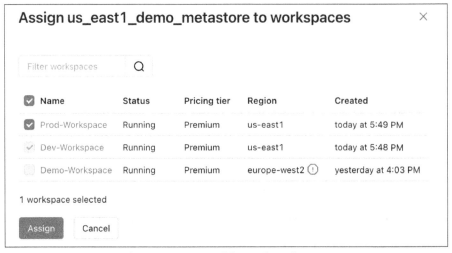

Figure 8-29. Assigning the metastore to additional workspaces

7. Scroll to the bottom of the dialog and click Assign.

8. On the confirmation dialog, click Enable.

After the assignment is complete, the newly assigned workspace(s) will appear in the metastore's Workspaces tab, ensuring they now have access to the data and governance policies defined in that metastore.

Running Unity Catalog workloads

Running workloads in Unity Catalog requires that your compute resources meet specific security and compliance requirements. Notably, clusters that were created prior to enabling Unity Catalog in your workspace do not meet these security standards. As a result, these pre-existing clusters cannot be used to access data or other objects managed by Unity Catalog.

Creating a UC-compliant cluster. To run Unity Catalog workloads, it is essential to create a new cluster after enabling your workspace for Unity Catalog. When configuring a new cluster, the compliance with Unity Catalog can be verified through the summary card in the cluster configuration, as illustrated in Figure 8-30.

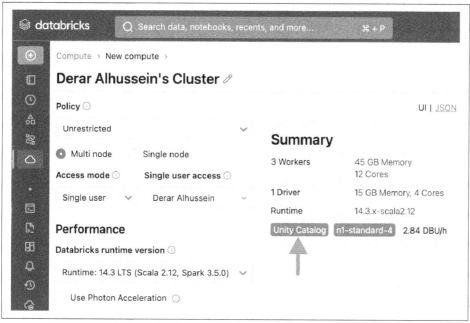

Figure 8-30. Creating a Unity Catalog–compliant cluster

Alternatively, you can use an SQL warehouse to run Unity Catalog workloads, as SQL warehouses are inherently compliant with Unity Catalog requirements.

Managing data catalogs. In Unity Catalog, managing data catalogs is an essential aspect that allows you to organize and secure your data across workspaces. You can create a new catalog in a metastore from any workspace linked to that metastore.

To follow along with this section, you will need to use Databricks SQL in a workspace enabled for Unity Catalog. Begin by navigating to the SQL editor located in the left sidebar of your Databricks workspace. Before executing any commands, ensure that your SQL warehouse is up and running.

Creating a new catalog. To create a new catalog, use the CREATE CATALOG command in Spark SQL. For example, to create a catalog named hr_catalog, execute the following command:

```
CREATE CATALOG IF NOT EXISTS hr_catalog;
```

This command will successfully create the catalog if your metastore is already configured with a root storage location. Otherwise, you will encounter the following error:

```
ERROR: Metastore storage root URL does not exist.
Please provide a storage location for the catalog (for example 'CREATE
CATALOG myCatalog MANAGED LOCATION '<location-path>').
Alternatively set up a metastore root storage location to provide a
storage location for all catalogs in the metastore.
```

This error indicates that a storage location is required for the managed tables in the catalog. To resolve this error, you have two options:

Set up a metastore-level storage location
> Update the metastore configuration to define a root storage location for the entire metastore. This location will serve as the default storage path for all catalogs within the metastore.

Provide a catalog-level storage location
> When creating the catalog, specify a default storage location by using the MAN AGED LOCATION clause, as demonstrated in the following command:

```
CREATE CATALOG IF NOT EXISTS hr_catalog
MANAGED LOCATION '<location-path>';
```

Each of these options requires pre-configuring the storage location path by creating an external location object and its associated storage credential object. This setup process is detailed in the Databricks documentation for your cloud provider and is beyond the scope of the certification exam.

Verifying the created catalog. After successfully executing the CREATE CATALOG command, you can verify the existence and proper creation of the catalog through the Catalog Explorer, as displayed in Figure 8-31.

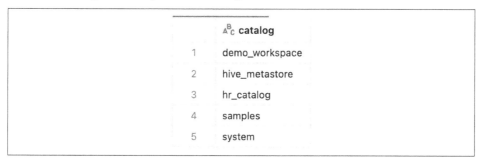

Figure 8-31. List of UC catalogs in the Catalog Explorer after creating hr_catalog

As shown in the figure, each newly created catalog contains a default database named default and a system database named information_schema. This information _schema database contains a set of views that reference system tables in the system catalog, offering catalog-level historical observability.

Alternatively, you can run the following command to show all catalogs in the metastore:

```
SHOW CATALOGS;
```

Figure 8-32 illustrates the output of this command, which lists all catalogs in the metastore, including our newly created catalog hr_catalog.

	ᴬᴮᵪ catalog
1	demo_workspace
2	hive_metastore
3	hr_catalog
4	samples
5	system

Figure 8-32. The output of the SHOW CATALOGS command after creating hr_catalog

What makes Unity Catalog particularly noteworthy is its ability to streamline access across various workspaces. Specifically, any workspace that is linked to this metastore will now have access to the hr_catalog. This unified access allows regional teams to seamlessly query and analyze the same datasets from a centralized repository whenever they have the appropriate permissions.

Granting permissions. Let's now grant permissions for creating schemas, creating tables, and using the catalog to all users on the account. These permissions can be combined in a single GRANT command, as shown here:

```
GRANT CREATE SCHEMA, CREATE TABLE, USE CATALOG ON CATALOG hr_catalog
TO `account users`;
```

This command grants the specified permissions to the group account users, which typically includes all users associated with the Databricks account. Similarly, you can assign permissions to other account-level groups or individual users.

After granting permissions, it is important to verify that the correct privileges have been assigned. This can be done using the SHOW GRANT statement, which displays the permissions associated with a specific catalog, schema, or table. To check the grants on the hr_catalog, you can run the following command:

```
SHOW GRANT ON CATALOG hr_catalog;
```

This command produces the list of grants on our catalog, confirming that all account users have the granted privileges, as illustrated in Figure 8-33.

$^{AB}_C$ Principal	$^{AB}_C$ ActionType	$^{AB}_C$ ObjectType	$^{AB}_C$ ObjectKey
account users	CREATE SCHEMA	CATALOG	hr_catalog
account users	CREATE TABLE	CATALOG	hr_catalog
account users	USE CATALOG	CATALOG	hr_catalog

Figure 8-33. The output of the SHOW GRANT command on the hr_catalog

Creating schemas. In addition to the default database in a catalog, we can create new databases using the CREATE SCHEMA command. To create a schema named hr_db within the hr_catalog, we execute the following command:

```
CREATE SCHEMA IF NOT EXISTS hr_catalog.hr_db;
```

After creating a new schema, we can verify its existence and ensure it has been properly added to the catalog using the Catalog Explorer. Alternatively, we can use the SHOW SCHEMAS command, which lists all schemas within a specified catalog. To list all schemas in the hr_catalog, we run the following command:

```
SHOW SCHEMAS IN hr_catalog;
```

Figure 8-34 illustrates the results of executing this command. The output includes a list of all schemas within the hr_catalog, including the newly created schema hr_db.

	$^{B}_{C}$ databaseName
1	default
2	hr_db
3	information_schema

Figure 8-34. The output of the SHOW SCHEMAS command in the hr_catalog

Managing Delta tables. Unity Catalog integrates seamlessly with Delta Lake, enabling the creation and management of Delta Lake tables. To create a Delta Lake table in Unity Catalog, you use the CREATE TABLE command with the three-level namespace in the format <catalog>.<schema>.<table>. This approach ensures that the table is appropriately placed within the catalog and schema hierarchy.

For instance, to create a table named jobs in the hr_db schema of the hr_catalog, you can execute the following command:

```
CREATE TABLE IF NOT EXISTS hr_catalog.hr_db.jobs
(id INT, title STRING, min_salary DOUBLE, max_salary DOUBLE);
```

Once the table is created, data can be inserted using the INSERT INTO command, as in the following example:

```
INSERT INTO hr_catalog.hr_db.jobs
VALUES (1, "Software Engineer", 3000, 5000),
    (2, "Data Engineer", 3500, 5500),
    (3, "Web Developer", 2800, 4800);
```

Afterward, we can view advanced metadata information about the table using the DESCRIBE TABLE EXTENDED command:

```
DESCRIBE EXTENDED hr_catalog.hr_db.jobs;
```

The output of this command reveals that our table is a managed table created in the root storage of the metastore, as illustrated in Figure 8-35.

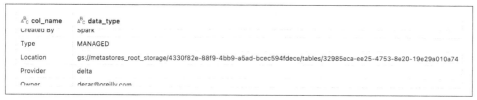

Figure 8-35. The output of the DESCRIBE EXTENDED command on the jobs table

Dropping tables. To drop a managed table, the `DROP TABLE` command is used, which effectively removes the table from the catalog. For example, to drop our `jobs` table, we run the following command:

```
DROP TABLE hr_catalog.hr_db.jobs;
```

Unlike traditional Hive metastore behavior, dropping a managed table in Unity Catalog does not immediately delete the table's directory from the underlying storage. Instead, Unity Catalog retains the data files for a period of 30 days before permanently deleting them. If you examine the root storage of the metastore in your cloud account, you'll find that the table directory and its data files remain present after dropping the table, as shown in Figure 8-36.

Buckets > metastores_root_storage > 4330f82e-88f9-4bb9-a5ad-bcec594fdece > tables > 32985eca-ee25-4753-8e20-19e29a010a74

UPLOAD FILES   UPLOAD FOLDER   CREATE FOLDER   TRANSFER DATA ▾   MANAGE HOLDS   EDIT RETENTION   DOWNLOAD

Filter by name prefix only ▾   ☰ **Filter**   Filter objects and folders

	Name	Size	Type	Created ❓	Storage class	Last modifi
☐	📁 _delta_log/	–	Folder	–	–	–
☐	📄 part-00000-f79bbd73-7b66-43f0-b...	1.1 KB	application/octet-stream	Aug 5, 2024, 2:19:34 PM	Standard	Aug 5, 202

Figure 8-36. The content of the jobs table directory, in a GCP bucket, after executing the DROP TABLE command

During a seven-day period after deletion, it is possible to recover a recently dropped table using the `UNDROP TABLE` command. This feature is particularly useful in scenarios where a table is accidentally deleted or needs to be restored for further use, enhancing data safety and management. To recover the `jobs` table, we run the following command:

```
UNDROP TABLE hr_catalog.hr_db.jobs;
```

After executing this command, you can query the table to confirm that it has been successfully recovered. For example, use the following command to verify the contents of the recovered table:

```
SELECT * FROM hr_catalog.hr_db.jobs;
```

This query should return the data that was present in the table before it was dropped, confirming that the recovery process was successful.

Conclusion

In conclusion, implementing data governance within Databricks through Unity Catalog represents a significant advancement in managing and securing data assets. Unity Catalog offers a comprehensive suite of governance features that streamline data management, enhance security, and ensure regulatory compliance. For organizations still using the legacy Hive metastore, Databricks strongly recommends transitioning to Unity Catalog to fully leverage these advanced capabilities. Adopting Unity Catalog will significantly enhance your organization's ability to govern and secure data effectively, better positioning you to meet both regulatory requirements and operational demands.

Sample Exam Questions

Conceptual Question

1. Which of the following represents the hierarchy of relational entities in Unity Catalog?

A. Metastore → Catalog → Table → Schema (Database)

B. Schema (Database) → Metastore → Catalog → Table

C. Metastore → Catalog → Schema (Database) → Table

D. Catalog → Metastore → Schema (Database) → Table

E. Schema (Database) → Catalog → Table → Metastore

Code-Based Question

2. A data engineer uses the following SQL query:

```
GRANT MODIFY ON TABLE inventory TO supply_team
```

Which of the following describes the ability granted by the MODIFY privilege?

A. It gives the ability to add data to the table.

B. It gives the ability to delete data from the table.

C. It gives the ability to modify data in the table.

D. All of the above abilities are granted by the MODIFY privilege.

E. None of these options correctly describes the ability granted by the MODIFY privilege.

The correct answers to these questions are listed in Appendix C.

Certification Overview

As you approach the final stage of your certification journey, it's time to prepare for the exam. In this chapter, we will provide a comprehensive overview of the certification exam, detailing its format, structure, and the key topics you need to focus on. We'll also offer a practical guide on how to register and what to expect on exam day. To further enhance your preparation, we will share valuable resources for practice exams, enabling you to assess your knowledge and skills effectively.

Exploring the Exam Format

Before taking the Databricks Data Engineer Associate exam, it's important to familiarize yourself with the exam layout. The exam typically consists of 45 questions that you are required to complete within a 90-minute timeframe. However, depending on the difficulty of specific questions, you may occasionally encounter an additional 4 to 5 questions, bringing the total number to approximately 50 questions.

The passing score has been established through rigorous statistical analysis, considering the varying levels of difficulty among the questions. Currently, the passing mark is approximately set at 75%. However, to increase your chances of certification, it's advisable to aim for at least 80%, which means correctly answering a minimum of 40 questions out of the potential 50.

Key Topics Covered

The questions expected during the exam are distributed across several core topics, ensuring comprehensive coverage of the platform's capabilities. The distribution is as follows:

1. *Databricks Lakehouse Platform—24%*

    11 questions out of 45 will focus on the use and benefits of the Databricks Data Intelligence Platform. This includes understanding its architecture and core components, particularly Delta Lake.

2. *Building ETL Pipelines—29%*

    13 questions will cover the creation of ETL pipelines using Apache Spark SQL and Python. This section emphasizes practical knowledge of transforming and processing batch datasets and working with higher-order functions and user-defined functions (UDFs) in Spark.

3. *Incremental Data Processing—22%*

    10 questions will delve into processing data incrementally. This topic involves understanding how to manage streaming data and design incremental medallion architectures.

4. *Production Pipelines—16%*

    7 questions will explore topics on constructing production pipelines and performing Databricks SQL analytics. This involves implementing DLT pipelines, creating end-to-end workflows, and visualizing data using Databricks Dashboards.

5. *Data Governance and Security—9%*

    4 questions will assess knowledge of data governance and security practices. This includes understanding access controls in Hive and Unity Catalog to ensure secure and compliant data management.

Figure 9-1 visually represents the distribution of exam questions across these essential topics.

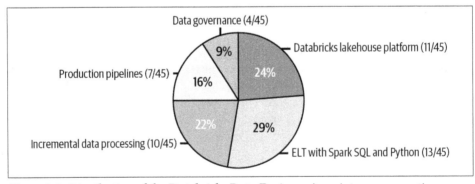

Figure 9-1. Distribution of the Databricks Data Engineer Associate exam questions

Rest assured, all these topics have been covered in depth throughout this book. The chapters are carefully designed to align with the exam topics, ensuring that you're fully prepared for the assessment.

Out-of-Scope Topics

While focusing on the key areas is crucial, it's equally important to recognize which topics will not appear on this Associate-level Data Engineer exam. The following subjects are considered out of scope:

Apache Spark internals
  Detailed mechanisms and underlying architecture of Apache Spark will not be tested.

Databricks CLI and REST API
  Knowledge related to the Databricks command-line interface and RESTful API is not required.

Data modeling concepts
  Questions concerning data modeling principles are excluded from the exam content.

GDPR/CCPA
  Regulations like the General Data Protection Regulation (GDPR) and California Consumer Privacy Act (CCPA) will not be assessed.

Monitoring and logging production jobs
  Practical aspects of tracking and logging in production environments are not included.

Dependency management and testing
  Topics related to managing dependencies in projects and testing methodologies are also not part of this exam.

By understanding both the key topics and those that are out of scope, you can tailor your study plan effectively, focusing on the areas that will enhance your chances of success in the certification exam.

Code Snippet Language

In code-based questions, data manipulation will primarily be demonstrated using SQL whenever applicable. If SQL is not suitable—such as in Spark Structured Streaming—code snippets will be provided in Python.

Familiarity with both SQL and Python will be essential, as it will enable you to navigate and understand the code effectively, ensuring you can correctly answer any code-based question.

Registering for the Exam

Before scheduling your exam, it's essential to understand the associated costs and policies. Understanding these details can help ensure a smoother registration process and better preparation for your exam experience.

Registration Fee

Each attempt at the certification exam requires a fee of $200, excluding applicable taxes. Candidates may retake the exam as many times as necessary to achieve a passing score. However, a fee of $200 is required for each attempt, and there is a mandatory 14-day waiting period between retakes. This policy is designed to allow sufficient time for review and preparation before retesting.

Exam Platform Overview

Databricks exams are conducted online through the Kryterion Webassessor platform, a globally recognized and secure online exam portal. The platform can be accessed directly via this link: *https://www.webassessor.com/databricks*. To register for the exam, you need first to create an account on the platform by clicking the Create New Account link, as displayed in Figure 9-2.

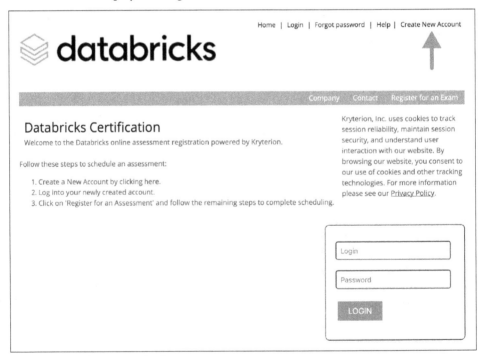

Figure 9-2. Webassessor platform sign-in page

You will be required to provide basic personal information, including your name, email address, and contact details. Once your account is set up, log in to your account to access the main dashboard of the Webassessor platform.

Scheduling the Exam

Once logged into your account, follow these steps to scheduling your exam:

1. Navigate to the exam registration page: Access the "Register for an Exam" option on the top bar of the Webassessor platform. This will open the page where you can view the available Databricks certification exams, as shown in Figure 9-3.

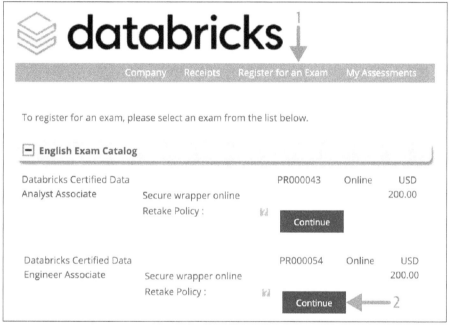

Figure 9-3. Register for the exam on the Webassessor platform

From this list, locate the Databricks Certified Data Engineer Associate certification and click Continue next to it to proceed to the scheduling page.

2. Select date and time: Next, you will be presented with a calendar where you can choose the most suitable date and time for your exam, as displayed in Figure 9-4.

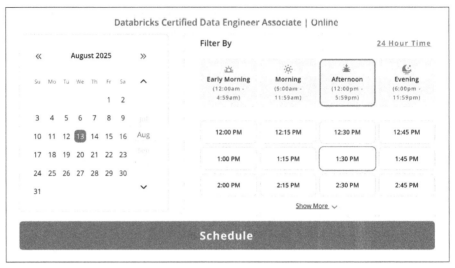

Figure 9-4. Exam date and time selection

Available slots will vary based on demand, so it is advisable to book your exam well in advance. After selecting the date and time, click the Schedule button to proceed to payment.

3. Completing payment: Follow the prompts on the payment page to enter your payment details and complete the transaction. Once payment is processed, you will receive an email confirmation with the details of your exam booking.

Troubleshooting and Support

The Kryterion support team offers assistance through a live chat feature, which allows for prompt resolution of any issues that arise before or during the exam. In the event of any technical problems, you can quickly contact the support team through the Kryterion Support Center, which can be accessed via this link: *https://kryterion.force.com/support*.

Once you have navigated to the support page, you will find a chat icon located at the bottom-right corner of the page. Clicking this icon will open a chat window where you can communicate with a support representative in real time.

This feature is particularly useful for resolving urgent issues that occur just before or during your exam. Whether you're experiencing difficulty with the exam scheduling or having trouble launching the exam, the live chat allows for immediate assistance without the need for email exchanges or long wait times.

Getting Ready for the Assessment

Before the day of your exam, review the instructions sent to you via a reminder email, and take the necessary steps to prepare your testing environment. On the day of your scheduled exam, it is recommended that you log in to your Webassessor account 15 minutes before your exam start time. This extra time will allow you to finalize your setup and ensure that your computer is ready for the assessment.

Once logged in, navigate to the My Assessments page from the top bar of the Webassessor platform. Here, you will find your scheduled exam listed, along with the date and time, as shown in Figure 9-5. From this page, you can launch your exam or, if necessary, reschedule or cancel it.

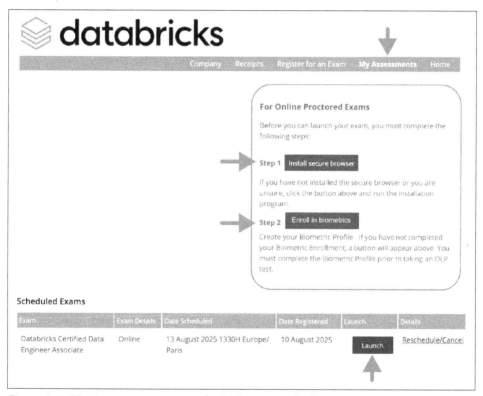

Figure 9-5. My Assessments page on the Webassessor platform

Before launching your exam, make sure to complete the following prerequisites if you haven't done so already:

- Installing the assessment software: Click the "Install secure browser" button to download and install the required assessment software. This program manages your exam environment and runs in full-screen mode, preventing access to other applications or files on your computer during the exam. Please note that some common corporate software may not function optimally within the secure test environment. Therefore, it is advisable to use a personal computer with a camera to avoid potential issues.

- Enroll in biometrics: Next, click the "Enroll in biometrics" button to verify your identity, a crucial step to ensure you are the person taking the exam.

Once these steps are completed, you can proceed by clicking the Launch button to start your exam.

Exam Proctoring

Databricks exams incorporate a strict proctoring process to ensure the integrity and security of the assessment. Understanding what to expect during the proctoring process will help you prepare appropriately and avoid any issues during the exam.

Webcam monitoring
Throughout the duration of the exam, you will be monitored in real time by a Webassessor Proctor via your computer's webcam. So, it is important to ensure that your webcam is fully functional prior to the exam.

Microphone and audio restrictions
In addition to webcam monitoring, your microphone must be operational for the entire duration of the exam. Please be aware that reading the exam questions aloud is strictly prohibited.

Testing environment requirements
No test aids are permitted during the exam. This means you will not be allowed to use notes, textbooks, or any other external resources. Your physical testing environment must be clean and free from any such materials. The proctor may inspect your testing area via the webcam before the exam begins to ensure it meets these requirements.

It is essential to understand that the proctor's role is to maintain fairness and security. While the proctor can assist with technical issues that may arise during the exam, they will not provide any assistance regarding the content of the exam. For example, if you encounter a problem with your computer or internet connection, the proctor can guide you through resolving the issue; however, they are not allowed to clarify or explain any of the exam questions.

Exam Result

Upon completing the certification exam, the grading process is both immediate and automated. As soon as you finish your test and submit your answers, the assessment software will instantly display your pass or fail result.

Although you receive your exam result immediately, the formal credentials—your badge and certificate—are not delivered instantaneously. If you pass the exam, your official certification will be sent to you via email within 24 hours. The email you receive will contain a link directing you to the Databricks Credentials platform, accessible at *https://credentials.databricks.com*. From this platform, you can manage, share, and verify all your certifications, as displayed in Figure 9-6.

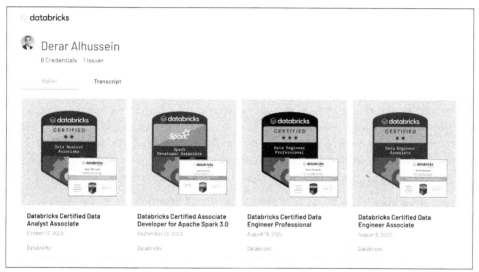

Figure 9-6. Databricks Credentials platform

This digital certification confirms your achievement and can be easily shared on social platforms or added to your professional profiles, such as LinkedIn.

Practice Exams

When preparing for certification, practice exams offer valuable opportunities to familiarize yourself with the exam format and types of questions, providing you with a solid foundation before taking the actual exam. To assist with your preparation for this certification, two valuable sources of practice exams are available: an official static practice exam from Databricks and interactive practice tests on various third-party learning platforms.

Official Databricks Practice Exam

One of the primary resources for exam preparation is the official Databricks practice test, which is accessible in PDF format. This static practice exam can be downloaded directly (*https://oreil.ly/practexam*).

This document contains 45 questions that are representative of the kinds of questions you will encounter in the real exam. However, these questions are no longer part of the current exam. Upon completing this practice exam, you can evaluate your performance by reviewing the answer key provided at the end of the document.

Interactive Practice Exams

For a more dynamic and immersive exam preparation experience, interactive practice exams are available on some popular learning platforms. One such resource is the Udemy course provided by the author, which offers a series of practice exams tailored to this certification. The course can be accessed here: *https://oreil.ly/Udemy-alhussein*.

These interactive practice exams simulate the live exam environment, providing a timed and structured approach to exam preparation. They allow you to experience the pressure and time constraints that come with the real exam. After completing a practice exam, you receive immediate feedback, including a pass or fail result. This feedback is invaluable, as it comes with detailed explanations for each question, helping you understand your mistakes and reinforce your knowledge.

To maximize your chances of success on the actual certification exam, it is recommended to aim for 100% accuracy in practice exams. By repeatedly taking these tests until you achieve a perfect score, you'll ensure that you are well prepared for the questions and scenarios presented in the real exam.

Seeking Assistance

If you have any concerns specific to Databricks certifications, such as exam content, registration issues, or credential inquiries, the best course of action is to reach out directly to the Databricks support team. You can contact them through their support page (*https://oreil.ly/C8t17*). This channel is specifically designed for certification-related inquiries and ensures that your questions are addressed by official support staff.

Final Thoughts

Congratulations on making it this far! This study guide was designed to help you on your journey to becoming a Databricks Certified Data Engineer Associate. You've now covered all the topics and skills needed for this certification exam. With a solid understanding of Databricks and data engineering concepts, you're ready to take the next step.

As you prepare for the big day, keep in mind that the secret to passing the exam is consistent practice. It's not enough to just read and understand the concepts; you need to put them into action. Take the time to review all the hands-on exercises in this book and apply them in your Databricks workspace to reinforce your understanding. Lastly, utilize the practice exams mentioned in this chapter to assess your knowledge and adjust your study plan accordingly.

It's often said that success is just 1% inspiration and 99% hard work. This is especially true when it comes to preparing for an exam. Your dedication and consistent effort will pay off, not only in passing the exam but in equipping you with valuable skills for your career. Stay focused, practice consistently, and trust in the work you've put in.

I wish you all the best in obtaining your Databricks Data Engineer Associate certification. I'd love to hear about your exam results, so feel free to share them with me on LinkedIn (*https://www.linkedin.com/in/deraralhussein*)!

Signing Up for Databricks

If you are new to Databricks, the company provides a 14-day free trial in your cloud account of Microsoft Azure, Amazon Web Services (AWS), or Google Cloud Platform (GCP). During this period, you have access to all the features available within the Databricks ecosystem, allowing for a thorough exploration of its capabilities. However, it's important to understand that while Databricks itself is free during this trial, the platform relies on cloud compute resources, which are billed separately by the cloud provider.

Most cloud providers offer promotional credits for new users, which can be applied toward these additional costs. To take advantage of these credits, you would need to sign up for the respective cloud provider's free tier using a credit card. For instance, when you sign up for the Microsoft Azure free tier (*https://oreil.ly/7bpR_*), you get a $200 credit valid for the first 30 days. This credit can significantly offset the costs associated with running Azure Databricks during your trial period.

Deploying Databricks on Microsoft Azure

Although Databricks offers similar functionalities across different cloud providers, its integration with Microsoft Azure stands out due to its native integration. On Azure, Databricks is offered as a first-party service known as Azure Databricks. This tight integration allows you to deploy Databricks using the same familiar Azure Portal interface that is used to manage other Azure services.

Here is a step-by-step guide to deploying Databricks on Microsoft Azure:

1. Access the Azure Portal: Begin by navigating to the Azure Portal (*https://portal.azure.com*). If you don't already have an Azure account, you'll need to create one to proceed.

2. Search for Databricks: Once logged in, use the search bar at the top of the Azure Portal to search for "Databricks." From the search results, select the Azure Databricks service, as illustrated in Figure A-1.

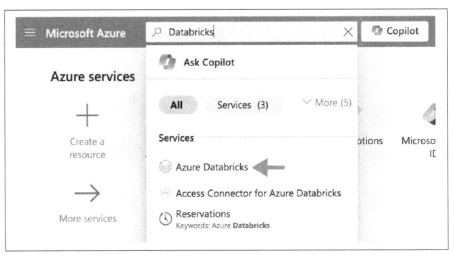

Figure A-1. Searching for Databricks service in the Azure Portal

3. Create a Databricks workspace: On the Azure Databricks page, click the Create button to start setting up a new Databricks workspace, as displayed in Figure A-2.

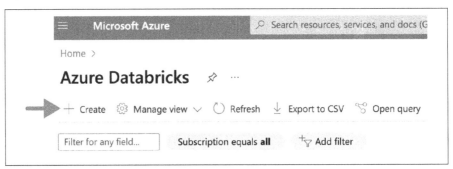

Figure A-2. Azure Databricks page in the Azure Portal

4. Subscription selection: You will be prompted to select your Azure subscription. If you have multiple subscriptions, choose the one under which you want to deploy Databricks, as shown in Figure A-3.

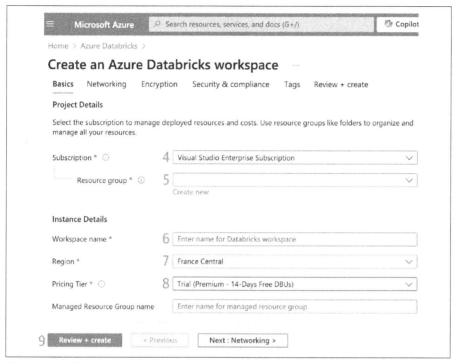

Figure A-3. New Databricks workspace configuration in the Azure Portal

5. Create a resource group: Next, you need to either select an existing resource group or create a new one. A resource group is essentially a container that holds related resources for an Azure solution. If you want to create a new resource group, click the "Create new" option below the resource group drop-down menu. It's a good practice to use a descriptive name, such as "databricks-demo-rg," which will contain all the resources associated with this demonstration.

6. Name your workspace: Enter a name for your Databricks workspace, such as "Demo-Workspace."

7. Choose a region: Select the Azure region where your workspace resources will be deployed. The choice of region can affect performance, cost, and availability of certain workspace features (*https://oreil.ly/p8XR_*).

8. Pricing tier: Azure Databricks offers two main pricing tiers: Standard and Premium. The Standard tier includes core Databricks features, while the Premium tier offers advanced features such as Databricks SQL, Delta Live Tables (DLT), and role-based access control (RBAC), which we use in this book. To explore the full range of Databricks capabilities, select the Trial (Premium - 14-Days Free DBUs) option. This will give you access to the Premium tier for the duration of the trial.

9. Review and create: After configuring your workspace, click the "Review + create" button to review your settings. If everything looks correct, click Create to begin the deployment process.

10. Deployment: Once you confirm the workspace creation, you'll be directed to the deployment page, as illustrated in Figure A-4. Here, you can monitor the progress of the deployment.

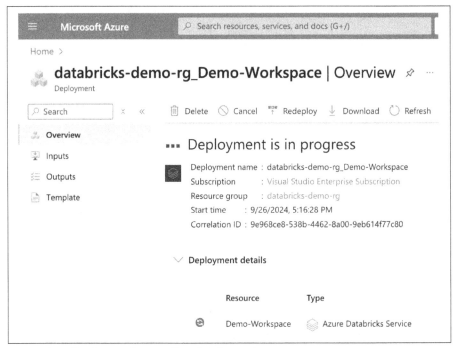

Figure A-4. Deploying the new Databricks workspace

11. Resource management: After the deployment is complete, you have the option to review the deployment details; otherwise, click "Go to resource," as displayed in Figure A-5 to access the overview page of your new Databricks workspace.

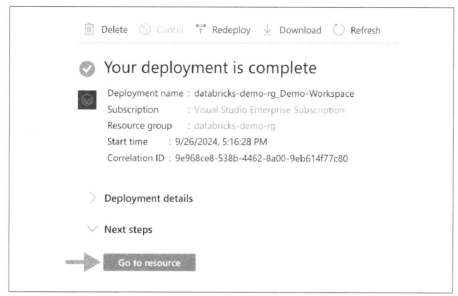

Figure A-5. Completed Databricks workspace deployment

Figure A-6 shows the overview page of your newly provisioned Databricks workspace. Along with this workspace, Azure has automatically set up a managed resource group to organize related resources efficiently.

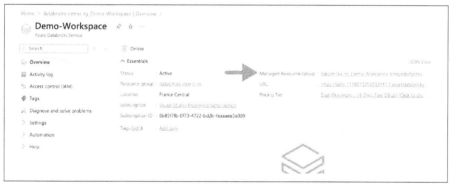

Figure A-6. The overview page of the new Databricks workspace

If you click the name of this managed resource group, you can explore the cloud resources associated with your workspace, as illustrated in Figure A-7.

Resources   Recommendations

| Filter for any field... | Type equals **all** × | Location equals **all** × | ⊤▽ Add filter |

Showing 1 to 5 of 5 records. ☐ Show hidden types ⓘ   No grouping

☐	Name ↑	Type ↑↓
☐	dbmanagedidentity	Managed Identity
☐	dbstoragegthzhc5vw2isu	Storage account
☐	unity-catalog-access-connector	Access Connector for Azure Databricks
☐	workers-sg	Network security group
☐	workers-vnet	Virtual network

Figure A-7. The managed resource group of the new Databricks workspace

This group contains the resources necessary for your Databricks workspace to function, such as a storage account used for the DBFS and associated network resources.

12. Launch your workspace: Go back to the resource overview page and click Launch Workspace, as displayed in Figure A-8, to open your Databricks workspace.

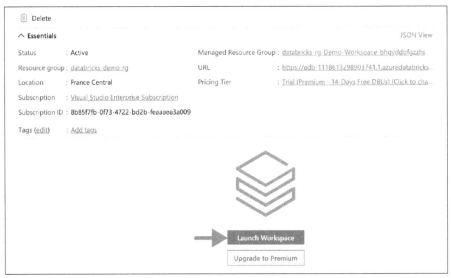

Figure A-8. Launching the new Databricks workspace

You will notice that the platform uses Azure Entra ID for single sign-on (SSO), simplifying the login process and ensuring that your workspace adheres to your organization's security policies. Figure A-9 illustrates the Databricks workspace showing its main interface and navigation options.

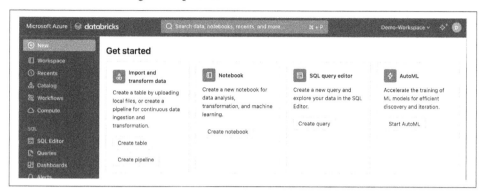

Figure A-9. The home page of the Databricks workspace

Congratulations! You have now successfully created your Azure Databricks workspace. This workspace serves as your central hub for performing data engineering, machine learning, and analytics tasks. In Chapter 1, we navigate the workspace interface and explore the various features that Databricks offers.

To create additional workspaces, simply navigate back to the Azure Databricks service page in the Azure Portal. From there, you can manage your workspaces and create new ones as needed.

Deploying Databricks on Amazon Web Services

If you're considering using Databricks on AWS, you can start with a free trial subscription available through AWS Marketplace.

Databricks workspaces operating on AWS incur additional costs related to the NAT gateway deployed with the workspace. Even if no clusters are actively running in your workspace, you will still be charged for the NAT gateway usage. You can review NAT gateway pricing on the AWS website (*https://oreil.ly/90Fyz*).

Here are detailed instructions for creating your first Databricks workspace via the AWS Marketplace:

1. Log in to your AWS account: Start by logging into your AWS account Console (*https://console.aws.amazon.com*).

2. Search for Databricks: In the AWS Console, use the search bar to look for "Databricks." Under the Marketplace tab, select "Databricks Data Intelligence Platform," as illustrated in Figure A-10. Alternatively, you can directly access the listing (*https://oreil.ly/FsBYX*).

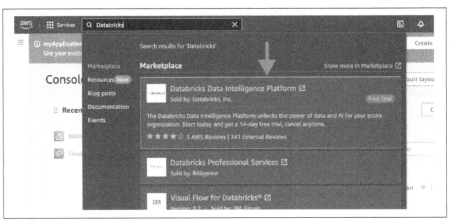

Figure A-10. Searching for Databricks product in the AWS account console

3. View purchase options: On the Databricks Data Intelligence Platform product page, click "View purchase options," as shown in Figure A-11.

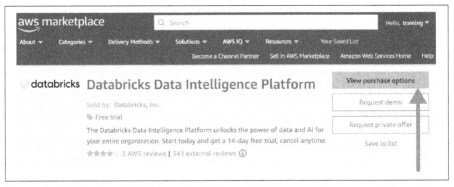

Figure A-11. The Databricks Data Intelligence Platform product page in the AWS Marketplace

4. Subscribe: At the bottom of the subscription page, click the Subscribe button, as displayed in Figure A-12, to begin the subscription process.

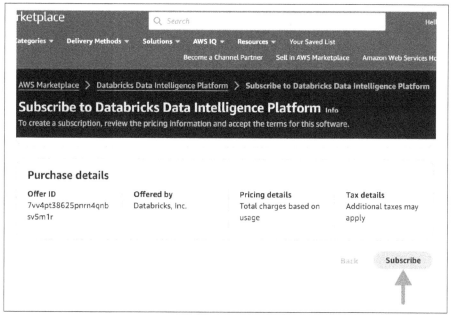

Figure A-12. Subscribing to Databricks Data Intelligence Platform product from the AWS Marketplace

5. Set up your account: Once the subscription process is completed, a confirmation message will appear at the top of the page, as shown in Figure A-13. At this point, click "Set up your account" to create a new Databricks account on the Databricks website.

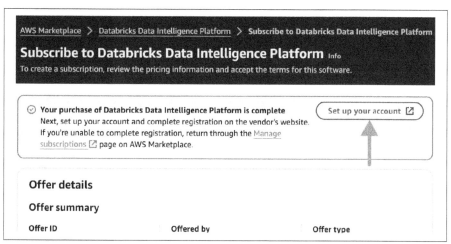

Figure A-13. The confirmation message for setting up a new Databricks account

6. Enter account details: As illustrated in Figure A-14, you need to provide your email address, first and last names, and company name (or "Personal" if using a personal email). Fill in these details, and then click "Sign up."

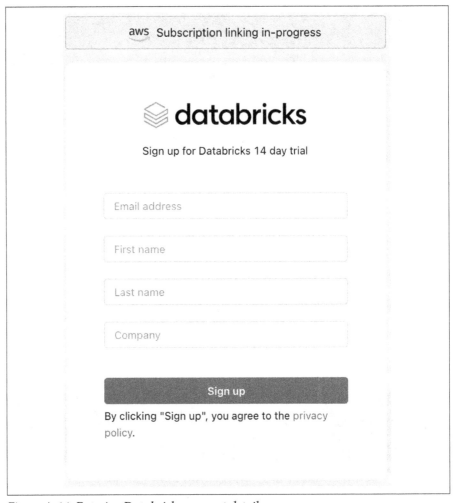

Figure A-14. Entering Databricks account details

7. Verify your email address: Open your email and use the provided login to complete the setup of your Databricks account.

8. Logging in to Databricks: Log in to your Databricks account console using your email address and a one-time password. This account console allows you to manage all your Databricks workspaces.

9. Workspace setup: In the setup page of the Databricks workspace, as displayed in Figure A-15, provide the following details:

   a. Enter a friendly workspace name: Provide a name for your workspace, such as "Demo-Workspace."

   b. Select the region: Choose the AWS region where your workspace will be deployed. The choice of region can affect performance, cost, and availability of certain workspace features (*https://oreil.ly/ns_dV*).

   c. Start quickstart: Click "Start quickstart" to initiate the setup.

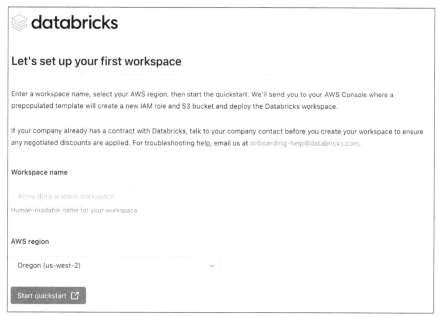

Figure A-15. Setting up your first Databricks workspace on AWS

10. Create CloudFormation stack: You'll be redirected to the AWS Console to continue the configuration using CloudFormation. On the stack creation form, scroll to locate and select the checkbox shown in Figure A-16 and then click "Create stack."

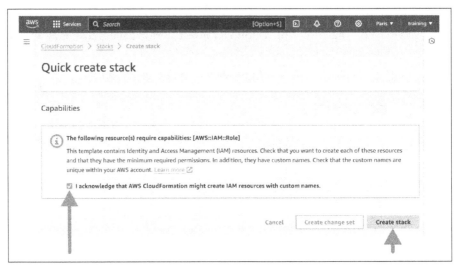

Figure A-16. Creating the CloudFormation stack on AWS for the Databricks workspace

11. Receive workspace URL: The successful completion of the stack creation, as illustrated in Figure A-17, means that your workspace is ready. You will subsequently receive an email containing the URL for accessing your new workspace.

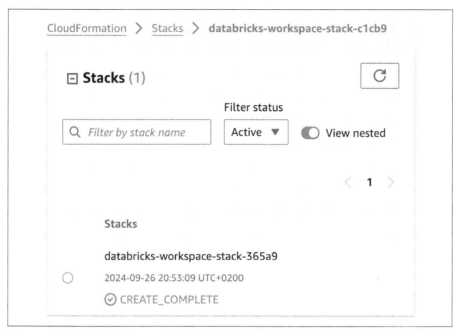

Figure A-17. Successful completion of the CloudFormation stack creation for the Databricks workspace

12. Log in to your workspace: Access your new Databricks workspace by using the workspace URL sent to you via email.

Congratulations! You have successfully created your Databricks workspace on AWS. To ensure easy access in the future, I recommend bookmarking the workspace URL in your web browser.

Additional Workspaces and Account Management

Once you've set up one Databricks workspace, you might want to create additional workspaces for different projects or teams. You can do this easily through the Databricks account console:

1. Access the Databricks account console (*https://accounts.cloud.databricks.com*).

2. Create additional workspaces: Under the Workspaces tab, click "Create workspace," as shown in Figure A-18.

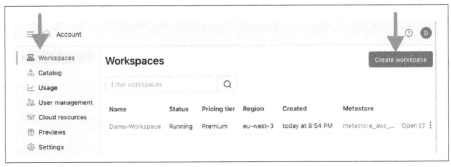

Figure A-18. Creating additional workspaces from the Databricks account console

3. Use the quickstart option by repeating steps 9 to 12 as outlined previously.

Deploying Databricks on Google Cloud Platform

If you're interested in exploring Databricks on GCP, you can begin with a free trial subscription available through Google Cloud Marketplace.

> Google Cloud applies an additional per-workspace cost for the Google Kubernetes Engine (GKE) cluster required to manage Databricks infrastructure in your GCP account. Even if no clusters are actively running in your workspace, you will still be charged for this GKE cluster. For detailed pricing information, visit the GKE pricing page (*https://oreil.ly/HXOJd*).

To create a free trial subscription of Databricks on GCP and create your first Databricks workspace, follow these steps:

1. Log in to Google Cloud Platform: Start by logging into your Google Cloud Platform account (*https://console.cloud.google.com*).

2. Select or create a project: Choose an existing Google Cloud project or create a new one. Ensure that billing is enabled for the project and that you have the Billing Account Administrator permission. Billing must be active to use Databricks.

3. Search for Databricks: Use the search bar in the Google Cloud Console to look for "Databricks," as illustrated in Figure A-19. Select the Databricks product from the search results. Alternatively, you can access the Databricks product directly (*https://oreil.ly/OPSaG*).

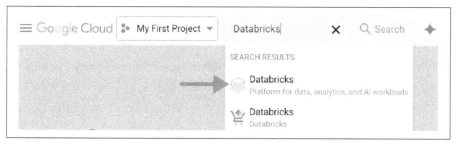

Figure A-19. Searching for Databricks product in the GCP account console

4. Subscribe to Databricks: Click on the SUBSCRIBE button to begin the subscription process, as displayed in Figure A-20.

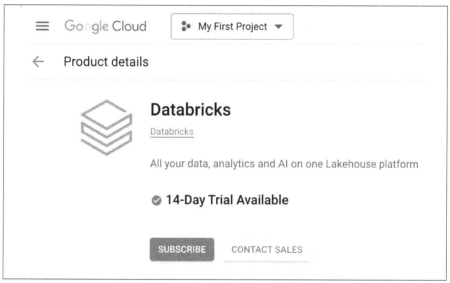

Figure A-20. Subscribing to Databricks from the Google Cloud Marketplace

5. Accept terms: Review the terms and conditions, and click SUBSCRIBE to agree, as shown in Figure A-21.

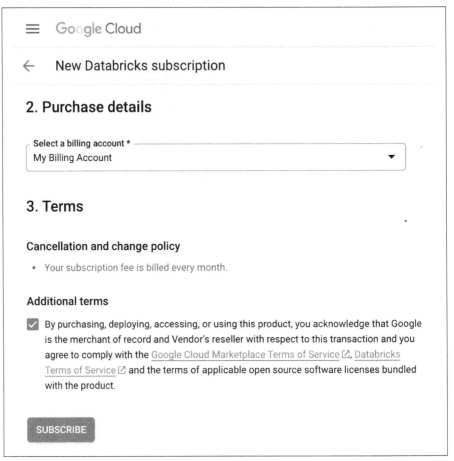

Figure A-21. Reviewing the terms and conditions for the Databricks subscription

Once your subscription request is sent, click GO TO PRODUCT PAGE to proceed, as shown in Figure A-22.

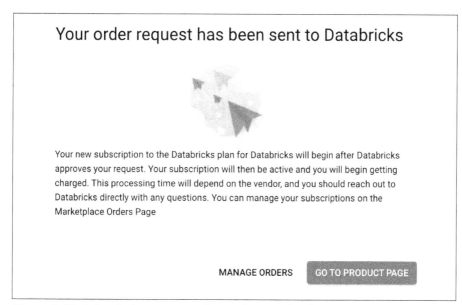

Figure A-22. *Subscription request submitted to Databricks*

6. Sign Up with Databricks: Click SIGN UP WITH DATABRICKS, as illustrated in Figure A-23, to create a new Databricks account.

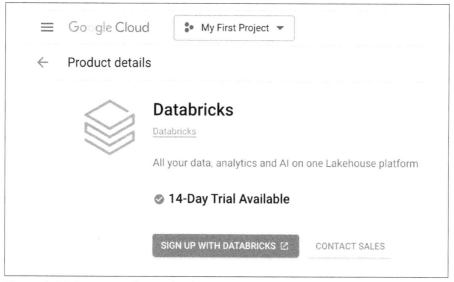

Figure A-23. *Sign up with Databricks*

7. Enter your company name if using a professional email, or type "Personal" if using a personal email. Then, click Sign in with Google, as illustrated in Figure A-24.

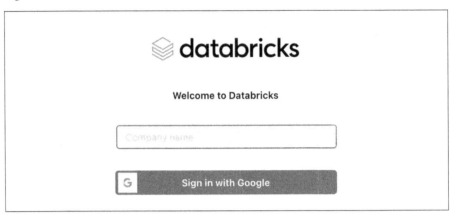

Figure A-24. Entering company name during Databricks sign-up

8. Manage your Databricks account: Click MANAGE ON PROVIDER, as displayed in Figure A-25, to access your Databricks account.

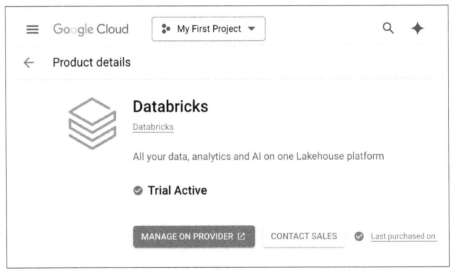

Figure A-25. Databricks trial is active

9. Select subscription plan: Choose the Premium subscription plan, as shown in Figure A-26, and click Continue to proceed with the premium features of Databricks.

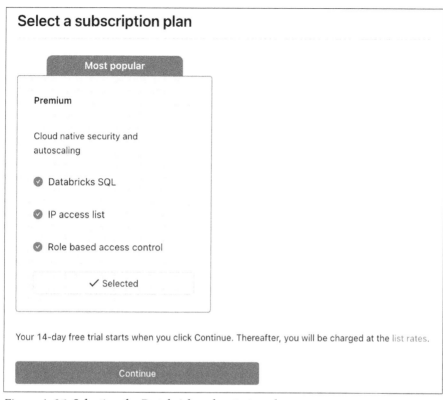

Figure A-26. Selecting the Databricks subscription plan

10. Create a Databricks workspace:

    a. Access Databricks console: In your Databricks account console, go to the Workspaces tab on the left sidebar and click "Create workspace," as shown in Figure A-27.

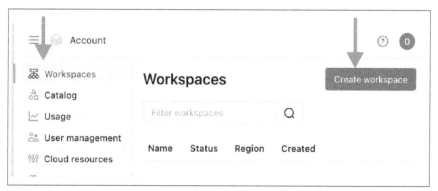

Figure A-27. Creating a workspace from the Databricks account console

This opens the workspace creation page, as illustrated in Figure A-28.

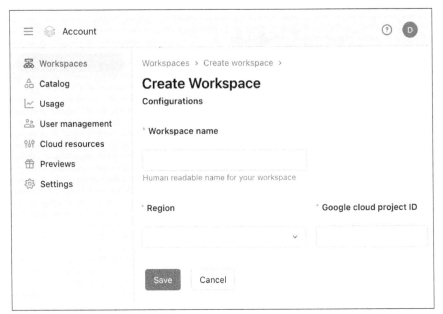

Figure A-28. Workspace creation page in the Databricks account console

b. Workspace configuration: Enter the following details:

   i. Enter workspace name: Provide a friendly name for your workspace, such as "Demo-Workspace."

   ii. Select region: Choose the target region where your Databricks workspace will be deployed. The choice of region can affect performance, cost, and availability of certain workspace features (*https://oreil.ly/-hLcN*).

   iii. Enter Cloud project ID: Input your Google Cloud project ID, which can be located on your project dashboard, as demonstrated in Figure A-29.

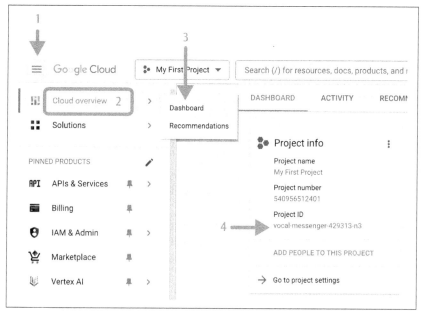

Figure A-29. Locating Google Cloud project ID on the project dashboard

c. Click Save to initiate the creation of your workspace.

11. Refresh and check status: Refresh the Workspaces page to check the status of your workspace creation, as displayed in Figure A-30.

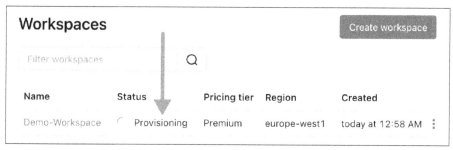

Figure A-30. Databricks workspace in provisioning status

12. Log in to your workspace: Once the workspace is ready, click Open, as displayed in Figure A-31, to log in to your Databricks workspace.

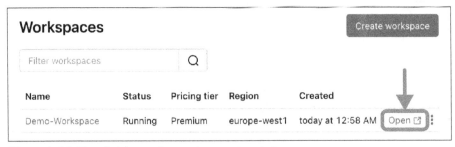

Figure A-31. Databricks workspace in running status

Congratulations! You've successfully created your Databricks workspace on Google Cloud. To ensure easy access in the future, bookmark the workspace URL in your preferred web browser. If you need to create additional Databricks workspaces, you can return to the Databricks account console at any time (*https://accounts.gcp.data bricks.com*).

Databricks Community Edition

Databricks Community Edition provides a free and accessible way for you to explore the capabilities of Databricks without the need for a cloud account. However, it is limited compared to the full trial available on cloud platforms like AWS, Azure, or Google Cloud. The full cloud-based trial provides access to production-grade functionalities such as Databricks SQL, Delta Live Tables, and Git folders, which are not included in the Community Edition.

If you do not yet have a cloud account, it is possible to create one at no cost. Major cloud providers generally offer free tiers, which allow you to explore their services within specified usage limits. This option provides an opportunity to experience the full capabilities of Databricks in a cloud environment, which is essential for understanding and preparation for the exam.

Nevertheless, the Community Edition remains a good starting point for anyone new to Databricks, offering an opportunity to explore the platform's core concepts and tools. To sign up for Databricks Community Edition, follow these steps:

1. Visit Databricks Community Edition: Start by navigating to the Databricks Community Edition sign-in page (*https://community.cloud.databricks.com*).
2. Sign up: Click Sign Up, as illustrated in Figure B-1.

Figure B-1. Signing up for Databricks Community Edition

3. Enter your details: Fill in your personal information, as illustrated in Figure B-2. Enter your full name, email address, and job title. In the Company field, enter your company name (or "Personal" if using a personal email); then click Continue.

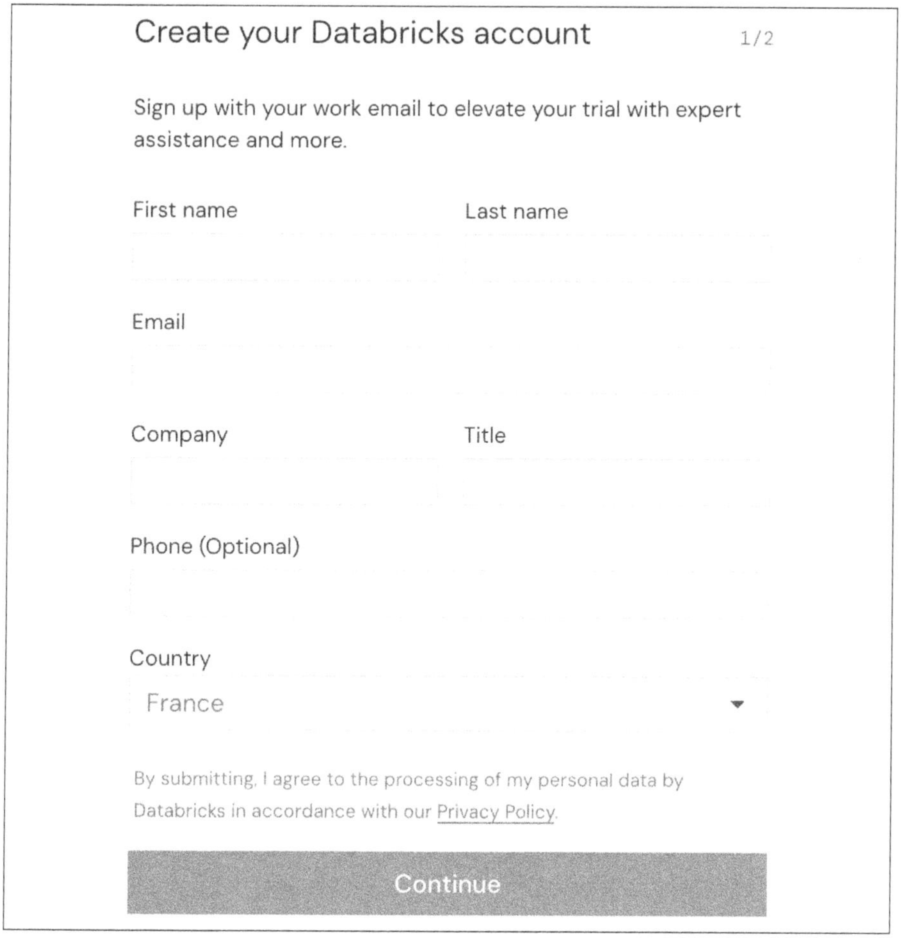

Create your Databricks account

Sign up with your work email to elevate your trial with expert assistance and more.

First name   Last name

Email

Company   Title

Phone (Optional)

Country

France   ▼

By submitting, I agree to the processing of my personal data by Databricks in accordance with our Privacy Policy.

Continue

Figure B-2. Sign-up form for Databricks account

4. Select Community Edition: At the bottom of the registration page, click "Get started with Community Edition," as displayed in Figure B-3.

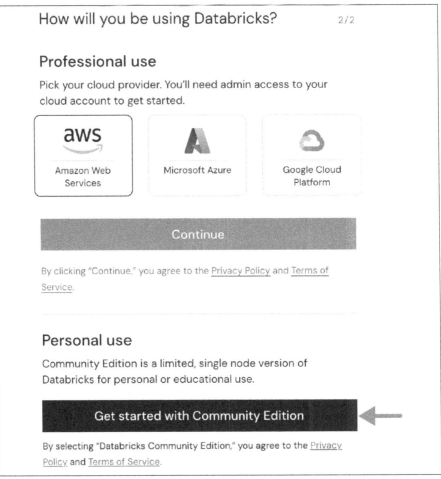

Figure B-3. *Getting started with Community Edition*

5. Complete security verification: Confirm that you are not a robot by solving the puzzle provided.

6. Verify your email address: Go to your email inbox and locate the verification email sent by Databricks. Click the link within the email to confirm your email address.

7. Set your account password: After verifying your email, you will be prompted to set a password for your new Databricks account, as shown in Figure B-4. Choose a secure password to complete the setup and log in to your workspace.

Figure B-4. Password setup for the Databricks Community Edition account

Congratulations! You have successfully created your Databricks workspace on the Community Edition. You can access your workspace at any time by visiting *https:// community.cloud.databricks.com* and logging in with the email and password you set during the registration process.

Answers to Sample Exam Questions

This appendix provides the correct answers to the sample exam questions from Chapter 1 to Chapter 8.

Chapter 1: Getting Started with Databricks

1. C
2. D

Chapter 2: Managing Data with Delta Lake

1. E
2. B

Chapter 3: Mastering Relational Entities in Databricks

1. D
2. C

Chapter 4: Transforming Data with Apache Spark

1. B
2. D

Chapter 5: Processing Incremental Data

1. B
2. E

Chapter 6: Building Production Pipelines

1. A
2. E

Chapter 7: Exploring Databricks SQL

1. C
2. A

Chapter 8: Implementing Data Governance

1. C
2. D

Index

VERSION AS OF keyword (SELECT * FROM), 67

versions
  notebook versioning, 37
  versioning with Git, 38-46

views, 100-107
  comparison of view types, 106
    accessibility, 107
    creation syntax, 107
  creating view on top of two tables by performing inner join between them, 100
  creating with Databricks SQL, 295
  dropping, 107
  live views in Delta Live Tables, 199
  materialized views in DLT, 198
  reviewing permissions assigned to, 298
  revoking privileges assigned to in Catalog Explorer, 302
  temporary views
    using with CTAS to create Delta tables from foreign data sources, 124
  types of, 102-106
    global temporary views, 105
    stored views, 102
    temporary views, 103-105
  view objects in Hive metastore, 286

violations of constraints, 200, 204

virtual machines (VMs)
  selecting VM size for worker nodes in clusters, 22

visualizations
  designing for new dashboard in Databricks SQL, 262-264

W

Webassessor platform
  logging into your account prior to exam, 333
  monitoring by Webassessor Proctor via computer's webcam, 334
  My Assessments page, 333
  overview of, 330
  prerequisites before launching into exam, 334
  scheduling certification exam, 331
  viewing available Databricks certification exams, 331

WHEN MATCHED clause (MERGE INTO), 131

WHEN NOT MATCHED clause (MERGE INTO), 131

WHERE clause, 61
  CHECK constraints and, 99
  use with FILTER function, 145

worker nodes (clusters), 16
  configuring for all-purpose cluster, 22

workflows, orchestrating, 234-251
  configuring job settings, 242-246
  creating Databricks jobs, 235-242
  debugging jobs, 249
  introduction to Databricks Jobs, 235
  running the job, 246-249

workspaces (Databricks), 4, 8-15
  Catalog tab, 59
  creating additional workspaces, 351
  Databricks SQL, 253
  enabling for Unity Catalog, 313
  importing book materials (example), 13-15
  management before and after adopting Unity Catalog, 305
  navigating to Compute tab, 19
  navigating workspace browser, 10-13
  overview of workspace interface, 8-10
  setting up, 7
  Unity Catalog metastore, assigning to, 316
  Unity Catalog metastore, existing, assigning to, 317
  verifying Unity Catalog enablement, 313
  Workflows tab
    Delta Live Tables, 205
  Workspace tab, creating notebook with, 26

WRITE FILES privilege, 310

writeStream method, 164

writing and reading data (Delta Lake), 54
  concurrent writes and reads, 56
  failed writes scenario, 57
  writing to tables, 126-133
    appending data, 129
    merging data, 130-133
    replacing data, 127-129

Z

Z-Order indexing, 70-73

About the Author

Derar Alhussein is a senior data engineer with a master's degree in data mining. He has over a decade of hands-on experience in software and data projects, including large-scale data projects on Databricks. Derar is a Databricks MVP and holds eight certifications from Databricks, showcasing his proficiency in the field. He is also an experienced instructor, with a proven track record of success in training thousands of data engineers, helping them to develop their skills and obtain industry-recognized certifications.

Colophon

The animal on the cover of *Databricks Certified Data Engineer Associate Study Guide* is a sacred kingfisher (*Todiramphus sanctus*). This striking bird has a bright turquoise back, head, and wings, contrasting with a white neck and chest. It can be found widely throughout Southeast Asia, Australia, New Zealand, and various Pacific islands. The sacred kingfisher's name is derived from its cultural significance in some Pacific Island societies. For instance, in Polynesian mythology, the birds were associated with the sea and fishing, and venerated for having control over the waves. Their bright feathers were also used in traditional crafts and apparel.

The kingfisher's long, pointed bill is ideal for catching prey. Unlike other kingfisher species that dive below the water to catch fish, the bulk of the sacred kingfisher's diet consists of animals it hunts on land, such as crustaceans, small reptiles, frogs, and insects. It is considered a medium-sized bird at about 8–9 inches long.

Sacred kingfishers are known for their aerial agility and distinctive mating calls, which are often described as as a piercing "kek-kek" sound. They are typically solitary but may be seen in pairs during the breeding season from September to January. The birds nest in burrows, which they excavate in riverbanks, hollow trees, or termite mounds. The female lays a clutch of 3–6 white eggs, and both parents share the incubation and chick-rearing duties. Typically, there will be two clutches in each breeding season.

While the sacred kingfisher's population is stable, many of the animals on O'Reilly covers are endangered; all of them are important to the world.

The cover illustration is by Karen Montgomery, based on an antique engraving from *Pictorial Museum of Animated Nature*. The series design is by Edie Freedman, Ellie Volckhausen, and Karen Montgomery. The cover fonts are Gilroy Semibold and Guardian Sans. The text font is Adobe Minion Pro; the heading font is Adobe Myriad Condensed; and the code font is Dalton Maag's Ubuntu Mono.

O'REILLY®

Learn from experts.
Become one yourself.

60,000+ titles | Live events with experts | Role-based courses
Interactive learning | Certification preparation

**Try the O'Reilly learning platform
free for 10 days.**

©2025 O'Reilly Media, Inc. O'Reilly is a registered trademark of O'Reilly Media, Inc. 718900_7x9.1875

www.ingramcontent.com/pod-product-compliance
Lightning Source LLC
Jackson TN
JSHW062113140625
86115JS00006B/157